MACAU, CHINA

*A Political History of
the Portuguese Colony's
Transition to Chinese Rule*

McFarland & Company, Inc., Publishers
Jefferson, North Carolina, and London

British Library Cataloguing-in-Publication data are available

Library of Congress Cataloguing-in-Publication Data

Shipp, Steve, 1937–
    Macau, China : a political history of the Portuguese colony's
transition to Chinese rule = [Ao-men Chung-kuo] / by Steve Shipp.
      p.   cm.
    Includes bibliographical references and index.
    ISBN 0-7864-0233-4 (library binding : 50# alkaline paper) ∞
    1. Macau—History. 2. Macau—Politics and government. 3. China—
Politics and government—1976–   I. Title.
DS796.M2S53   1997
951.26—dc21   96-47117
                                                CIP

Manufactured in the United States of America

McFarland & Company, Inc., Publishers
Box 611, Jefferson, North Carolina 28640

To the memory of my parents,
Guy and Ina Shipp

Contents

Preface		1
Introduction		3
Maps		5
1	Portugal Opens an Ocean Route to the Far East	11
2	The Portuguese Settle at Macau and Expand Trade with China	17
3	Portugal Establishes a Colony at Macau	32
4	Dutch Attacks Threaten Macau	42
5	Macau and the Portuguese Restoration	50
6	British Artists Discover the South China Coast	56
7	The British Offer "Protection" for Macau	64
8	Macau Defends Its Territory Against China	71
9	World War II in Macau	81
10	Rioting Breaks Out in Macau	87
11	China and Portugal Sign Secret Agreements on Macau	94
12	Talks with China on the Future of Macau	102
13	Portugal and China Agree on the Future of Macau	107
14	Macau in the 1990s—Growth and Optimism	121

Appendices

A.	*Sino-Portuguese Joint Declaration*	129
B.	*The Basic Law of the Macau Special Administrative Region of the People's Republic of China*	143
C.	*Antonio Fialho Ferreira's Account of His Journey to Macau with News of the Restoration*	172
D.	*The Organic Statute of Macau*	178
E.	*Chronology of Events Relating to Macau*	194

Notes	203
Bibliography	213
Index	219

Preface

One of history's most unusual instruments for the transfer of people and property from one country to another, a document that resembles the agreement to return Hong Kong to China in 1997, is the 1987 Sino-Portuguese Joint Declaration to return Macau to China in 1999. The Hong Kong accord, involving 6 million people and 415 square miles, was negotiated between China and Great Britain over a two-year period ending in 1984. The Macau agreement, involving 450,000 people and just over 9 square miles, was worked out between China and Portugal in four negotiating sessions over nine months during 1986–87. Just as Hong Kong will become "Hong Kong, China," Macau will become "Macau, China."

Portugal first started settling at Macau in 1557, beginning 442 years of administration of the Asian outpost which at one time was one of the world's most important trading ports. Over the centuries, Macau became a place of intrigue, a place of refuge, and an interesting mix of Portuguese and Oriental culture in its architecture, food, and politics. Then, in the 1990s, while approaching its return to Chinese rule on December 20, 1999, Macau developed into an important alternative to Hong Kong as a gateway to the booming economic growth within the People's Republic of China.

This book is designed to present the relationship of Macau to China, from its early days as an important entrepôt to its more recent development as an important business link to mainland China. Events from the mid-sixteenth century are presented in sequence, with occasional emphasis on specific personalities and situations which led to changes in the enclave.

Some of Macau's illustrious past is reviewed in the Introduction, but is then presented in more detail in the opening chapters. Chapter 1 tells of Macau's early history, as Portuguese explorers reached the Far East by sea and attempted to begin trading with China. Chapter 2 focuses on the first Portuguese settlers at Macau and their successful attempts to expand trading. This chapter also includes a look at the early influence and growth of the Jesuit brotherhood in Macau.

Portugal's formal establishment of Macau in 1557 is described in Chapter 3, along with the development of its "golden era" as a trading center. Chapter 4 focuses on Macau's valiant and sometimes desperate defense against

Dutch invaders, while Chapter 5 reviews Macau and the restoration of the Portuguese Crown in 1640.

The interest of art and artists in Macau is taken up in Chapter 6, while Chapter 7 tells of the British withdrawal from Macau, their subsequent settlement in Hong Kong, and the Opium Wars of the mid–nineteenth century. Chapter 8 describes the successful Portuguese efforts to strengthen their possession of Macau amid conflicts with China, followed by its years of decline in worldly importance except as a place of refuge.

Macau's responses to World War II, the Korean War, and China's Civil War are taken up in Chapter 9, while Chapter 10 reflects the influence in Macau of China's Great Proletarian Cultural Revolution. Chapter 11 describes significant secret agreements between China and Portugal on Macau in the 1960s and 1970s, while Chapter 12 outlines formal negotiations between China and Portugal on Macau's future in the 1980s.

Chapter 13 reviews the 1987 Sino-Portuguese agreement to return Macau to China on December 20, 1999, while Chapter 14 reflects the growth and optimism of the people of Macau as they approach the 1999 handover of their little enclave to the People's Republic of China.

Appendices include the 1987 Joint Declaration, the Basic Law of Macau for post–1999, an announcement of Portugal's Restoration in 1640 as delivered to Macau, and the Organic Statute governing Macau during its last 23 years as "a Chinese territory under Portuguese administration."

Steve Shipp
Fall 1996

Introduction

Macau, a tiny peninsula with two adjoining islands on the southern coast of China that has been administered by Portugal since 1557, was formally given up in 1987 through an agreement allowing the resumption of Chinese sovereignty over the Portuguese enclave on December 20, 1999. In the beginning, China had granted "permission" for Portugal to colonize Macau in return for Portuguese efforts to reduce piracy in Chinese waters. Within a few years, it had become one of the most important sea-trading ports linking Southeast Asia and Europe. Macau enters the twenty-first century with another worldly distinction: This little territory of 450,000 people, expanded in size through recent land reclamation to just over 9 square miles, has become the most densely crowded place in the world, with more than 50,000 people per square mile.

Despite frequent early conflicts with the Spanish, Dutch, and British between 1580 and 1808, Macau enjoyed a relatively stable history under Portuguese administration, serving as an important trading outpost between East and West until the mid-1800s. The last serious threat to Portuguese rule occurred in 1808 when the British occupied Macau to "protect" the enclave from "possible" French invasion. China quickly joined Portugal in successfully pressuring the British to withdraw and move to Hong Kong, which then became one of the world's great trading seaports.

By the closing years of the twentieth century, Macau had become a favorite destination for tourists and gamblers attracted to its nine casinos, hotels, horse racing, dog racing, and jai alai. By the 1990s, more than 70,000 Macau residents were directly employed within the gambling industry, while most commercial ventures in the enclave benefited from the constant flow of tourist dollars. Toy production accounted for about 10 percent of Macau's exports by the 1990s, with a lesser percentage for other exports such as electronics, plastics, and garments. Fishing was revived in recent years as a small but important industry, but farming never was a viable possibility, because only about three percent of the land is suitable for growing crops.

In the late 1970s, Portugal offered three times to return Macau to China, which declined to accept its return until after it had settled the question of Hong Kong with Britain. After the 1984 Joint Declaration on Hong Kong, an accord scheduling its return to China in 1997, Portugal and China began formal negotiations which led to a similar agreement on Macau in 1987. Many of the terms for the Macau and Hong Kong agreements were similar, with sovereignty going to China in return for a guarantee of fifty years of continued capitalism and current life-style and a promise of no change in social, economic, and legal systems. After additional negotiations in the early 1990s, the Basic Law for Macau was adopted by China in 1993, defining terms and guidelines effective on December 20, 1999.

One of the most controversial elements in the Macau handover was Portugal's granting of full citizenship rights for ethnic Chinese residents of Macau and their descendants after 1999. This meant Portuguese citizenship for between 100,000 and 150,000 Macau residents—a promise which helped avert mass migration from Macau before the 1999 handover. The Portuguese promise was disputed by the Chinese leaders, however, who maintained that Chinese citizens in Macau after 1999 would not be allowed to hold dual citizenship and definitely would not be permitted to pass along Portuguese nationality to their children after 1999.

A degree of tentative confidence developed during the closing years of Macau as a Portuguese territory. Many local residents and business executives would be monitoring China's handling of the Hong Kong reversion in 1997 before deciding how to deal with their own pending reversion in 1999. Meanwhile, new investment in the early 1990s produced strong demands for residential housing and business space, enhanced by the construction of a new bridge in 1992 linking the Macau peninsula with adjacent Taipa Island, improved highways from Macau into neighboring Zhuhai, one of China's Special Economic Zones, and the opening of Macau's International Airport in December 1995. Through it all, it has seemed as if Macau is coming full circle—once again becoming one of the world's most important cities, particularly through its unique and unexpected end-of-the-century link to the booming economic changes in mainland China.

The enclave of Macau is located on the southeastern coast of China, just south of Guangzhou (Canton) and west of Hong Kong.

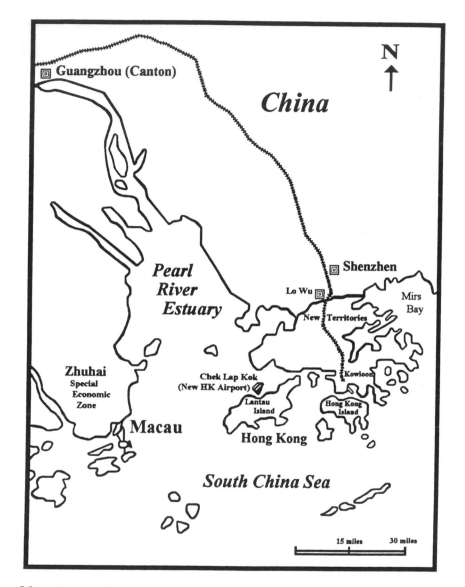

Macau is situated at the southeastern end of China's Zhuhai province, forty miles west of Hong Kong (across the Pearl River Estuary) and about 90 miles south of Guangzhou (Canton).

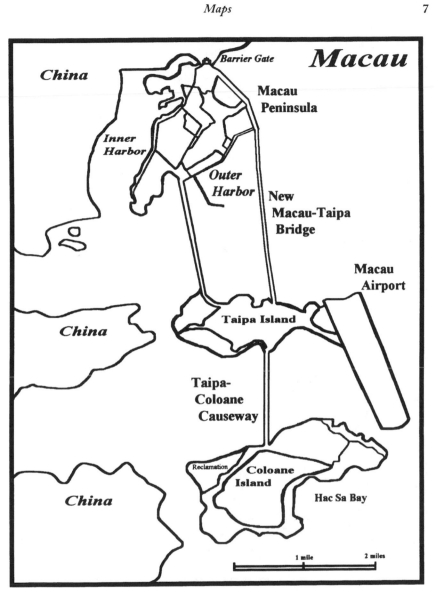

Map of the Macau peninsula and its two islands

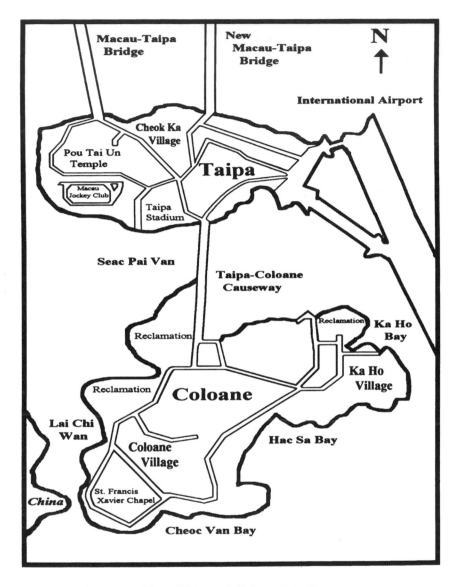

Map of Taipa and Coloane Islands

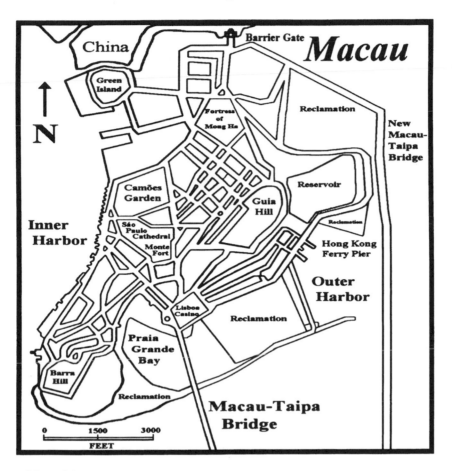

Map of the Macau peninsula, location of the enclave's main business district

Chapter 1

Portugal Opens an Ocean Route to the Far East

The course of Macau's future cannot be charted without understanding her past. —PROFESSOR T.K. LIN[1]

The ocean-going Portuguese, generously supported by the resources and vision of their royal leaders in the early sixteenth century, were the first European traders to experience the lure and promise of profit-making with the Far East by sea, beginning with the famed explorations of Vasco da Gama.

By the mid-fifteenth century, Portugal's Dom Henrique the Navigator had already commissioned successful expeditions to Madeira, the Azores, and the Cape Verde Islands. These voyages led to a growing and lucrative trade relationship between Portugal, England, and other European countries. Dom Henrique also commissioned several exploring expeditions down the western seacoast of India, believing strongly in the possibility of opening a sea-route to India.

Although an expedition led by Gil Eanes managed to round the southern tip of Africa (Cape Bojador) in 1434, most later expeditions were forced to turn back because of violent storms and adverse weather conditions. One of the Portuguese explorers, Bartholomeu Dias, finally reached the southern tip of Africa in 1488, giving it the vividly descriptive name "Cape of Storms." In another seaborne effort in 1490, a fleet of ships commanded by Pedro Álvares Cabral, reached the eastern coast of South America, making the first sanctioned exploration of coastal areas of Brazil, which subsequently led to its colonization by Portugal.

Portugal's King João II, who renamed the treacherous southern tip of Africa the "Cape of Good Hope," was more optimistic than his predecessors about the potential sea-route to India around southern Africa and encouraged his country's explorer-navigators to continue their perilous journeys. Finally, under commission of Portugal's King Manoel I, the Da Gama brothers, Vasco and Paolo, commanding three ships, were commissioned in 1497 to sail around the dangerous waters of the Cape of Good Hope to establish commercial and

11

political relations with Calicut, Cochin and Goa on the west coast of India. All three of the ships under the command of the Da Gama brothers, namely the *Berrio*, *São Rafael*, and *São Gabriel*, were heavily defended with cannons in case force was needed to ensure the safety of their journey.

Vasco da Gama reached the Indian coast in 1498, making port at Goa, Cochin, and Calicut; he quickly established Goa as a primary base for Portuguese traders, whose superior ships soon replaced merchant traders from India, Malaya, and the Arab countries. It was the beginning of a bountiful "golden era" for Portugal in trading between East and West, and Macau was to be one of the most important ports of this commerce until nearly the mid-seventeenth century.

Lisbon Establishes the "Portuguese State of India"

Realizing his goal of achieving an ocean trade route between Europe and the Far East, Vasco da Gama returned to Portugal in late 1498 with an impressive cargo of precious stones and spices, including pepper, ginger, and cinnamon. The spice trade would prove to be a valuable enterprise for future Portuguese merchant traders. Vasco's brother, Paolo da Gama, was not quite so fortunate. Paolo, along with at least half his crew of 148, suffered fatal complications of scurvy and died during the mission.

At that time, the spice trade with the Arab countries in the Mediterranean region was highly lucrative because of the great demand in European countries for pepper, cinnamon, camphor, ginger, and a variety of Eastern luxury items. Pepper, for example, was extremely valuable, worth nearly its own weight in silver; it was frequently used to offset customs duties and to purchase land.[2] The spice trade in the Mediterranean was effectively dominated by the Italians, however, who excluded Portugal from this profitable commerce.

Afonso de Albuquerque strengthened Portugal's domination in India through his forced conquests of the island of Goa in 1510, Malacca in 1511, and Ormuz in 1515, thus establishing the "Portuguese State of India." In Goa, the Portuguese Crown appointed a viceroy whose responsibilities included administrative control over the city and its colonization, including construction of churches, seminaries, and fortresses.[3] The Portuguese conquest also included the removal of the sultan of Malacca, an island which had until then enjoyed a modest but regular trade with China. The Portuguese then scheduled regular trading voyages from Lisbon to its controlled Far East ports of Goa, Malacca, and Ormuz, becoming exceedingly prosperous while at the same time reducing the reliance of European countries on trading in the Mediterranean.

The Portuguese "Discover" China

In the early years of the sixteenth century, Portugal also learned of early trading by the Chinese in India, particularly at Malacca. As dramatic proof, Vasco da Gama brought back some Chinese porcelain with him when he returned to Lisbon. Expeditions to Malacca were then directed to continue and expand their trading in spices but also to investigate trading with China.

The area around Macau was first visited in 1513 by the Portuguese, who were seeking to expand their domination of worldwide trading and open new markets with the great land of China. By the end of the sixteenth century, the tiny outpost of Macau had become the richest entrepôt in the world and the primary ocean stop between Japan and India.

In June 1513, Jorge Álvares, the treasurer (*feitor*) of the Malacca Trading Post, became the first European to reach China by sea, landing at the Bay of Tuen-mun near what is now known as Castle Peak, one of the many islands around Hong Kong. Tuen-mun was subsequently referred to as Tamão by the Portuguese. Álvares established a base on Neilingding Island, about three miles from Nantou off the southern Chinese coast, one of the very few places where foreign trading merchants were tolerated by the highly protective Chinese. One of Álvares' children died on Neilingding Island, and Álvares himself died there in 1521 (the same year that China expelled the Portuguese from the island). A special monument to honor Álvares was commissioned in 1953 by the government of Macau.

The Portuguese enjoyed a modest trade during the period 1513 to 1521 from voyages between Neilingding Island and Malacca. This comfortable relationship also encouraged the Chinese to relax their isolationist policies, which in turn allowed some growth in trading activities with the Portuguese. In addition, the Chinese even allowed extended visits to the tiny ports of Nantou and Quanzhou for trading in the provinces of Fujian and Guangdong. This enlivened and profitable trade situation between China and Portugal continued for about eight years, though it was interrupted by frequent hostilities caused by problems and differences between the Portuguese traders and their Chinese counterparts. These hostilities finally led to a renewal of Chinese prohibitions against trade with foreign countries, mainly Portugal, that resulted in the ordered expulsion of the Portuguese from Neilingding Island in 1521.

Tome Pires Commissioned to Secure
Trade Relations with China

A second Portuguese expedition to China was led in 1515 by Rafael Perestrelo, a relative of New World discoverer Christopher Columbus. Perestrelo sailed to the southern China coast and up the Pearl River for a considerable distance. This led to a decision in 1517 by Lopo Soares de Albergaria, the viceroy of Goa, to dispatch Tome Pires, a pharmacist by profession, as an ambassador to negotiate an official relationship with China and to secure permission for the Portuguese to settle on Chinese territory.

Pires, sailing with a fleet led by Fernão Peres de Andrade, reached Tamão (now Tuen-mun, a small island within the region of Hong Kong) in mid-August of 1517 before going on to Guangzhou [Canton], where he assigned Jorge de Mascarenhas to arrange trade agreements with local Chinese authorities. Pires was forced to wait in Guangzhou for two years before gaining permission to travel to the city of Nanjing for a meeting with Emperor Chang Te, who granted approval for him to journey to Beijing. Although the meeting in Nanjing was moderately successful, the death of Emperor Chang soon after this meeting was quickly followed by a reversal of the Chinese attitude towards Portugal's diplomatic efforts.

There were reasons for the change of the Chinese attitude. The Portuguese already had acquired Malacca by force, dethroning the sultan of Malacca, who subsequently sent a representative to China to protest the action. This protest came at an opportune time for the Malaccan envoy, because of some recent problems at Tamão between the aggressive Portuguese and Chinese. It seems the Portuguese, under the direction of Simão Peres de Andrade (brother of fleet captain Fernão Peres de Andrade, who had transported Tome Pires to Tamão en route to Guangzhou and Beijing) had constructed a fortifying palisade at Tamão without permission from the Chinese. In addition, Simão Peres de Andrade was accused of attacking Chinese ships in the area around Tamão. These actions were interpreted by the Chinese as an aggressive and open attempt by the Portuguese to occupy the island.

After learning of the actions of Simão Peres de Andrade at Tamão, the Chinese responded by arresting Tome Pires during his return trip from Beijing to Guangzhou. He was placed in a prison at Guangzhou, where he died in May 1524. Some 60 other Portuguese died in the Guangzhou prisons around this time.[4] Most of the Portuguese prisoners had been captured in 1522 during a violent skirmish with the Chinese, who overran and destroyed their Guangzhou trading center. In 1523, the Chinese issued a ban on all sea-trading between China and Portugal, hoping to persuade the Portuguese to return authority over Malacca to the dethroned sultan. Ignoring the directive about Malacca and the trade ban, however, the persistent Portuguese established another trading center at Lappa, a large island near Macau, from which they conducted business with obliging Chinese merchants through the remainder of the 1520s.

In 1530, the Chinese allowed foreign trading to resume at Guangzhou, but specifically prohibited any trading there by the Portuguese. In 1535, Portugal formally petitioned China to allow it to resume trading at Guangzhou, but its effort was unsuccessful. The Portuguese ignored the ban, however, and continued trading at other points along the southeastern China coast, mainly in Zhejiang and Fujian provinces. By 1540, becoming even more confident, the Portuguese were regularly spending winters at the tiny port of Ningbo on the south China coast. Then, in efforts to expand their trading, the Portuguese opened illegal trading centers upstream from Ningbo near the mouth of the Youngjiang River. They were now trading in earnest at the ports of Ningbo and Quanzhou, where they were still in an illegal position, but tolerated. China's trading merchants were also frustrated by their country's isolationist policies and wanted the benefits of trading with foreign countries.

Chu Yuan Takes Action Against Portuguese Traders

The Chinese, in a dramatic show of courage, finally managed to expel the Portuguese from their trading activities near Ningbo in 1544, at least temporarily. The ban on sea-trading with Portugal became even stronger in 1547 when Chu Yuan, the new governor of Zhejiang and Fujian provinces, was again ordered by the Chinese authorities to prohibit illegal trading in his region, and particularly any trading with the Portuguese. Even though China's leaders decided to forcefully ban the illicit trading, Chu's actions weren't entirely supported by local Chinese citizens, especially those living along the coast, whose lives and life-styles had been considerably improved through increased trading with the Portuguese.[5]

Supported by the official prohibition, Chu Yuan ordered an attack on Portuguese vessels at Ningbo in 1548 and destroyed their trading center there. The Portuguese then decided to move south to trading posts in Guangdong province, which they generally operated during the months of August to November. These annual trading centers were based during 1549 to 1553 at Shangchuan Island, and then during 1553 to 1557 at Lampacau, an island near Macau. Among the most desired items purchased at Lampacau were Chinese silks, which later became important in trading with Japan. The coastal traders were of course upset by Chu Yuan's 1548 actions of attacking Portuguese ships and forcibly strengthening China's ban on trading with foreigners. As a result, the traders complained loudly and effectively, subsequently forcing the dismissal of Chu Yuan as governor. This humiliating decision was blamed for Chu Yuan's suicide in 1549.

In a related event, which eventually became very important during Macau's golden age, Portuguese deserters "accidentally discovered" the country of Japan.[6] The Portuguese had already become aware of occasional Japanese traders at Malacca and also realized that numerous instances of Japanese piracy had led to a strict prohibition of trade between China and Japan. This meant a potentially lucrative opportunity for the Portuguese to act as middlemen in trade activities involving an exchange of desirable products, in particular silks and silver, between the two countries.

Following Chu Yuan's death, trading again was tolerated along the Fujian-Zhejiang coastal region, and the Portuguese turned further south of their destroyed trading center at Ningbo, eventually settling in 1555 at Macau's Haoching Bay, located on the eastern coast of the tiny peninsula. Their presence at Macau was somewhat more tolerated and was even welcomed by China following successful efforts by the Portuguese to reduce piracy in the South China Sea. Within a short time, Portuguese traders were even more firmly settled at Macau, which seemed to be acceptable to the Chinese. Another favorable factor for the Portuguese settlement at Macau was that their continued presence there (through informal agreements and sizable fees to local trading merchants) was not immediately announced to Chinese authorities in Beijing.

Thus, by the mid–1500s, Portugal's erratic trading relationship with China was finally becoming more solvent, leading to the establishment of the historic settlement of the Portuguese at Macau.

Chapter 2

The Portuguese Settle at Macau and Expand Trade with China

What value could this little toehold in China have possibly been [in the 1500s]? Today, it is hard to see the answer, but Macau's importance at the time was tremendous, simply tremendous, and it lasted for centuries, for centuries. —FATHER MANUEL TEIXEIRA, Portuguese priest in Macau[1]

The Portuguese, bolstered by their off-and-on trading successes of the early sixteenth century in Asia, became even bolder and more successful towards the middle of the century. Beginning in 1550, they began conducting business during annual trading seasons from temporary centers on the Chinese islands of Lampacau and Shangchuan, near the southern China coastal province of Guangdong.

With the quiet approval of local Chinese merchant-traders, the Portuguese erected simple mat-sheds for use as shelters against the weather, completed their trading, and then set off for either Malacca or Japan. In fact, it was the rapidly growing trade with Japan that encouraged the Portuguese to step up efforts to secure a more permanent trading base near Guangzhou. Such an agreement was reached in mid–1555 following several months of negotiation between Captain-Major Leonel de Sousa, who headed a Portuguese expedition of seventeen vessels from Goa to Japan, and Wang Po, a representative of Guangdong province and acting commander (the *haitao*) of the regional Chinese coast-guard fleet. The agreement between Leonel de Sousa and Wang Po, although verbal, allowed the Portuguese to continue their trading from the islands of Lampacau and Shangchuan and to resume trading at Guangzhou and other nearby ports.

Terms of the agreement were stated in a letter from Leonel de Sousa dated January 15, 1556, that was forwarded to the Infante Dom Luiz of the Portuguese monarchy in Lisbon. "In this manner I made peace," De Sousa wrote in his letter, noting his satisfaction that Portuguese traders could now "carry on their business as they please without being troubled."[2] The agreement came with a price: The Portuguese had to pay license fees, customs taxes, and a yearly lease sum (along with numerous well-placed gifts to their Chinese contacts), and they also had to allow monitoring of their activities by Chinese authorities. Thus, by 1555, the Portuguese were becoming firmly established at Macau and were gradually improving their trading activities with the Chinese. In any event, the agreement between Leonel de Sousa and the Chinese haitao, Wang Po, set the stage for legal Sino-Portuguese trade, and it led directly to a more permanent settlement of the Portuguese at Macau in 1557.

Much of the trade with China at this time centered around spices, silk, musk, ivory, porcelain, and aromatic woods, which, as noted by Friar Gaspar da Cruz in a 1556 letter, "a man may well live without."[3] Thus, much of the early trade with China, though small in volume, had great value and demand in terms of luxury and trading profits. Friar Gaspar characterized this luxury trade being conducted by Portugal as "so little in comparison of the great traffic of the country, that it almost remaineth as nothing and unperceived."[4]

One of the most enduring stories regarding the early Portuguese settlement at Macau arises from an incident in 1556 in which some 500 Portuguese participated in a sea battle against pirates off the southern coast of China. The Chinese were much impressed by the Portuguese effort to repel the pirates and began considering these "foreign devils" in a more favorable manner.

Early Days at Macau

There were only a few Chinese living at Macau when the Portuguese, with confidence and in rapidly growing numbers, began frequenting the tiny peninsula in 1555 and 1556. Following the agreement negotiated by Leonel de Sousa, the Portuguese traders began settling at Macau, successfully culminating the decades of temporary outposts, mixed hostilities, and diplomatic efforts. Many of the earliest Portuguese settlers at Macau were involved in sea-trading, and they were often accompanied by mistresses and slaves from Malacca and Goa.

One common sight for the early Portuguese visitors and settlers were small Chinese shrines and temples, which often served as combination sanctuaries and inns for travelers from mainland China seeking physical rest and spiritual peace. The Kun Iam Temple, for instance, is first mentioned in records surviving from the Yuan dynasty, which ranged from 1279 to 1368. The Lotus Temple, or Lin-Font, was a combination temple-inn established around 1500 near the present border of Macau and mainland China. The most famous of all, however, is the A-Ma Temple, which began as a shrine during the early years of the Ming (1368–1644) dynasty and developed into a temple during the reign of Wan-Li. By the mid-1500s, all three of these early main temples

Spiral coils of joss hang from the roof of Macau's Kun Iam Temple, which dates from the late Chinese Ming dynasty period. Dedicated to the Goddess of Mercy, it is a classic example of the art, architecture, and religious life-style of a traditional Chinese Buddhist temple.

were Buddhist, because Wan-Li was an ardent follower of Buddhism.[5] The A-Ma Temple, located at the southern entrance of Macau's Inner Harbor, looks out to sea from the southwestern edge of the peninsula and is nestled against an outcropping of granite on a hilly slope.

According to historian Cesar Guillen-Nuñez:

> The A-Ma Temple, more than any other temple in Macau, was intended to harmonize perfectly with nature in the classical Chinese manner. Its layout made use of a rugged hillock in a way that is unique to Macau. The pilgrim's spirit was uplifted as he climbed the rocky paths on which the four main pavilions are built, the jade-colored tiles of the roofs emerging amidst the yellow and green bamboo groves or the venerable old trees, whose colors changed with the seasons. The whole was set off by the flowing muddy waters of the river delta below."[6]

Most of the Chinese inhabitants at Macau in 1555 were involved with fishing. There was virtually no agriculture activity taking place on the peninsula at that time. The peninsula itself (often compared to early Rome) was dominated by hills (long-ago volcanoes), which the Portuguese subsequently named "Montanha Russa," "Guia," "Mong-Ha," "Penha," "Sao Geronimo," "Sao Paulo," "Patane," and "Dona Maria." More recently, the adjacent island-hill known as "Ilha Verde" (Green Island) was adjoined to the northwestern

The A-Ma Temple, Macau's most famous temple

portion of the peninsula through reclamation. These little mountains, combined with the surrounding islands, provided natural barriers against the wind and water, "configurating a geography which was destined to provide a haven for those who arrived at its shores."[7] At the northernmost part of the Macau peninsula was a narrow isthmus (just over a half-mile long) bordering the

The A-Ma Temple, a popular tourist attraction

mainland Chinese county of Zhongshan ("fragrant mountain"), actually a very large island in the Pearl River Delta. At times, the river waters moving into the sea along the east and west sides of Macau are quite still and muddy, which led to one early description of the area as "the Peninsula of the Sea Mirror."[8]

Bust of Luís de Camões, Portugal's epic poet

Luís de Camões Arrives in Macau

The Portuguese poet Luís de Camões was among the first official arrivals at Macau. Camões had gone to India in 1553, spent some time at Goa in 1554, where he distinguished himself by participating in a battle against forces of the king of Pimenta to successfully recapture an island along the Malabar Coast on behalf of the king of Cochin, who was allied to Portugal. He was assigned to Macau in 1556 as the Portuguese government official responsible for collecting and dispersing the effects of Portuguese citizens, absent or deceased. During his nearly three years at Macau, Camões composed his epic poem *Os Lusiadas* (*The Lusiads*), which told of Portugal's glorious history, including the significant sea voyages of Vasco da Gama to the Far East. Interestingly, *Os Lusiadas* contains no apparent reference to Macau, an exclusion which has defied explanation by historians.[9] Currently, one of the most popular tourist locations in Macau is the "Luís de Camões Grotto and Garden," located just east of the Inner Harbor. Over the centuries, this famous poet and his epic poem have achieved a high level of importance among Macau's international visitors, of whom most have probably never read *Os Lusiadas*.

Camões' assignment to Macau was ended when he incurred the wrath of a superior, who ordered him returned to Goa for trial. En route to Goa, however, the ship Camões was sailing on experienced problems and went down near the coast of Cambodia. He swam to shore carrying the only copy of his long manuscript above his head. Camões managed to secure accommodating treatment from local natives and spent several months making his way to Goa. He was held for a time because of his problems at Macau, but was released when a judge declined to uphold the charges. Camões returned to Lisbon in April 1570, and his *Os Lusiadas* was published in 1572, for which he received a modest pension from the Portuguese king. The pension was renewed in 1578, though he was living in near poverty when he died two years later in 1580.

Portuguese Macau Attracts Trading Merchants and Missionaries

Portuguese vessels sailing to Indian and Chinese ports during the early sixteenth century carried numerous trading merchants who negotiated purchases and sales, but they also carried pioneering Jesuit priests eager to spread the word of God to the people of the Chinese empire. It was a challenging prospect, one which they believed would truly be rewarding. The strong links between early trading merchants and missionaries were noted by a Portuguese Jesuit missionary named António Vieira in his book *History of the Future*: "If there were not merchants who go to seek for earthly treasures in the East and West Indies, who would transport thither the preachers who take heavenly treasures? The preachers take the Gospel and the merchants take the preachers."[10] Three of those missionaries accompanied Afonso de Albuquerque when he claimed Malacca as a Portuguese base in 1511. They were Álvaro Margulhão, Domingos de Sousa, and João Alemão. It is generally acknowledged that Álvaro Margulhão, who arrived on the South China coast in 1521, was the first Christian priest to visit China.[11] He later died there. Another pioneering priest was Estevao Nogueira, who was assigned in 1542 to Ningbo as the vicar of a Portuguese Christian community which may have numbered around 1,200 at the height of the annual trading seasons.[12]

One of Portugal's most famous priests was Father Francis Xavier, the "Apostle of the Far East," whose prestigious rise was assisted and encouraged by his strong and early professional relationship with St. Ignatius of Loyola, the noted founder of the Jesuit order known as the Society of Jesus. Father Xavier was assigned in the 1540s to conduct missionary work at Portuguese-dominated port regions of India and the Spice Islands. This missionary work resulted in thousands of conversions to the Catholic church and included courageous efforts to expose and denounce activities of local administrators and others which he declared unjust in their effect on the general population.

Following his inspiring successes in Goa, Malacca, and the Spice Islands, Father Xavier departed in April of 1549 for Japan, arriving in August at the Japanese port city of Kagoshima, and again he was especially influential in his efforts to introduce Catholicism to local inhabitants. Despite his success in spreading the religious philosophy of the Jesuit order, however, Father Xavier disagreed with certain elements of the activities and life-styles of the Buddhist monks in Japan and finally determined that perhaps his dream of converting the Far East might be better served from China. Father Xavier applied in 1551 for permission to enter China, and in 1552 he began sailing down the southernmost coast of China to await entry. He stopped at the island of Shangchuan, where the Portuguese then had a seasonal trading post. Rather suddenly, however, he was stricken with a fever, and he died on December 3, 1552, without realizing his highly ambitious missionary plans for China.

Father Xavier was originally buried on the island of Shangchuan, though his body was later moved to Malacca and then to its final resting place at Goa. Shangchuan subsequently became a popular attraction for visitors interested in the history of Father Xavier. The island was closed to tourists and visitors in 1949 by order of the Communist leadership of the People's Republic of China. The travel ban to Shangchuan Island was finally lifted in 1986. The achievements of Father Xavier provided considerable inspiration for others who followed in later years, hoping to continue working towards his goal of spreading Christianity in China. Five missionaries arrived in 1555 at Lampacau and Shangchuan islands, and Jesuit priest Melchior Nunes Barreto stopped briefly at Macau in 1555 en route to Japan. Another early visitor was Father Gaspar da Cruz, who stopped at Guangzhou in 1555. Also, a Spanish priest

St. Francis Xavier Chapel, located on Coloane Island, a popular pilgrimage destination dedicated to the Portuguese missionary who introduced Christianity to southern Japan.

named Father Gregorio Gonzalez arrived in Macau around 1557 and remained there for twelve years.[13]

Father Francis Xavier may have been given more credit than he deserved in the founding and settling of Macau by the Portuguese. Many believed the early agreements permitting the Portuguese to become established at Macau were actually a direct result of spiritual intervention initiated by Father Xavier rather than diplomatic efforts and superior military strength. As noted by Father Valignano in 1601: "The Portuguese took it that this license had been obtained through the prayers of Father Francis Xavier himself, it being of such great benefit not only for the Portuguese but also for Christianity in Japan and China.[14]

Early Influence of the Jesuit Order in Macau

The influence of the Jesuit order gradually developed during the early years of the Portuguese settlement at Macau, complementing the community with a strong Christian foundation, at least among the Portuguese merchant residents, their servants, and increasing numbers of converted Chinese. One indication of the heightened Christian influence was reflected in the number of recorded Catholics in Macau, totaling about 600 in 1561 and rising to 5,000 by 1568.[15] Several priests arrived soon after the 1557 "founding" of Macau, and their numbers increased in the early 1560s, as they arrived by sea on the annual trading voyages from Goa and Malacca. Another Jesuit, Father Baltasar Gago, arrived at Macau in May of 1561. Father Luís Fróis, a Jesuit who achieved recognition for his writings, arrived in 1562, as did Father John Baptist del Monte, who went on to Japan in 1563. In that same year of 1563, three more prominent Jesuits sailed from Goa to Macau—Brother André Pinto, Father Manuel Teixeira, and Father Francisco Perez. In the mid–1550s, Father João Soares, representing the bishop of Malacca, was named vicar of Macau's Church of St. Maria.

Another one of the influential early missionaries was Melchior Nunes Carneiro of Lisbon, a Jesuit priest who had first visited Macau in 1555 while en route to Japan and then returned to Macau in 1568. He was instrumental in establishing several medical and charitable institutions serving both Chinese and Portuguese. He also played a major role in the 1576 establishment of the diocese of Macau. Father Nunes Carneiro's official Jesuit title was "Apostolic Administrator of the Far East Missions." In 1569, he opened the Hermitage of our Lady of Hope (later renamed the Church of São Lázaro), a special institution for people afflicted with leprosy. He also founded Macau's Hospital of St. Raphael and helped develop smaller institutions such as the Santa Casa da Misericordia, with its stated purpose "to provide for all the poor."[16] Father Nunes Carneiro died in 1583.

The Misericordia is an ancient charitable institution peculiarly associated with the Portuguese Crown and the development of its colonies around the world. The Misericordia at Goa, long overlooked by historians, has been characterized as "one of the redeeming features of Portuguese imperialism in Asia.... In succoring the needy and oppressed, befriending the orphan, and guarding the patrimony of the widow and the fatherless, this organization performed a truly merciful task, and performed it very well."[17] The institution itself, originally founded in 1498 as the "Holy House of Mercy," was established at the request and support of Queen Dona Leonor of Portugal. The Misericordia at Goa, based on the same charitable principles as the Lisbon institution and supported almost entirely by private donations and bequests, was opened soon after the successful conquest of Goa in 1510 by Afonso de Albuquerque. The number of Misericordias in Portuguese Asia eventually totaled twenty, of which the Misericordia at Macau was the most important.[18]

Misericordias were administered by a brotherhood ranging up to 300 in number, guided by 14 primary responsibilities, of which 7 were spiritual in nature and 7 were related to day-to-day necessities.

The Santa Casa de Misericordia, the oldest institution in Macau, was founded in 1569 to provide for the poor, the sick, and orphaned children.

The seven spiritual responsibilities included:

1) Giving good advice
2) Teaching the ignorant
3) Consoling the sorrowful
4) Punishing evil-doers
5) Pardoning injuries received
6) Suffering our neighbor's shortcomings
7) Praying to God for the living and the dead

The seven practical responsibilities included:

1) Giving food to the hungry
2) Giving drink to the thirsty
3) Clothing the naked
4) Visiting the sick and prisoners
5) Giving shelter to the weary
6) Ransoming captives
7) Burying the dead[19]

There also were certain basic qualifications to belong to the Misericordia Brotherhood, whose members were primarily supposed to be "men of good conscience and repute, obedient to God, modest, charitable and humble."[20] Failure to meet any of the following qualifications could mean "instant expulsion on detection":

> 1) Purity of blood, without any taint of Moorish or Jewish origin
> 2) Freedom from ill repute in word and deed
> 3) Of a suitable age, and not under 30 years old if unmarried
> 4) Not suspect of serving the Misericordia for pay
> 5) Of sufficient intelligence and able to read and write
> 6) In sufficiently comfortable circumstances to obviate any temptation to embezzle the funds of the Misericordia, or any others to which they have access
> 7) To accompany only the Bier of the Misericordia and no other[21]

As the community of Macau developed, so did its religious institutions and churches. Through the financial support of the Jesuits, the Church of São Lourenço (St. Lawrence) and the Sé Cathedral were established during the 1560s. Our Lady of Hope was established in 1569, as was Our Lady of the Visitation, followed in 1580 by Our Lady of the Angels, in 1586 by Our Lady of Grace, and in 1587 by Our Lady of the Rosary. One of Macau's most distinguished architectural complexes, the Seminary and Church of São Paulo (St. Paul) was established by the Jesuit order in the early years of the seventeenth century. The Seminary of São José (St. Joseph) was established in 1728 to train missionaries for assignment in mainland China.

Father Matteo Ricci Arrives in Macau

Father Matteo Ricci, an Italian-born member of the Jesuit order since 1571, reached Macau in 1582, and rose to become one of the best-known and most influential of the Jesuits involved in Chinese missionary work. Father Ricci had achieved early recognition as an educator, astronomer, scientist, and mathematician at the Jesuit College in Rome and Coimbra University in Portugal. He was assigned to Goa in 1578 and then went on to Macau in 1582 and finally to Beijing in 1601. Father Ricci's successful efforts in China were enhanced by his proficiency in speaking Chinese, which he had learned at the Seminary of São Paulo in Macau. The Seminary of São Paulo, founded by the Jesuits in 1594, was expanded into a university institution in 1597, offering degrees in theology, rhetoric, philosophy, humanities, and the languages of Latin and Greek.

After much preparation, Ricci and fellow Jesuit missionary Diogo de Pantoja traveled to Beijing in 1601 for a meeting with the Chinese emperor Wan-li, who granted Ricci permission to establish a Christian mission in China. His successful meeting was probably aided by his gifts, which included two chiming clocks which apparently intrigued the emperor.[22] Ricci and other

Macau's most famous landmark is the façade of the Church of São Paulo (St. Paul), all that remains from a disastrous fire in 1835.

Jesuit missionaries were well aware of the value of gifts to their Chinese hosts, especially gifts related to their scientific and intellectual interests. The range of these gifts included glass prisms, clocks, gauges, horological instruments, astronomical devices, and mathematical instruments, plus religious, literary, geographical, and architectural books.[23]

Because of his facility with the Chinese language, his outstanding background in astronomy and science, and his familiarity with Chinese literary classics, Ricci was generally accepted by his Chinese counterparts in Beijing.

The graceful façade of St. Dominic's Church in Macau, first established by the Portuguese Dominicans in the 1590s, reconstructed in 1767, and extensively renovated in the 1990s.

Another helpful factor was that he adapted the garments generally worn by Chinese Confucian scholars. Over the next few years, besides his preaching and religious lectures, Ricci also wrote and translated into Chinese a number of books focusing on science and religion. His friendships with Chinese scholars helped him produce these translations. Some of Ricci's assistants assisted in correcting the Chinese calendar, while others were officially appointed as state astronomers by Emperor Wan-li. The titles of Ricci's books include *Elements of Geometry of Euclides*, *Work on Trigonometry*, *Treatise on Geometry*, and *Treatise on the Celestial Bodies*.

Matteo Ricci was regarded not only as an "outstanding cultural link between China and the West," but also as "the pioneer of European science in China."[24] He also developed a map of the world for the Chinese, diplomatically placing the Chinese Empire at the center. Following Ricci's death in May 1610, other Jesuit missionaries assigned to Beijing faithfully continued his work in astronomy, science, mathematics, and education. Despite the inroads made by Matteo Ricci, however, the Chinese remained suspicious of the intentions of the missionaries, particularly their insistence on the exclusivity of Catholicism. Many missionaries suffered degrees of persecution during their assignments to China. This persecution was directed principally towards the Christian missionaries, although the Chinese leadership also maintained close regulation on Buddhism, Taoism and, to a lesser degree, Neo-Confucianism. Even so, the Jesuit order continued to send missionaries into China on a regular basis, virtually without competition for many years. Other religious orders soon began sending their own representatives, however, as the Dominicans arrived in 1631, the Franciscans in 1633, the Augustinians in 1680, and the Paris Foreign Missions in 1683.

The production of books was greatly facilitated by a new printing press with movable type that was installed at the Jesuit College in 1588. The Chinese, already interested in Macau's development of new types of firearms and the Portuguese methodology regarding artillery, regarded this press as "a radical improvement on the original Chinese invention of woodblock printing."[25]

Chapter 3
Portugal Establishes a Colony at Macau

One of the most fabulous stories in the Far East is that of a small place on the South China coast, the name of which only entered history in 1555—Macau. —ROLF DIETER CREMER[1]

The year 1557 is generally acknowledged as the formal settlement date for the Portuguese of their colony at Macau, but the Portuguese actually began frequenting the tiny peninsula in 1553. The number of visits rose sharply after the 1555 verbal agreement between Captain-Major Leonel de Sousa and Wang Po, the Guangdong Province *haitao,* an agreement which cleared the way for resumption of foreign trading at Guangzhou.

Even so, the Chinese retained considerable control over these people they characterized as "foreign devils" by constructing in 1573 a barrier wall with one gate (the "Portas do Cerco") across the narrow isthmus to prevent their access into mainland China. In this manner, the Chinese retained tight physical control over the little peninsula, along with strict supervision of legal and financial matters.

It is also generally acknowledged that early permission for the Portuguese presence at Macau required a sizable amount of unrecorded "fees" passed along to Chinese officials. These fees were subsequently replaced by an annual rental payment, thereby legalizing the granting of permission for the Portuguese to use Macau as a base for their trading operations. The only exception from China's absolute jurisdiction in early Macau related to matters involving Portuguese subjects, which were generally dealt with by the Portuguese themselves. This virtual Chinese jurisdiction over Macau continued until 1849, when Portugal demanded the right to resolve all matters within the confines of Macau. The jurisdictional question was finally resolved by the Protocol of Lisbon in 1887, in which Macau was formally recognized by China as a territory of Portugal.

The famed Portas do Cerco, or Barrier Gate, where people have crossed between Macau and mainland China for more than four centuries.

Macau Becomes a Major Stop on Trading Voyages

After the "founding" of Macau by the Portuguese in 1557, Portuguese trading in the Far East began to expand considerably, with Macau as the primary stop on three major voyage routes between the West and the Far East. These voyages included (1) Macau to Malacca to Goa to Lisbon, (2) Guangzhou to Macau to Nagasaki, and (3) Macau to Manila to Mexico. Thus, for the next 80 years, Macao was the shining centerpiece of highly profitable voyages linking Portugal with India, China, Japan, the Philippines, and Mexico.

Trading ships left Lisbon in March and arrived at Goa in September, carrying such European goods as cut glass, mirrors, decorative items, metalware, and wines. After loading cotton textiles at Goa, the vessels departed the following spring for Malacca, where they took on muslin and high-quality cotton from local merchants. When they arrived at the Spice Islands, they traded the cotton textiles for spices (especially pepper). The ships then headed for Macau, generally arriving by May, pushed by the late spring southwest monsoon winds. When they arrived at Macau, Chinese customs officials inspected the goods of each vessel and collected taxes and other fees. Items designated for the Portuguese at Macau (wines, textiles, oil, and consumer goods) were then unloaded and the ships proceeded to Guangzhou to purchase porcelain, metal goods, and silk before returning to Macau en route to Nagasaki in Japan.

The Guangzhou-Macau-Nagasaki voyage was highly profitable and was conducted exclusively under the administration of a captain-major appointed by the Portuguese Crown. It was truly an example of supply-and-demand. The Japanese wanted quality Chinese silks, and the Chinese wanted Japanese silver. Most of the trading conducted by Portuguese ships between China and Japan during the years 1560 to 1640 concentrated on this lucrative exchange of silk and silver. The third major voyage, from Macau to Manila to Mexico, focused largely on transporting a variety of goods from China and Macau to Manila in exchange for silver coins.

Meanwhile, the population of Macau climbed from about 400 in 1557 to an estimated 900 in 1564; the latter number included Portuguese merchants and Chinese residents along with African and Indian slaves and servants who had been transported to Macau by the Portuguese. By the end of the 1560s, Macau's population had swelled to nearly 5,000.

One major event during the late 1560s occurred in July of 1568 when the Portuguese successfully battled an attack by pirates. The pirate force estimated at between 3,000 and 4,000 men was armed with 1,500 guns and transported on about 100 vessels.[2] Following this attack, the Portuguese requested and received permission from the Chinese to construct fortifications at Macau as a defense against possible future attacks by pirates.

King Philip II of Spain Rules over New Dual Monarchy

Meanwhile, Portugal's King Dom Sebastião was killed in 1578 while participating with Portuguese military forces at the battle of Alcácer-Quibir in Morocco. Dom Sebastião, who was only in his mid-twenties at the time of his death, had been "idealistic but irresponsible."[3] According to historian Cesar Guillen-Nuñez: "Even at age 24, his only reaction to Portugal's dilemma was a determined effort to escape reality. He roamed the Kingdom with his court, settling nowhere, like a medieval knight in search of a cause."[4] Upset over reports that the Moors were openly harassing coastal towns in southern Portugal, "Sebastião became obsessed with a private scheme to defeat the infidel."[5]

Despite strong advice against military reprisals, King Dom Sebastião went to Morocco in June 1578, leading "a badly organized army of 24,000 made up of Portuguese soldiers and Italian, Spanish and German mercenaries. At the plain of Alcácer-Quibir, the enemy, outnumbering and brilliantly outmaneuvering the Portuguese army, massacred most of them. Amidst the carnage lay the body of Dom Sebastião."[6] His death led to the establishment in 1580 of a dual monarchy, with the leadership of both Spain and Portugal given to King Philip II of Spain, a grandson of a previous Portuguese king named Dom Manoel I. This dual monarchy continued for 60 years, spanning three kings named Philip, and adversely affected the economic and political ties of Portugal to its Far East colonies.

Portugal's famous poet Luís de Camões is often recalled for an agonizing statement which he wrote in a letter before his death: "I loved my country so much that I shall die with her."[7] Within the next few months, King Philip II's armies entered Portugal to establish the Union of Crowns and Camões died, "poverty-struck, according to every testimony, and certainly heartbroken, on June 10, 1580."[8]

Macau and the Union of Crowns

Macau's "golden age" spanned the decades from 1580 to 1640. It was a time of great promise, great prosperity, and great expansion of world trading—with Macau and its unique location playing a significant role. This also was the period of the "Union of Crowns," the dual monarchy in which Macau was subject to Spanish rule.

Although the Union of Crowns uniting Spain and Portugal was formally established in 1580, the news of the change did not reach Macau until 1582. Upon receiving the announcement from a Spanish priest dispatched from Manila, Macau's captain-major, Dom João de Almeida, promptly wrote a long letter to the governor of Manila saying that he had been properly advised that King Philip II of Spain was now also the crown head of Portugal and that he declared "his willingness to recognize the dual monarchy."[9] In his letter, De Almeida described Macau as being "relatively large and prosperous" and cautioned the new Spanish rulers against disrupting the trading voyages between Manila and Macau in order to avoid causing problems with China, upon which Macau was dependent for many foodstuffs and supplies.[10] Despite Dom João de Almeida's "willingness to recognize," historian C. R. Boxer notes that news of the accession of King Philip II arrived in Macau at the end of May 1582 but authorities delayed taking the oath of allegiance to their new monarch until December 18, "and even then they dispensed with the prescribed public solemnities for 'fear of the Mandarins and other Chinese dignitaries.'"[11]

Macau's first legislative body, known as the Senado da Camara (Municipal Senate), was established in 1583, possibly at the urging of Father Nunes Carneiro, who died that year after successfully establishing several charitable institutions in Macau. Another influential supporter of the Senado da Camara was Dom Leonardo de Sá, who was installed in 1583 as the first bishop of the diocese of Macau.

The Macau diocese had been formally created in January 1576 through a papal bull issued by Pope Gregory XIII. The diocese originally had juris-

Leal Senado building in Macau's main plaza

diction over a wide region of the Far East, including Japan, Formosa, Korea, and Indochina. Japan was removed from the Macau diocese in 1588 through the creation of the diocese of Funai, later the city of Oita in Kyushu, which was given jurisdiction over all of Japan.[12] Upon founding the diocese of Macau, the Vatican pledged to establish more than 600 dioceses in Asia.[13] The prophetic projection was stated by a Spanish Jesuit, Father Alfonso Sanchez, when he read the papal bull creating the Macau diocese. Over the next 360 years, more than 600 dioceses were in fact created in Asia.[14] Through this early foundation in Macau, the Jesuits and other denominations spread their gospel to the Koreans, Japanese, and Chinese. The church also played a significant part in the development of science and education in the Far East, largely through its activities at the Seminary of São Paulo in Macau, which had been established shortly after the Portuguese were allowed to settle in Macau and was expanded into a major influential institution of learning in the 1580s.

Macau's Senate was actually a form of democracy in which local citizens (*moradores*) voted to elect six representatives, who in turn would nominate three persons as aldermen (*vereadores*). The three aldermen, along with three legal officials and a secretary, formed the Senate. The Senado da Camara was the true governing body of Macau, assuming the role of the captain-general, whose responsibilities then became limited to military matters. Senate members served three-year terms, with the presidency of the body passing to each of the aldermen for a one-year period. Issues before the Senate were debated in sessions open to the public and were then decided by a majority vote. Expenditures approved by the Senate, such as defense projects and diplomatic missions, were financed almost entirely through the collection of import and export duties on goods passing through Macau.[15]

In addition to the Senate and the captain-major, Macau also was governed for a time by a judicial representative known as an *ouvidor*, whose functions were sometimes confused with those of the captain-majors. The ouvidor, serving by appointment of the Portuguese Crown, had jurisdiction over criminal matters during the times when the captain-majors were away from Macau on their trading voyages.[16] The legislature was renamed the Loyal Senate (Leal Senado da Camara) in 1809 after it had offered some military assistance to the Portuguese Crown leadership during a period of unrest when the court was forced to flee to Brazil.[17]

In 1586, upon formal request of the Senado da Camara, the viceroy of Portuguese India issued a decree which formally declared Macau to be a "city," with the same "privileges, liberties, honors and pre-eminences" as the Portuguese city of Évora.[18] Until then, Macau had been known as the "Settlement or Port of the Name of God in China." The new classification, approved in January 1587 by King Philip II of Spain and Portugal, designated Macau as "City of the Name of God in China" (Cidade de Nome de Deus da China).

Portuguese Trading Voyages in the East

Trading conducted by the Portuguese expanded to a grand scale during the early years of Macau's golden age. For many years the trading ships were giant "carracks" (nãos do trato) capable of carrying several tons of goods in their annual voyages from Goa (in Portuguese India) to Macau to Japan, back to Macau, and then to Malacca and back to Goa. The voyage, always dependent on monsoon winds, usually required about 18 months or more, sometimes as long as three years.

The oversized carrack was commanded by a captain-major, a *fidalgo*[19] whose profits from a successful voyage on the Goa-Macau-Nagasaki-Malacca run could amount to a considerable fortune, generally enough to give him wealth sufficient to last a lifetime. Captain-majors had divided responsibilities, commanding their trading fleets while at sea and overseeing activities of Macau when in port, generally during the monsoon period, which could last for several months. Although captain-majors were appointed for the Japan voyage by the Portuguese Crown, they could sell their rights to the appointment or auction the rights to the highest bidder, which later became a frequent practice in Goa.

The term *fidalgos*, once limited to persons with aristocratic ancestry, began taking on a broader meaning after the Portuguese began exploring and colonizing in the fifteenth century. By the time Macau was established in the mid–sixteenth century, the term *fidalgos* referred to leading Crown administrators, merchants, missionaries, and sailing fleet commanders such as captain-majors and captain-generals. As noted by historian C. R. Boxer: "Once around the Cape of Good Hope, every Portuguese gave himself the airs and graces of a *fidalgo*."[20]

The first phase of the voyage, from Goa to Malacca, would usually leave in midspring, perhaps in April or May, with a cargo of Portuguese wines, scarlet cloth, calico, cotton piece-goods, Flemish clocks, glassware, crystal, woolens, and Indian chintzes. In Malacca, some of the goods would be exchanged for items such as deerhides and sharkskins (from Siam), sandalwood and spices, a valuable trading commodity at that time because of their demand in Europe. Sandalwood, in demand throughout much of Asia, was derived from the "santalum album," a small tree which flourished in the Lesser Sunda Islands, which included the ports of Solor and Timor. It had varied uses and purposes, ranging from body ointments to bathing lotions, scents and essences, medical treatments and cosmetics; it was also carved for statues, coffins, wood objects, and furniture.[21] The demand for sandalwood also brought enormous profits. Bishop F. Pedro da Silva of Cohin, in a letter written in 1590, said the profit rate of the sandalwood trade from Macau to China at that time was 100 percent. And this increased to between 150 and 200 percent by 1630.[22]

After Malacca, the carrack (aided by northeast monsoon winds) would sail to Macau, where it would make port for several months, often close to a year. While the large carrack remained at anchor in Macau, smaller ships, lighters known as "lanteas," would sail up the Pearl River from Macau to Guangzhou to purchase finished and raw silks from Chinese suppliers. The silks were then taken by barge to Macau and placed in larger vessels for transporting to Goa, Japan, and other locations. High profits from the Japan voyage were derived mostly from the high demand there for Chinese silks, which would be exchanged for silver bullion.[23] Upon return to Macau, the silver would be removed from the vessels and used to finance purchases of silk in advance of voyages scheduled in the following year. While in Macau, the ships would also take on porcelain, ivory, pearls, gold, musk, and Chinese silks for eventual sale in Goa. Besides the rich cargoes of silver, gold, and silk, the giant carracks occasionally transported peacocks, Bengal tigers, and Arabian horses.[24]

These trading ventures to Guangzhou were always accompanied by generous gifts or large sums of money to leading authorities, usually the city's viceroy or the governor, both upon arrival and upon departure. It was a necessary business expense designed to ensure permission for the traders to deal with the Chinese merchants. The Guangzhou trading fairs were conducted twice each year, in January and June; traders brought back goods to load onto the large carrack, which usually arrived at Macau between June and August. The next phase of the journey would begin the following summer (with the southwest monsoon), when the carrack, with its cargo of goods from China, would depart from Macau for Nagasaki, a voyage requiring from two weeks to a month. After unloading its cargo of goods from India and China, the carrack would take on silver bullion (and sometimes gold) from Japan, along with such "curiosities" as furniture, gold-leaf paper screens, lacquered cabinets, crafted boxes, kimonos, and swords.[25]

The oversized, slow-moving carracks, generally ranging from 800 to 12,000 tons or more, were able to transport great amounts of cargo. But they also were highly vulnerable to damage or sinking during violent storms and were easy targets for the aggressive Dutch, whose frequent capture of the ships at sea forced the Portuguese to begin using smaller and faster ships known as "galiotas" in 1618. The swift-moving galiotas, ranging from 200 to 400 tons, became the primary vessel for the Portuguese trading merchants for the rest of the seventeenth century and most of the eighteenth century.[26]

In later years, copper also became one of the major exports from Japan. The copper became vital in the casting of bronze cannons at Goa. Its use became even more important after 1629 in Macau at the noted gun-foundry of Manuel Tavares Bocarro, whose production of heavy weapons dominated the industry for two decades.

One of the main reasons why the Portuguese traders profited from these voyages was that China had prohibited direct trade with Japan, thereby allowing the Portuguese the good fortune of acting as middlemen. Macau itself enjoyed a regular flow of revenue through a *caldeirao*, a three-percent tax levy which the Portuguese assessed on profits earned from the Japanese voyage; this tax was used to finance the administrative needs of the city.

Portugal Benefits Through China Ban on Trade with Japan

China's "favoritism" towards the Portuguese in the early 1600s was in large part a result of its decades-long ban against direct trade with Japan; China maintained that the Japanese were behind most of the piracy which occurred along the China coast. The result for the Portuguese was a virtual monopoly of trade in products desired by China and Japan. This trading domination also effectively hampered persistent efforts by the Dutch and British for trading with China in the early 1600s.

For many years, the basis of the highly lucrative trading routine involved the ports of Macau, Guangzhou, and Nagasaki, providing a regular exchange of Japan's copper and silver for China's gold and silks. In addition, at least for a brief time, a two-way voyage between Macau and Manila added to the trade. Another profitable commodity was tobacco, which grew in popularity as the Chinese acquired increasing desire and demand. Besides all the regular trading exchange of copper, gold, silver, silks, and tobacco, the Portuguese also brought both religion and firearms to China and Japan. Finally, the Japanese became concerned about the long-term intentions of Portugal and Spain and began persecuting Japanese Christians. These concerns led to Japan's complete prohibition against foreign trade in 1637, which shut off what had been a lucrative source of income for Portuguese traders for nearly a century.

Meanwhile, in 1635 the British began making progress in their pursuit of trade with China when the English East India Company sent a British vessel to Guangzhou, supported by a squadron of British ships under the command of Captain John Weddell, an aggressive, blustery, and confident Yorkshireman. The fleet arrived at Macau in June 1637, where it experienced a cool reception from the Portuguese, and it continued up the Pearl River on its journey to Guangzhou. The Chinese at Guangzhou promptly detained six British merchants, but promised to release them when Weddell agreed to leave. Nevertheless, "after 'a cross and costly voyage,' Weddell's ships were able to collect a reasonable cargo, 600 tons, mainly of sugar ('very good, smelling like roses'), but also green ginger, cloves, gold and porcelain, which was as much as he might have expected."[27]

The Trading Fairs of Guangzhou

From the founding of Macau in 1557, the Portuguese enjoyed a fragile and highly regulated trade relationship with China, but it was, nevertheless, a relationship that other nations such as Japan, Holland, and Great Britain were unable to secure until well into the seventeenth century. Relations between China and Portugal, already restrictive, tightened further in the 1620s, however, when the Chinese began giving the Portuguese trading access to China's products only at Guangzhou and only twice a year at "trading fairs" in January and June.

In preparation for these trading fairs, several influential and wealthy Portuguese merchants from Macau would travel up the Pearl River to a small island near Guangzhou and request permission from provincial authorities to initiate trading negotiations. This request was accompanied by a sizable gift to the person responsible for granting such permission. After gaining permission, the Portuguese representatives would spend up to five months contracting, negotiating and purchasing gold, porcelain, metals, silk piecegoods, raw silk, and other products. The traders, supported by their contracts, would then negotiate with Chinese merchants for the latter to produce agreed-upon quantities of goods, particularly of the silk products, and then the traders would petition local authorities (to whom they gave more gifts) to open the trading fair officially. Following an official announcement that the trading fair was open, all Chinese merchants were then allowed to make contact with the Portuguese representatives and offer their merchandise and other products for possible sale.

With the Portuguese representatives overseeing the trading exchanges, the purchased products were loaded onto small vessels for the return trip down the Pearl River to Macau. Before departing, however, the Portuguese had to request permission to leave, which required more gifts. They also had to pay duty fees on their cargo before finally being allowed to depart in a convoy of ten to fifteen small vessels, all of them well guarded by armed soldiers to protect them against pirates during the journey back to Macau.

Meanwhile, the population of Macau at the beginning of the 1600s had risen to several thousand, of whom about one thousand were Portuguese. The population also included local Chinese, along with Japanese and mixed-race individuals from Malacca, plus many Indian, Malaysian, and African slaves serving their Portuguese masters. Many of the local Chinese were associated directly with the trading profession. In addition, some worked the streets as hawkers, while others were employed as servants and laborers.

Historian Austin Coates, in his 1978 book *A Macao Narrative*, offers a colorful description of Macau as it might have appeared around 1600:

> Trees had grown up on the two southern hills of Barra and Penha; high-walled gardens surrounded a few large houses and churches on the ridge, the gentle slope separating the two harbors. Around the bay of the Outer Harbor, the Praia Grande was lined with well-built stone houses. Approached from the open sea, this long crescent of buildings with squat towers and low domes of classical churches rising behind them, so gave the appearance of a Mediterranean city that it was difficult to imagine oneself in China.[28]

One of the vital aspects of life in Macau in the early 1600s concerned the medical work of the Jesuits' St. Raphael's Hospital, whose doctors and physicians often treated patients without adequate funds to pay for their treatment. Nor was this "open-door" policy limited to the poor and needy; it was occasionally extended across China's border to Beijing in response to medical needs of Chinese leaders of the time.[29] Portuguese physicians in Macau also took it upon themselves to gather and publish books "describing the herbs used by the Chinese and other Oriental peoples, in an attempt to acquire some knowledge of Chinese and Oriental pharmacopoeia."[30]

Chapter 4

Dutch Attacks
Threaten Macau

The guns at Monte Fort [in Macau], today forever pointed at some invisible enemy, remind us that by the turn of the [seventeenth] century, war—often in the form of sudden raids from the sea—had become prevalent in the Iberian world, and was as much a part of life as the plague or the Inquisition. —CESAR GUILLEN-NUÑEZ[1]

The Portuguese settlement which developed at Macau in the late 1500s was envied greatly by other European nations, especially England and Holland, who both were becoming more and more aggressive in their efforts to develop trading with China. The emerging commercial growth of the Netherlands, especially after the establishment of the Dutch East Asia Company (Vereenigde Oost-Indische Compagnie, or VOC) in 1602, gave the Dutch heightened confidence and interest in carving out a share of worldwide trading from the dominating Portuguese and Spanish traders. These persistent efforts by the Dutch also gave competitive encouragement to the development of worldwide trading by the English.

Differences between Portugal and Holland took a dramatic and violent turn in 1601 when the Portuguese captured 17 Dutch seamen on a vessel near the coast of Macau. The Portuguese accused the Dutch seamen of participating earlier in an attack by a small armed fleet on a Portuguese trading post in the Moluccan port of Tidore. The captured Dutch prisoners were subsequently "barbarously murdered, despite a unanimous last-minute conversion to Catholicism."[2]

Macau thus became a prime target for Holland. The Dutch retaliated with some minor exploratory attacks on Macau in 1602 and 1603, apparently with heightened resolve to drive out the Portuguese from the tiny Chinese peninsula, which they envisioned as their own future Far East base for the lucrative trade routes between China and Japan. Bolstered by increasing self-confidence, the Dutch formally requested permission to trade at Guangzhou in 1604 and 1607, only to be turned down by the Chinese leadership. Pinning blame on the Portuguese for these setbacks, the Dutch stepped up their attacks on Macau from the sea, hoping to take over the tiny peninsula as their own Asian possession and to use it as a base for trading with both China and Japan. Realizing the Dutch intentions required serious defensive efforts, the Portuguese constructed a wall in 1606 which completely surrounded the Jesuits' Madre de Deus College and Seminary of São Paolo. After a few more small attempts at capturing Macau, the Dutch mounted a major attack in 1607 that was successfully turned back by the Portuguese.

A measure of relief in the conflict between the Dutch and Portuguese over Macau was promised in 1609 with the signing of the Truce of Antwerp between the Netherlands and Spain. The document pledged twelve years of peace, but the Dutch continued to challenge Portugal's trading domination in Asia and to threaten Macau's uneasy existence as a Portuguese trading base. This led to more defensive efforts on the part of the Portuguese, who constructed the São Tiago fortification and closed entry to Macau's primary streets.

By 1609, the Dutch had established a trading outpost at the small Japanese fishing village of Hirado. Even with this foothold, however, the Dutch were unable to loosen the Portuguese domination of trading between Macau and Nagasaki. Attempting the same backdoor approach, British traders also maintained a trading outpost at Hirado during the years 1613–23. Both nations were effectively shut out of trading with China by the Portuguese, who profited especially from their ability to provide Japan with regular shipments of raw silk and silk fabrics from China.

Unable to develop trading arrangements in Chinese ports, the Dutch were forced to continue dealing with tiny trading posts along the Indian seacoast. In addition, they captured a modest amount of trading goods from Chinese and Portuguese vessels in the China Sea. Although their primary targets were Chinese and Portuguese vessels, the Japanese began protesting that the Dutch were acting as pirates, not traders.

The 1622 Attack on Macau by the Dutch

After several more minor attacks against Macau during the twelve-year course of the Truce of Antwerp, which expired in 1621, the Dutch mounted a significant invasion in 1622. Although the 1622 incursion was seemingly well organized and was carried out almost according to plan, it also was repulsed, and in a manner that thoroughly embarrassed the militaristic-minded invaders. Plans for the invasion began to unfold in Batavia around a fleet of eight ships commanded by Captain Cornelis Reijersen, who was ordered to incorporate other vessels when possible and to secure a permanent base on the south China coast. The possibility of actually attacking Macau was a matter to be decided by Captain Reijersen.[3]

The fleet arrived near Macau on June 21, 1622, where it was joined by two other Dutch vessels and two British ships. Altogether, Reijersen now had 13 ships and 1,300 men under his command. The two British ships subsequently withdrew from the group, however, after being advised their crews would not be permitted to keep anything looted from the Portuguese colony.[4]

Reijersen assigned three men and a Chinese guide to go ashore on June 22 to determine whether the residents of Macau would fight, surrender, or remain neutral if the Dutch were to put on a show of force. The four men, unable to make any determination, returned to their ship. On June 23, Reijersen and some of his senior officers rowed close to shore in a launch to survey possible landing sites along the eastern portion of the tiny peninsula; they finally decided to send the bulk of their military force to Cacilhas Beach on the following day. As a diversion, three ships anchored off the southeastern coast of Macau began bombarding the São Francisco battery and surrounding area, attempting to distract attention from their intended landing invasion farther north at Cacilhas Beach. According to historian C. R. Boxer: "During this artillery duel, the Dutch crews shouted to the battery's defenders that next day they would be masters of Macau, and would rape the women after killing all the men over twenty years old."[5] The bombardment ended at sunset, with the three Dutch ships moving away from shore, but the Dutch "celebrated the expected victory by blowing trumpets and beating drums all night."[6]

Macau's captain-major, Lopo Sarmento de Carvalho, spent the night visiting his forts, reminding his defenders, who included volunteer Portuguese citizens and a sizable number of Negro slaves, that they could expect no mercy from the Dutch invaders. He also made clear that they could not expect refuge with the local Chinese, since most of them had already fled the city.[7] As expected, two Dutch ships renewed their bombardment of the São Francisco battery at daybreak on June 24, the feast day of St. John the Baptist. The Portuguese defenders managed to cause serious damage to one of the ships, which had to be removed from the area. About two hours after sunrise, 32 launches carrying 800 men landed at Cacilhas Beach, northeast of the main section of Macau. They went ashore under protective fire from two ships, plus a thick blanket of smoke conveniently produced by "drifting smoke from a barrel of damp gunpowder which had been fired to windward—perhaps one of the earliest instances of the tactical use of a smokescreen."[8]

The 800 invading military combatants met a defensive force of 150 Eurasians and Portuguese, one of whom fired a musketshot into the smokescreen and hit the leader of the Dutch invaders in the stomach, forcing him to be returned to his ship. The Dutch, under a replacement senior officer, managed to rout the Macau defenders from their trenches bordering Cacilhas Beach, but at least 40 of the invaders were killed during the landing. After assigning several dozen men to guard their launches at Cacilhas Beach, about 600 Dutch invaders continued working their way towards the center of Macau, skirmishing with the retreating Macau defenders as they went and firing their muskets with "precision and dexterity."[9]

As the Dutch moved closer, they were fired upon from the unfinished cathedral of São Paulo with a large cannon manned by Father Jeronimo Rho, an Italian Jesuit and mathematician. One of Father Rho's cannonballs landed directly in a barrel of gunpowder "which exploded in the midst of the Dutch formation with devastating results."[10] The fortuitous cannonball hit disrupted the advance of the Dutch, who withdrew briefly and then decided to advance against a different hill guarded only by some thirty defenders. The Dutch were unable to progress because of the natural rocky protection on the hill, however, and were perhaps short on gunpowder; they withdrew again and decided to return to their ships.

When the Macau defenders realized the Dutch were retreating, they took up the chase. Back at Cacilhas Beach, the guards of the launches panicked at seeing the retreating Dutch invaders and began moving their boats into the ocean without waiting for their passengers. As a result, "many of those who escaped the cold steel of the Portuguese were drowned or shot down in the sea. So complete was the panic, that the entire force would probably have been exterminated, save for the fact that many of the Negro slaves abandoned the pursuit of the flying foe in order to strip and plunder the bodies of the dead."[11] The retreating Dutch also abandoned hundreds of weapons in their rush to return to their ships.

Accounts of casualties have varied according to different sources. The Portuguese claimed they had killed more than 300 of the Dutch invaders, though the official Dutch version showed 136 killed and 126 wounded. Four Portuguese and 2 Spanish defenders died, and perhaps 20 defenders were wounded. Several Portuguese slaves also were wounded in the skirmishes, but the number was never accurately determined.

Almost immediately after the Dutch were chased off the shores of Macau and back to their ships, the Portuguese ordered freedom for all slaves held by Macau residents as a reward for their assistance. Seven years after the battle, in March 1629, the Union of Crowns bestowed a knighthood on Lopo Sarmento de Carvalho for his role in leading the Macau defenders to victory over the Dutch.

Macau's defenses were strengthened considerably during the 1620s and 1630s, beginning with the arrival in 1623 of Macau's first governor, Francisco Mascarenhas, who was "determined to turn Macau into a great fortress."[12] Using his own money, Mascarenhas expanded existing forts, built a new fort on Guia Hill and constructed a series of walls linking the forts. He also initiated construction of a cannon and gun foundry, which was established in 1623 by Manuel Tavares Bocarro. A gunpowder factory also was established, which enjoyed considerable success in dealing with several Chinese regional militant groups. São Tiago was developed further as Macau's second major fort

The Penha Church and adjoining Bishop's Residence crown the crest of Macau's Penha Hill. It was originally built by Portuguese sailors in 1622 who believed their prayers for help against threats by Dutch marauders had been answered.

and was completed in 1629. Other fortifications included Nossa Senhora do Bomparto in 1622, São Francisco in 1629, Monte Fortress in 1626, and Guia Fortress in 1638. The fortresses were connected by a series of walls, and each included a chapel, reflecting the strong influence of Christianity in the development of Macau by the Portuguese.

After failing in their 1622 invasion of Macau, the Dutch decided to establish a base on one of the Pescadores Islands near Taiwan (Formosa). From this new base, the Dutch continued to threaten Macau with occasional attacks, but these forays were always rejected by the Portuguese, who had gradually developed better defenses. The Dutch also began developing modest trading with small coastal ports along southeastern China. This continued until Chinese authorities finally forced the Dutch to leave the Pescadores Islands in 1624, after which they established a more permanent base and trading post on the west coast of Taiwan. This settlement also included construction of the Zelandia Castel fortress. Despite their previous attacks on Macau and their problems with China, Dutch merchants on Taiwan believed they were in a good position to conduct trading between Japan and the East Indies. They also continued pushing for better relations with China, at least until 1662, when the local regional ruler Koxinga ordered them to leave Taiwan.

Cannon at Macau's Monte Fortress, constructed in the 1620s by the Jesuits near the Seminary and Church of São Paulo (St. Paul).

Macau Traders Search for New Business

The end of Portuguese trade with Japan in 1639 posed a major existence crisis for Macau. Local trading merchants were forced to develop business elsewhere, constrained by the growing domination of sea-trading by the Dutch East India Company. Macau also was affected by an extremely depressed economic situation in China that was produced by a continuing feud between the Manchu and Ming forces seeking territorial and political control of mainland regions in the southern part of the country. The fact that the Portuguese supported the Ming leadership did not set well later when the Manchus became victorious. All of these elements were working against the efforts of the Portuguese to maintain their little outpost at Macau. Its golden era was already over, and it would never again reach the same level of worldwide importance.

The situation for Macau worsened in 1641 when Malacca was captured by the Dutch, thereby disrupting trading voyages between Macau and Goa, which was Macau's main port of call in Portuguese India. Since it had been forcefully taken by Afonso de Albuquerque in July 1511, Malacca had been under the administrative control of a Portuguese-appointed captain-major, who in turn was responsible only to the viceroy of Goa. Without Malacca, Macau was effectively isolated from the security and protection of the Portuguese Empire.

As a result, the port of Macassar (in the kingdom of Goa) became a primary market for the Portuguese based at Macau. Macassar, situated in the southwestern Celebes group, was then at its peak of influence in the eastern Indonesian archipelago and had been frequented regularly during the 1630s by the Portuguese. It was one of several markets pursued by Macau in the colony's effort to reduce its dependence on trading in various ports bordering the South China Sea and at the same time develop trading business in ports not dominated by the Dutch East India Company. By this strategy, Macau also hoped to disrupt seriously the flow of Chinese products in Macassar and similar markets, which in turn might adversely affect trading by the Dutch in those markets and eventually in Japan. Country traders from Macau increased their voyages to Macassar during the 1640s and 1650s, but after that period the number of voyages declined.

Macau also enjoyed a secondary reciprocal relationship with Macassar, providing needed weapons and munitions to the sultan of Macassar, who used them successfully in defending his region against military incursions. The benefits of this cooperative relationship were fully understood by both Macassar and Macau and clearly aided their trading exchanges during the mid-seventeenth century. In one significant example, to evade potential disruption by the Dutch in the 1630s, the Portuguese frequently disguised their ships as vessels operated and owned by the rulers and merchants of Macassar as a convenient means of dealing for sandalwood at Timor. This strategy was later expanded to include trading voyages between Macassar and Manila.

It should be noted, however, that Macau was not completely in dire straits. Trading voyages embarked regularly to the Lesser Sunda Islands' ports of Solor, Flores, and Timor, ports around the Indochina peninsula, the port of Macassar, and Manila (lucrative trading with Manila continued despite its prohibition by the Dutch). Macau's traders gradually developed Macassar as a central port to store sappenwood and sandalwood brought from the Lesser Sunda Islands. Traders also exchanged or bought spices such as pepper and cloves at Macassar and sold gold, silk, and porcelain there.

One indication of Macau's prosperity at the time is contained in an official message conveyed by the Municipal Senate of Macau to Spain's King Philip in 1640:

> This city has seventy large cannon mounted in four Royal Forts and five bulwarks, firing shot from 12 to 40 lbs.; another 20 fieldpieces, and good material for works of fortification, redoubts and trenches; a good foundry for all kinds of metals, and spacious gunpowder mills. Married Portuguese number about six hundred, and their sons who are capable of taking arms, somewhat less. The native born are over five hundred, including married men and soldiers. Slaves number

about five thousand, so that altogether we can surely reckon on putting two thousand good musketeers in the field.[13]

Historian C. R. Boxer has noted the "exaggerated" characterization of Macau's prosperity by another chronicler (not identified), who estimated the Chinese population in Macau at 20,000. He added that "everyone was abundantly rich, without there being a single person who was known to be poor. This notorious opulence led to many persons, not only adventurers and refugees but highly respectable people, leaving India and even Portugal to settle down and live in this place, marrying here owing to the enormous dowries then in vogue."[14]

In an attempt to calm hostilities, Portugal and Holland signed a ten-year truce in 1642. The agreement was generally ignored, however, by the Dutch East and West Indies Companies, whose directors were intent on further expanding Dutch influence in the Far East.[15]

Chapter 5

Macau and the Portuguese Restoration

The period 1560 to 1640 marked Macau's zenith as an economic center. Indeed, it is no exaggeration to say that Macau at that time was the focus of all trade between East Asia and Western Europe.
—RICHARD LOUIS EDMONDS[1]

The dual monarchy of Portugal and Spain came to an end in December 1640 when the duke of Braganza ascended to become King João IV of Portugal. Known as the Restoration, King João IV's installation as the Portuguese monarch was secretly "arranged" by a small group of people interested in breaking Portugal's six decades of subjection to the Spanish Crown. The next concern was informing Macau and other Portuguese colonies, who had deliberately been kept in the dark about the change until it was successfully carried out.

The duke of Braganza was an intelligent and personable member of the Portuguese nobility who was a competitive hunter with a passionate love for music. He is credited with composing the melody for "Adeste Fideles."[2] His accession to king in December 1640 was a carefully arranged revolution orchestrated by a small group of influential Portuguese lawyers, clerics, and others, whose efforts were supported by the duke's wife, Dona Luisa de Guzman. Despite her Spanish ancestry, Dona Luisa was obsessed with "a burning ambition to become a reigning Queen."[3]

News of Portugal's successful break with Spain, ending "sixty years' captivity"[4] under jurisdiction of the Spanish Crown, was carried to Macau by Antonio Fialho Ferreira, who had served as a captain-major of the Macau-Manila voyages in the early 1630s. Fialho Ferreira had returned to Lisbon in 1638 and was in the right place at the right time when King João IV was proclaimed head of Portugal on December 1, 1640. Fialho knew that time was of the essence in advising Macau about the new king, in order to prevent Spain from declaring Macau as its territory. Through an apparently successful self-promotion effort, Fialho managed to achieve his prestigious appointment as "royal envoy" on January 24, 1641, with instructions to deliver the news to Macau that Portugal had broken with Spain and was now headed by King João IV.

Antonio Fialho Ferreira departed Lisbon in late January 1641, going first to England to board a ship operated by the English East India Company heading to the East. He later joined a vessel operated by the Dutch (who apparently believed that it would be better to deal with the Portuguese rather than the Spanish), and he arrived in Macau on May 31, 1642 (disguised as a Portuguese prisoner released by the Dutch). He promptly requested a meeting of local leaders, including the current captain-general and the governor of the bishopric, and delivered the news that the dual monarchy of Portugal and Spain had been broken and that King João IV had been proclaimed the royal head of Portugal.

The Restoration Is Celebrated in Macau

News of the Restoration was overwhelmingly accepted in Macau, which immediately began ten weeks of almost nonstop celebration, hampered only by above-normal rainstorms during the spring monsoon season. The celebrating included a series of religious and military processions through the streets of Macau, numerous gatherings of thanksgiving in all of the churches and religious institutions of Macau, several Portuguese-style bullfights, frequent fiestas ("festas" in Portuguese), and a series of parades in honor of King João IV. Brightly colored decorations covered houses, churches, and other buildings, many of which were illuminated by fire at night.

The weeks of celebrating culminated in a special public gathering in the town square in which Macau's captain-general at the time, Dom Sebastião Lobo da Silveira, took the formal oath of allegiance to the restored Portuguese Crown:

> I, Dom Sebastião Lobo da Silveira, Gentleman of His Majesty's Household, and Captain-General of this stronghold of Macau, City of Name of God in China, swear fealty and homage, on the oath of the Holy Evangelists, to obey, defend and maintain as my own lawful, native, and true King of the Kingdoms of Portugal, His Majesty the King Dom João, the fourth of this name, who God preserve; and for this loyalty, I offer myself on behalf of his honor, credit and reputation, freely to give my life, blood and property, even in the uttermost regions of the earth, as an example of Portuguese loyalty; and on this same oath, I swear loyalty and homage after his most happy days to the Prince Dom Theodosio, his heir-apparent, and to all of his descendants in the Crown of Portugal.[5]

Following the solemn taking of the oath by Dom Sebastião Lobo da Silveira, a guard of honor fired their muskets, which in turn led to the organized firing of cannons at all of the forts of Macau. It was, indeed, a glorious celebration and one that invited participation by all the residents of Macau, wealthy and poor, merchants and servants, Portuguese and Chinese.

The governors of Macau, serving by appointment of the Portuguese Crown, were expected to be firm administrators on the little colony. Some of the administrators carried their firmness to severe levels, however. In one example, Dom Sebastião Lobo da Silveira, already linked to several disputes during his term, was accused of murdering Diogo Vaz Freire, the Crown administrator assigned to Macau. Authorities said Vaz Freire had been kept chained in Lobo da Silveira's basement for eight months before being beaten to death on May 4, 1643. According to the story, the governor denied his victim's request to be given final sacraments before his death and even strangled a young slave who begged the governor for mercy on behalf of Vaz Freire. Governor Lobo da Silveira then removed Vaz Freire's body to the entrance of the Misericordia during the night, where it was discovered the following morning by witnesses who said the body was "covered with sores and weals, and with one eye hanging out from its socket."[6] The governor, in a communication sent to Lisbon, maintained he committed the murder because "it was convenient for His Majesty's credit, the honor of the Portuguese nation, and safety of his [Lobo da Silveira's] own life."[7]

Needless to say, the Crown ordered the arrest of Lobo da Silveira and his return to Lisbon for trial in the murder of Diogo Vaz Freire. With the help of some highly placed friends, however, he managed to delay the deportation until February 1647, when he was finally taken to Goa and placed on a ship sailing to Lisbon. The ship was wrecked near a desolate coastal section of Natal (southern Africa) during the voyage. Everyone aboard the ship survived the wreck, but Lobo da Silveira died while attempting to walk to a coastal port.

Another problem involved a Macau governor who came to power in August 1646—Dom Diogo Coutinho Docem, the son of a nobleman who was killed in a battle against the Dutch near Malacca. According to historian C. R. Boxer, soon after young Dom Diogo reached Macau, the soldiers of the garrison at Macau mutinied because of delays in their pay; they seized the Guia Fortress and aimed the fort's cannon on the Senate House. "The citizens, on their part, took up arms and, in the ensuing free-for-all fight which followed, stormed into Government House and cut to pieces the unfortunate captain-general [Dom Diogo Coutinho Docem], whom they found cowering under the staircase."[8]

Foreign Trading at Guangzhou Expands in the 1700s

The Portuguese monopoly on trading with China ended in 1685 when the emperor of China issued a directive that foreign commerce would be allowed at all Chinese ports. The first to benefit was the English East India Company, which was granted permission to engage in trading at Guangzhou. English ships began arriving with increased regularity from 1699. By 1715, the

English East India Company was doing well enough to justify assigning representatives to set up offices in Macau and Guangzhou. Other countries, hoping to share in the potentially lucrative profits, also began sending ships to Guangzhou, including France in 1698, Denmark in 1731, Sweden in 1732, Russia in 1753, and the United States in 1784.

Sailing from Macau to Guangzhou was an eighty-mile journey requiring three to five days. A variety of complications along the route helped the Chinese defend their territory. Historian Frank Welsh provides a description of the journey as it would have occurred in the late 1700s and early 1800s:

> About thirty miles above Macao, the channel narrows to a few hundred yards into the strait known as the Boca Tigris, the aptly named Tiger's Mouth, commonly known as the Bogue, or Humen, where the passage is commanded by the guns of the Ch'uen-pi and Ty-lok-to forts. Between Ch'uen-pi and the Second Bar, for rather less than twenty miles, a ship has to stick to the channel, never out of range of the shore. At the Bar, a sea-going vessel has to wait for a tide to help it over the shallows. The First Bar, just below Whampoa, is even more restrictive. Whampoa, some seven miles below Canton, is therefore the limit for ocean-going ships of any size. Canton [Guangzhou] itself is accessible only by shallow-draft vessels.... A hostile man-of-war, if it braved the gauntlet of the forts in the Tiger's Mouth, would in most conditions find herself stuck at Whampoa, unable to bring Canton within the range of her guns, with only the ship's boats able to penetrate farther upriver.[9]

Most of the successful trading at Guangzhou at the end of the seventeenth century depended on an exchange of fees, a result of constant and necessary private bargaining which traders were forced to accept in order to continue doing business there.[10] Then, in 1702, in an attempt by China to develop more consistent regulation, an "emperor's merchant" was appointed to deal with the foreign traders. This arrangement soon proved to be unsatisfactory for the traders, however, because they were unable to appeal any decision made by the emperor's merchant. In addition, they were unable to trade freely with the particular Chinese merchants with whom they wanted to trade, and they were not permitted to employ Chinese as servants within the confines of their designated living and trading areas. They were even restricted in purchasing ordinary provisions at Guangzhou for their living areas and their ships. It was a frustrating situation for the visiting traders, who were decidedly overwhelmed by regulations and restrictions.

Development of the Co-hong

Guangzhou merchants also were dissatisfied because they too were affected by the constantly changing and complex tight regulations and restrictions set down by the emperor's merchant. Finally, in 1720, the local merchants formed a representative committee of twelve (later thirteen[11]) known as the "Co-hong," which was designed to establish uniform prices and monitor the exchange of products among the foreign trading representatives, who became familiarly known as the "hongs." The Co-hong, headquartered at Consoo Hall on Thirteen Factory Street, thus replaced the emperor's merchant, apparently with the sanction of local Chinese officials. Most controls on trade continued as before and generally became even more restrictive, but there was more general uniformity. All sides now had a better idea of what to expect.

One significant example of early strict monitoring began in 1736 with the assigning of one Chinese merchant to each arriving foreign trading ship. This representative had a wide-ranging responsibility, including arrangements for the sale of imports and exports involving his assigned vessel, plus any other matters relating to the ship during its stay in port. In other words, a Chinese merchant representative monitored every operation, no matter how insignificant, from the arrival to the departure of his assigned vessel.[12]

An imperial decree issued in 1755 required that the merchants assigned to "secure" foreign trading vessels had to be members of the Co-hong. Through this ordered change, the Co-hong security officials themselves replaced the Chinese merchant representatives in dealing directly with the foreign traders.

On the surface, the Chinese leadership said the change was intended to make sure that foreign traders "observed the rules of the government." Also, the Co-hong was "to act as the sole medium of communication between the government and the foreign traders."[13] It was an effective means of governmental control and a lucrative source of income beyond that gained through normal trading revenues. Every activity, exchange, inspection, and invoicing related to the Chinese merchant traders was accompanied by a variety of fees, of which the Co-hongs extracted a profitable percentage before sharing them with upper echelon superiors in Beijing

One of the most famous of the Co-hong merchants at Guangzhou was Hou Qua II, a millionaire with banking links to New York and London who rose to become the leader of the group. An American trading merchant from Philadelphia, Nathan Dunn, said in 1838 that he believed Hou Qua II was probably the world's "richest commoner."[14] Hou Qua II, highly regarded for his honesty, developed "strong financial links and warm friendships" with several Western merchants and bankers. He presented many of these businessmen with replicas of his portrait, which was painted by George Chinnery, an English artist who lived in Macau from 1825 until his death in 1852.

Enter the "Hoppo"

All foreign trading merchants at Guangzhou also had to deal with the "Hoppo," the customs commissioner, who had almost absolute control over trading activities in the port.[15] The Hoppo, whose appointment usually lasted for three years, also had absolute jurisdiction over the Co-hong and was even more powerful than the governor of Guangzhou.

Indeed, the Hoppo was a subject of vital concern for the governor, whose own modest income was dependent on added revenues generated by the activities of the Hoppo. Author Frank Welsh noted one calculation suggesting that "the ratio between the official remuneration of a governor and that obtained— to put it politely—irregularly, was 7 percent and 93 percent."[16] A governor, assuming he wanted to retire in prosperous comfort, could never allow himself to underestimate the importance of the Hoppo.

Even though the Hoppo was designated by appointment, he paid dearly for the privilege. During his first year in office, the Hoppo usually earned enough to recoup his purchase price, his second year yielded enough to meet "extra" demands by his superiors, and the income from his third year was his to keep as the profit from his appointment as Hoppo.[17]

During the 1700s, the Chinese exerted considerable control over the activities of Macau. In 1732, the Manchu dynasty leaders established a second customs house in Macau (supplementing one which had been operating since 1688) and permanently assigned an official government representative to Wangxia, a Macanese village near the Barrier Gate. A Chinese decree in 1744 ordered that the Wangxia representative would have jurisdiction over criminal cases involving Chinese citizens and any foreigners involved in those criminal cases. Chinese restrictions continued to escalate, even to the point where building a house or making house repairs in Macau required permission from China.

In a move to return authority in Macau to the Portuguese, Dona Maria I began a series of directives in April 1783 that raised the powers of the Macanese governor, opened a Portuguese customs house, and sent a 150-man garrison to Macau from Goa. By 1789, the Loyal Senate (already recognized by the Chinese as a proper agency in the carrying out of Macau affairs) was given more latitude in decision-making.

Chapter 6

British Artists Discover the South China Coast

In the quaint world of the sketches and paintings of George Chinnery, the picturesque image of Macau is the subject for a type of cityscape such as had been popularized in England by Italian painters.
—CESAR GUILLEN-NUÑEZ[1]

Two British artists, Thomas Daniell (1749-1840) and his young nephew William Daniell (1769-1837), were among the first Europeans to conduct extensive landscape sketching along the South China coast. The Daniells began their extended visit at Macau in 1785 with a long-term plan to produce sketches which would be engraved following their return to London. Both of the Daniells also made meticulous notes in journals, dutifully explaining what they observed while pursuing their Oriental landscapes. After arriving at Macau, the Daniells went on to visit Whampoa and Guangzhou, then returned to Macau before going on to India in the summer of 1786. They remained in India for another nine years, producing hundreds of sketches before returning to England, after which they spent years selecting sketches to be engraved and published in a series of several volumes entitled *Oriental Scenery*.

Popular scenes of Macau also attracted other artists during the closing years of the eighteenth century. One prominent view was the Mage Temple (Ma-Kok), one of many Macau scenes drawn by John Webber, the draftsman for the famed Captain James Cook of England. Webber's sketches of specific subject matter such as temples, parks, and port settings were indicative of similar interests by European artists, both professional and amateur, who visited Macau in the nineteenth century. Port scenes at Macau, particularly depicting the Praia Grande, were pursued extensively by William Alexander, an accomplished draftsman who accompanied Great Britain's George Macartney embassy to the Chinese Court of Qianlong during 1792-93.

Looking south over the Macau peninsula, c. 1835. Engraved by S. Fischer; artist unknown.

The Demand for China Coast Paintings

The production of China coast paintings began in the early 1800s, offering Chinese scenes in a manner that appealed to the interest of foreign visitors. Many of these works depicted specific Asian events such as festivals and military scenes, but they were influenced by artistic styles derived from European reproductions in order to give them a familiar appearance for prospective buyers. Seaport views were especially popular and were painted over and over again, often with little variation, to meet the strong demand for them by the merchant visitors. Popular subjects also included sporting events, hunting and military scenes, festivals, traditional celebrations, and municipal gatherings for specific purposes. Sometimes the China coast paintings focused especially on a current event with historical meaning. Many of these paintings depicted ornamental terraces of lavish homes, pavilions, flower gardens, and tea houses, often located on Hainan Island in the Pearl River between Whampoa and Guangzhou. Millionaire businessman Hou Qua II owned several estates on Hainan Island, which was also the home of the famous Fa-tee Flower Gardens. One example of a title for the popular paintings of this time was "Hou Qua's Tea Gardens and Pleasure Pavilions on Hainan Island."[2]

Paintings of Macau were also in much demand, perhaps because merchants, seamen, businessmen, foreign government representatives, and others spent time there while waiting to conduct business in Guangzhou. Artists

The Praia Grande on the southeastern edge of the Macau peninsula, looking towards Penha Hill, c. 1835. Engraved by W. H. Capone from a drawing by Thomas Allom.

usually depicted Macau "from unusual angles from mountaintops and promontories. But, more significantly, they explored it and studied it from within, its picturesque churches and squares, its mansions, temples and inhabitants."[3] There were four main panoramic vistas depicting Macau: "from the North end of the Praia Grande looking South; from the South looking North; from Penha or another height at the southern end of the peninsula looking down at both harbors; and the frontal views of the Praia Grande or the Porta Interior."[4]

Before the outbreak of the First Opium War in 1840, artists found a lucrative return from producing a series of familiar port scenes. These sets were highly popular with the visiting merchants, who wanted meaningful souvenirs of their presence in the Far East. These works, always in watercolor, were generally categorized as "China trade paintings." The most popular set included scenes of Macau, the Boca Tigris, Huangpu, and Guangzhou. Later in the 1840s, Hong Kong was added to the set, replacing the Boca Tigris, or the set was expanded to include both Hong Kong and Shanghai. Scenes from other trade ports were added in later years.

George Chinnery Arrives at Macau

English artist George Chinnery had already gained considerable prominence through his portrait commissions in Dublin, Ireland, before going to

The Praia Grande, looking towards Guia Hill, c. 1835. Artist and engraver unknown.

India in 1802, where he lived in Madras and Calcutta. He had already turned fifty when, escaping from creditors and his wife, he left India and voyaged to Macau in 1825. By that time, it should be noted, Macau "had long outlived its heyday and reflected but a mere shadow of its former prosperity."[5]

George Chinnery was the only acclaimed European artist ever to live permanently in the Portuguese colony. His influence among local Chinese artists was so great that many works produced in the region during the mid-1800s have been categorized as "Chinnery School" paintings, and sometimes simply as "Chinnery" paintings. At times, even China coast paintings have been characterized as "Chinnery School." Over the decades, the Chinnery School term has been applied so broadly that it covers works by both local and visiting foreign artists, and even a few artists who produced their paintings before Chinnery arrived at Macau.

Chinnery was an artist with an abundance of "behavioral oddities, [but] he was a noted and popular personality in Macau, called upon by virtually everybody who wanted a portrait painted."[6] Historians Henry and Sidney Berry-Hill have given an unusually apt description of the artist:

> [Chinnery] had become paunchy towards the end of his stay in India, and now, with his untidy mop of greying hair and with his spectacles poised halfway down his nose, he became a popular figure in the streets, merging easily among the cosmopolitan community…. Perhaps occasioned by his peculiar proclivities, his looks apparently became a topic of local gossip…. His activities gradually developed

The Grotto of Camões, a memorial to Portugal's epic poet, c. 1835. Engraved by S. Bradshaw from a drawing by Thomas Allom.

into a routine. Early morning would see him settled in a [sedan] chair, carried by coolies, on sketching trips. He would stop for any particularly scene which caught his eye, when inevitably a knot of natives would materialize out of thin air to gather round and marvel at the speed of his pencil. Even this trivial and empty tribute gratified him. He followed some such produce with more or less regularity, but an oversize chair with four bearers became necessary when he grew unduly heavy. He indulged a voracious appetite.[7]

During his daily outings, which hardly ever varied in their routine, Chinnery produced hundreds of sketches that were intended as preparation for oil paintings. According to historian Cesar Guillen-Nuñez: "Today we can still trace the painter's artistic itinerary from his home behind São Lourenço [St. Lawrence] Church. He turns down São Lourenço Street, then heads for Santo Agostinho or the British East India mansions along the Praia Grande, and finally explores the Senate and São Domingos Square. Together with the A-Ma Temple and other stops along the Porta [*sic*] Interior, these all became favorite haunts of professional or amateur painters visiting Macau."[8]

Chinnery didn't send any of his works to London's Royal Academy for exhibition during his twenty-three years in Goa, and he lived in Macau for five years before finally submitting works to the Royal Academy to be exhibited in 1830. He continued sending works to London for exhibition until 1846. In addition, though he lived permanently in Macau, Chinnery made extended sketching visits to Guangzhou in 1826, 1827, 1828, and 1829 and remained in Guangzhou for more than eight months in 1832. During his last decade in Macau, Chinnery also spent time in Hong Kong, which had been colonized by the British following the First Opium War in 1840–42. Throughout nearly all of his time in Macau, Chinnery lived in a house located behind the São Lourenço Church.

After arriving in Macau, Chinnery took on a number of assistants, who subsequently profited considerably from their association with him. One of the most talented of these assistants was a Chinese artist named Lam Qua, who worked with Chinnery for about five years. He was highly prolific in producing copies of Chinnery's portraits and developed into a talented portraitist in his own right.

Lam Qua later opened his own studio and commercial gallery on Old China Street in Guangzhou, a favorite shopping attraction for visiting foreign merchants during their trading seasons. He painted original works but enjoyed a lucrative income through guiding his low-paid assistants in producing endless copies of popular scenes to meet the insatiable demand of visiting merchants and wealthy businessmen. Lam Qua was the only Chinese artist of that time to have one of his works accepted for exhibition at the Royal Academy in London.

Another Chinnery assistant was Protin Qua, whose work was said to be of high quality, though no painting has ever been specifically attributed to him.[9] Lam Qua and Protin Qua also took on many assistants, who in turn helped expand and promote the "Chinnery School" through their paintings, which included landscapes, narratives, genre scenes, interior conversation pieces, and China coast paintings.

George Chinnery's most prominent patron was William Jardine, a wealthy merchant he had first met in Goa. Jardine was influential in sending prospective clients to Chinnery to have their portraits painted. In later years, when Jardine and James Matheson formed the famous Hong Kong company known as Jardine Matheson, Chinnery was designated as their official painter.[10] The generous patronage of Jardine and Matheson helped Chinnery to live and work almost as he pleased. Many of Chinnery's surviving works owe their preservation to the care provided by Jardine and Matheson.

A distinguished French painter, Auguste Borget (1808–77), visited Chinnery in Macau in 1838-39, spending about six months in the Portuguese colony. Borget, a close friend of French author Honoré de Balzac (1799–1850), had studied painting in France with the prominent artist Jean-Antoine-Theodore Gudin (1802–80). Chinnery's influence was shown in Borget's sketches of life in Macau, Guangzhou, and Hong Kong that were published in Paris in 1842 under the title *La Chine et Les Chinois*. Additional sketches from his journey to China and India were published later in other books.

During Borget's visit to Macau, he and Chinnery were joined by British artist William Prinsep (1794-1874), who had studied with Chinnery in Calcutta. Borget, who was traveling and sketching around the world at the time, had planned to remain longer in Macau, but decided to leave when it appeared the Chinese and British were going to war over the opium situation. After leaving Macau, Borget went to Calcutta, where he became seriously ill and was cared for in the home of William Prinsep and his wife, Mary.

One of Chinnery's non–Chinese students was Harriet Low (1820–77), an American from Boston who was the niece of shipping executive William Henry Low, Sr. When Low moved to Macau in 1829 to administer business activities for Russell and Company, he asked Harriet to accompany him and assist in caring for his invalid wife. During her four years in Macau, Harriet kept a journal of her daily activities, which included her art sessions with Chinnery along with some of her observations about the artist. The Lows returned to America in 1834, and two years later Harriet married John Hillard of Boston. Their daughter, Katherine Hillard, edited and published her mother's account in 1900 under the title *My Mother's Journal*. The book describes how Harriet "became a constant visitor to his studio, where she improved her amateur painting and listened to stories of his strange experiences in India, interlarded with epigrams, as much entertaining as philosophical.... He taught her to paint, which lightened the boredom of endless lonely hours, until she made a circle of friends."[11]

Rise of the Chinnery School of Art

Many Chinese artists, encouraged by Chinnery's popularity, began imitating his style. When the First Opium War concluded in 1842, numerous Chinese artists flocked from Guangzhou to the new British Crown Colony of Hong Kong, attracted by the increasing demand and ready market for Chinnery School paintings. Because of the popularity of these paintings and the proliferation in their production, "Chinnery is linked with many more canvases that he did not paint than with those he did."[12] Among other artists in the area was Marciano Baptista (1826–96), who was born in Macau and began copying Chinnery drawings in the 1840s. Baptista moved to Hong Kong in 1857, promoting himself as a student of Chinnery and producing scenic watercolors which returned a lucrative income.

Chinnery visited Hong Kong for several months in the late 1840s, hoping to develop his many sketches of the new British colony into commissioned oil paintings. While in Hong Kong, he also experimented with photography, along with scene painting for stage productions. Despite his optimism, Chinnery was unable to develop a new market for these paintings, though he continued to produce commissioned portraits. After returning to Macau, he produced several oil paintings from his Hong Kong sketches, but with only modest success in sales.

One of Chinnery's leading patrons was his doctor, Thomas Boswall Watson, who moved from Scotland to Macau and opened a practice in the 1840s.

Dr. Watson, "already an enthusiastic sketcher," also studied with Chinnery, "sometimes adding color to Chinnery's outline drawings."[13] Watson's wife, Elizabeth, also produced several drawings and copies of Chinnery's works. Following Chinnery's death in 1852, Dr. Watson moved his practice to Hong Kong in 1856, and he returned to Great Britain in 1859.

Chinnery was an unusual personality, even for an artist. Among his close friends and companions, for instance, he was particularly noted for two interesting characteristics: "one of being an enormous eater; the other of never drinking either wine, beer or spirits. His sole beverage was tea, oftener cold than hot."[14] According to historians Henry and Sidney Berry-Hill: "Chinnery was indeed unique from all aspects, whether artistic, romantic or adventurous, but because of his long absence from England he was virtually forgotten there, and when he died in distant Macau on the 30th May 1852, his reputation had become so shadowy that the event was hardly noticed."[15]

Chapter 7

The British Offer
"Protection" for Macau

During ten days of its annual life-cycle, the seed-box of the white poppy exudes a milky juice of extraordinary chemical complexity, not yet fully understood, and from this is derived a bitter, brown, granular powder: commercial opium. —JACK BEECHING[1]

English military vessels began making port at Macau just after 1800, when Napoleon was expanding his European territorial claims through military force. The suggestion was that Macau probably needed "protection," but Macau's governor, J. Machado Pinto, realized the British were thinking occupation rather than protection and asked Beijing for support in preventing such a move. The English fleet under Lord Wellesley wisely departed Macau and returned to India. Another fleet from England arrived at Macau in October 1807, however, after Napoleon and his military force had entered Portugal, again on the pretense of "protecting" the tiny Portuguese territory.

Despite strong protests of then Macau governor Bernardo Aleix de Lemos e Faria, the British fleet and force headed by Admiral William Drury occupied the Macau fortresses of Bomparto, São Francisco, and Guia. Governor Lemos, in a letter to Admiral Drury dated October 30, 1808, said the people of Macau were allied only to the Portuguese Crown and would not support efforts to shift their sympathies to the British. In his letter, Lemos advised Drury that Macau's Senate was encouraging the Chinese to consider improving their relations with the British, and he added firmly: "As I have already told you and now repeat: Of the Macanese, not a single one but gives his allegiance to the House of Braganza."[2]

About that time, conveniently, the Portuguese successfully fought and subdued a pirate force from Japan a feat that impressed the Chinese leadership. In that action, six Portuguese warships with 730 men and 118 artillery guns withstood a fleet of 300 junks with 20,000 men and 1,500 guns headed by Gan Baoshi and forced him to surrender.[3] Shortly thereafter, influenced by persuasive negotiations by a Macanese judge, Miguel de Arriaga, the Chinese

64

emperor, Jiaqing ordered the English military fleet to leave Macau, which it did in late December 1808. Judge Arriaga was often characterized as "heroic" because of his efforts to persuade the Chinese to side with the Macanese in forcing the British to leave Macau. His reputation was enhanced further in 1810 when he successfully negotiated the surrender of a "notorious" Chinese pirate known as Kam Pau-said.[4]

Meanwhile, the British were among the leaders when China allowed more participation by foreign nations in trading at Guangzhou in 1799. The United States proved to be a strong rival in the lucrative tea trade business, however, even though American vessels were smaller and fewer in number than those of the British. During the 1805–06 trading season, for instance, 37 American ships exported 11 million pounds of tea from Guangzhou, compared with exports of 22 million pounds by 49 British ships.[5]

Macau became an important place for the British and other foreign merchants to live temporarily while waiting to conduct business with the Chinese. As trade expanded between China and Britain in the early decades of the nineteenth century, the British Parliament created a new position of chief superintendent of trade. The first appointee to the post, in December 1833, was William Napier, whose designated responsibilities included negotiating with the Chinese leadership and protecting the interests of British merchants. In addition, he was directed to live in Guangzhou, which was strictly forbidden by the Chinese government. And he was told to deal directly with Chinese officials, instead of communicating through the Co-hong, as required of all foreign representatives.

Napier arrived at Macau in July 1834 and ten days later, despite full awareness of the conflict between his orders and Chinese customs, "attempted to bypass the Co-hong and deal directly with the Viceroy at Canton."[6] His aggressive efforts were almost completely ignored. As noted by historian Frank Welsh: "Dispatched at great expense to secure the China trade, Lord Napier had succeeded only in having it stopped."[7] He was replaced in December 1836 as chief superintendent of trade by Captain Charles Elliot, who had accompanied him to Macau in 1834. Napier, who had become ill with a fever, was transported back to Macau in a Chinese boat and under Chinese escort. "To the exultant clash of gongs and the bang of firecrackers, the sick peer was slowly taken down to Macau under military guard—precisely in the manner used by Chinese to convey criminals."[8] The carefully orchestrated and humiliating journey took five days. After arriving in Macau, Napier was near death for the next five weeks; he complained that his nerves were unable to cope with the noise of church bells in the city. He died on the night of October 11, after the Portuguese "had obligingly stopped ringing their bells on his account."[9]

In an unusual twist of historical irony, Napier had proposed from Guangzhou that the British consider occupying "the island of Hong Kong, in the entrance of the Canton [Pearl] River, which is admirably adapted for every purpose."[10] The British did, indeed, settle at Hong Kong, later forcing the Chinese to concede "in perpetuity" the island and its deep sheltered harbor at the conclusion of the First Opium War. Napier's proposal may have been made at the suggestion of the British merchant William Jardine, since Napier had not visited the island himself.[11]

Ban on Religious Orders

A series of events in the early 1800s, following the French Revolution, led to serious problems for the Catholic church, which in turn led to a Portuguese government directive in 1834 suppressing activities by religious orders in Portugal and its territories overseas. The order, supported and encouraged by the Portuguese prime minister, Joaquim Antonio de Aguiar, included immediate government possession of convent buildings and other properties in Macau. The suppression also led to widespread persecution of Christians in the Far East and the deaths of numerous Christian missionaries.

Macau's Legislature Pronounced the "Loyal Senate"

Portugal's Prince-Regent João, who later rose to become King João VI, announced in 1810 that Macau's governmental body would thereafter be designated as the "Loyal Senate" (Leal Senado). The pronouncement was a reward for Macau's continued allegiance to Portugal during the Union of Crowns ("dual monarchy"), when it was subject to Spanish rule.

Legislators conducted their business in a distinguished building known as the Leal Senado, "aptly described as one of the finest examples of colonial architecture in Macau."[12] The structure, with its elegant façade and grand courtyard, is located several blocks east of the Inner Harbor on the Avenida Almeida Ribeiro, facing a public square known as the Largo de Senado.

The Factories at Guangzhou

Foreign trading involving China was centered during the early 1800s at Guangzhou, a walled city of one million inhabitants and the capital of two Chinese provinces, Guangdong and Guangxi. While at Guangzhou, each country's representatives were confined just outside the city under strict Chinese control to "a stone block of offices and warehouses between the city walls and the river frontage."[13] This combined series of buildings, linked by courtyards and covered corridors, extended about 1,000 feet along the river and became known as "the Factories," since it was the location where the foreign merchandising factors conducted their business transactions. Lower levels were used for storing merchandise and cargo for both import and export, while upper levels included living areas and rooftop vistas that were frequently depicted in "Hongs of Canton" paintings. From the rooftops of the factories, viewers could look at the landscape beyond Guangzhou, "green as far as the eye could see, until it merged in the distance into bluish hills, with pagodas sprouting on the far horizon. Balconied and gaily adorned villas belonging to wealthy mandarins were spaced along the river edge."[14]

During two trading seasons each year, foreign merchants resided within the factories and dealt with local Chinese trading representatives. Some of the foreign merchants, such as the British, Americans, Swedish, Dutch, and Spanish (representing a company from the Philippines), raised and lowered their national flags each day. The French merchants joined in this ritual in the early 1830s.

Restrictions for foreign merchants of the factories were almost unbearable, but these rules were tolerated because of the profit potential of the trading activities. Foreigners were not allowed to visit the city of Guangzhou or to engage the services of Chinese servants (although many were nevertheless so engaged through payments of money to certain Chinese officials for the privilege). Foreigners were not allowed under any circumstances to bring their wives or women friends to the factories of Guangzhou. These women were required to remain at Macau during the trading seasons.

Most of the British business at Guangzhou focused on the purchase and export of Chinese tea. Traders would make their deals and arrange for the chests of tea to be loaded onto Chinese barges and transported downriver to ships anchored in deep water. Historian Jack Beeching notes that, despite the severe Chinese restrictions, the East India Company staff members at Guangzhou had a reasonably agreeable life, "sweetened by the chance of making a small fortune." According to Beeching: "Memoirs of the time agree on the splendor of their dinners, when 30 or so sat nightly around the mahogany table under a huge chandelier, indulging in English meals of beef and mutton and boiled vegetables.... The digestive stroll after dinner was limited to the Factory courtyard—known as Jackass Point—and was taken under the gaze of dozens of inquisitive Chinese. Regulations allowed a foreigner to be rowed, three times a month, across the 500-yard-wide Pearl River, to stretch his legs in the gardens on Hainan Island, but not in a group numbering more than ten, and only on the understanding that all concerned came home sober, and before dark."[15]

Opium and the Asian Trade

Opium was among the imports allowed by China from the late 1600s, because of its medical use to relieve pain and relieve dysentery. As a painkiller, opium was swallowed raw. From 1678 to about 1760, fewer than 200 chests were imported annually into China. Although the smoking of opium became more and more popular through the decades, it was discouraged both officially and personally. As noted by historian Jack Beeching, opium smoking was "strongly condemned in China since, according to Confucian morality, the smoker's body was not his own, to demolish exactly as he chose, but had been entrusted to him by his ancestors as their link with his descendants."[16] Beeching also noted: "Intelligent Chinese saw opium in extreme terms—as a social poison introduced by foreign enemies."[17]

The Chinese leadership issued an order in 1729 forbidding the smoking of opium, but it was largely ignored. In 1799, China issued an imperial decree prohibiting both the import of opium and the smoking of opium. By then, however, the number of opium chests imported to China had increased to 4,000 annually. According to the imperial edict: "Foreigners obviously derive the most solid profits and advantages.... But that our countrymen should pursue this destructive and ensnaring vice ... is indeed odious and deplorable."[18]

China's ban against the opium trade presented a critical problem for the British East India Company, whose trading representatives were interested in the cash return for opium received in China and realized that demand for opium was continuing to grow. But they realized that the trade for Chinese tea was more important because of its related tax revenue received by the British government. There was no choice: The British East India Company issued orders prohibiting its representatives from transporting opium. But despite the cosmetic appearance of "official orders," sales of opium continued to be a mainstay at British East India Company auctions in Bengal, and this opened up opportunities for a profitable venture by "country traders."

Country traders conducted regular voyages between the East Indies, China, and India, traveling in their picturesque teak replicas of seventh-century galleons known as "country wallahs."[19] They were encouraged to purchase opium at the British East India auctions, which they transported to several small coastal bays near Macau that were safe from Portuguese and Chinese surveillance.[20] In this manner, for some twenty years after the issuance of the second imperial ban in 1799, the British East India Company could officially claim that it had no responsibility for the trading of opium in China. So, despite the official ban, imports of opium chests into China over the next twenty years continued to number more than 4,000 annually and sometimes exceeded 5,000.[21]

Many of these chests of opium, disguised as some other product, were kept in warehouses in Macau and moved to other locations when deemed necessary to avoid discovery. Others were stored in permanently moored and protectively covered "opium hulks" at Macau, awaiting opportune occasions to transport them to Guangzhou and regional Chinese mainland smuggling ports

Historic treaty table at Macau's Kun Iam Temple, where the United States and China signed their "Treaty of Friendship and Trade" on July 3, 1844.

and islets. These familiar opium hulks were frequently depicted by artists at Macau during the early 1800s.[22] By 1830, the opium trade at Guangzhou was "probably the largest commerce of its time in any single commodity, anywhere in the world."[23] The number of opium addicts in China in 1835 was estimated at two million.[24]

The British East India Company continued to maintain its monopoly on the trading of tea until 1833, when the British Parliament voted to end the company's domination in the interest of free trade. The result was immediate and very beneficial to British citizens, with the amount of tea imported to Great Britain increasing by 40 percent in 1834 and the price of tea declining. Along with this new era of free trade, opium imports also increased in China. The number of opium chests imported, estimated at nearly 19,000 in 1830, exceeded 30,000 by 1836 and more than 40,000 by 1839.[25] It was a lucrative paradise, promising instant prosperity for the growing number of traders who "began arriving at Macau like bees to a honeypot."[26]

Commissioner Lin Takes Action Against Opium Traders

By the 1830s, the illegal importing of opium into China was creating serious economical problems in China, where the traditional copper coins used for day-to-day purposes were being converted to silver to purchase opium and pay taxes. This led to a shortage of silver, which had always been in abundance in China and welcomed by opium traders. With silver now becoming more valuable than copper, the Chinese government was facing a sharp reduction in tax revenues. To resolve this crisis, Imperial Commissioner Lin Tsu-hsu was ordered to Guangzhou in 1839 and empowered to take whatever action he believed necessary to end the illegal importing of opium. Commissioner Lin wasted no time. Within one week after his arrival, Lin ordered the confiscation of all opium in the possession of foreign traders at the factories and arrested all foreign traders who were linked to the confiscated opium. All of the opium, totaling nearly 20,000 chests (mainly from British and American traders), was surrendered through Captain Charles Elliot, the designated superintendent of British trade, who had come from Macau to Guangzhou to negotiate with Commissioner Lin. Elliot also arranged for the release of the imprisoned British foreign traders and their safe return to Macau. Interestingly, the American traders were allowed to remain at Guangzhou and profit heavily by arranging for the import of British cargoes from Macau. The confiscated opium was valued at several million dollars (in American money) and "to the astonishment of the foreign community ... was mixed with salt and lime, and sluiced into the river."[27]

Many of the British traders, now based in Macau, continued to pursue their illicit and lucrative trading in opium. The relentless Commissioner Lin, capitalizing on his successful action in Guangzhou, threatened to bring an end to the opium trade in Macau by using military force. Governor Silveira Pinto of Macau, fearing a massacre of his citizens, wisely responded to Lin's pronouncement by ordering the entire British community to leave.[28]

Chapter 8

Macau Defends Its Territory Against China

When people think of China, they don't think of Macau. We seem to be a place with a big past, but only a small future. —C. Y. FOK, Macau banker[1]

Following the First Opium War (1840–42), in which China granted Hong Kong Island to Great Britain "in perpetuity," Chinese leaders moved to strengthen their dominating representation in Macau and reduce Macau's already small area. These moves were challenged by the incoming governor, João Ferreira do Amaral, who actually expanded Macau's minuscule region and ordered a number of defensive changes. Ferreira do Amaral, a distinguished Portuguese naval officer, was named as governor of Macau in 1846 and was directed by Lisbon to resolve Portugal's official status over the little peninsula and to reestablish Macau as a free port.

In one of his first actions after becoming governor, Ferreira do Amaral directed that Chinese fishermen in Macau would have to begin paying taxes. It was truly a dramatic change for the little Portuguese outpost, in which the Chinese had maintained virtually absolute control over judicial, fiscal, and territorial matters since it was established in 1557. The Portuguese had been permitted responsibility only over situations involving Portuguese subjects.[2]

Ferreira do Amaral then ordered the shutdown and destruction of China's two customs houses, thereby removing the powerful Hoppo customs officials, who had been operating in the territory since 1783. Finally, he formally annexed Taipa Island, situated directly south of the Macau peninsula. But he didn't stop there. The governor suspended Macau's annual lease payment to China (*foro do chao*), constructed new roads (for planned city expansion) that damaged Chinese graveyards, drained swamp regions, destroyed small farms, rooted out squatters, and occupied the area between Macau's city walls and the Barrier Gate. He also increased fortifications on Taipa Island, which had a clear view to Macau's Inner Harbor, and increased fortifications on the peninsula itself, particularly on Guia Hill, Wangxia Hill, and Dona Maria Hill.

71

These were dramatic changes, and ones that raised tensions between mainland China and the Portuguese at Macau.

Ferreira do Amaral's brief but stormy period as governor also included an international incident between Portugal and Great Britain. The crisis erupted in June 1849 when a Protestant teacher from St. Paul's College in Hong Kong, James Summers, was attending a regatta in Macau. The regatta featured warships from both the United States and Great Britain. Just before the regatta competition began, the Jesuit order conducted a Corpus Christi procession, an event in which observers were expected to remove their hats as a form of respect. Summers declined to remove his hat for the procession, even after a priest directed him to do so. Governor João Ferreira do Amaral, noticing the visitor's lack of respect, also ordered him to remove his hat. When Summers again refused, the governor directed authorities to place him in jail.

Efforts to secure the release of Summers were made by Captain Henry Keppel, a senior British officer, who maintained that as a British citizen, Summers was not subject to certain regulations of Macau. Captain Keppel's arguments were duly overruled by officials in Macau. Keppel then took matters into his own hands by leading a group of his men in storming the jail and removing Summers. During the skirmish, Keppel achieved his goal of getting Summers out of jail, but his men shot and killed one of the jailers and wounded several others. The incident was resolved later through a series of diplomatic exchanges which resulted in a formal apology from Great Britain, the censure of Keppel, and the awarding of a lifetime pension to family relatives of the murdered jailer.[3]

Governor Ferreira do Amaral's removal of the Hoppo produced much consternation and bitterness in the neighboring Chinese province of Guangdong. Authorities in Guangdong complained openly of his actions, and reward posters for retribution against the governor began appearing on streets of Guangdong villages.[4] Finally, on the afternoon of August 22, 1849, seven "beggars" approached Ferreira do Amaral while he was riding his horse on an inspection tour of construction projects near the Portas do Cerco. The seven rushed Ferreira do Amaral before he realized what was happening, pulled him off his horse, murdered him, and quickly moved across the border into China, taking his head and left hand as evidence of the assassination.

The Hero of Passaleong

Responding to the murder of their governor, Portuguese leaders in Macau formed an interim Council of Government and ordered a Portuguese garrison to occupy the Portas do Cerco. Within three days of Ferreira do Amaral's death, the garrison was formed and ready. Observers could see, however, that an estimated 2,000 Chinese soldiers were preparing for battle at the nearby

Chinese fort of Passaleong. Thereafter occurred one of the most heroic military episodes in the history of Macau. As they were viewed with astonishment by both sides of the conflict, Lieutenant Vicente Nicolau de Mesquita and a select group of 36 Macanese soldiers moved across the one-mile distance from the Portas do Cerco to the Passaleong Fort, ignoring a heavy barrage of Chinese gunfire.

With Nicolau de Mesquita leading the attack, the force of 36 men caused the 2,000 Chinese soldiers to abandon the Passaleong Fort, retreating in panic and confusion. The Portuguese force then blew up the Chinese fortress. It was a victory long savored by the Portuguese of Macau, and Vicente Nicolau de Mesquita is recalled in Portugal's history books as the "Hero of Passaleong." In 1940, the Macau government erected a monument near the Loyal Senate to commemorate him. The monument was destroyed during a Communist-inspired demonstration in 1966, however.

Portugal took more interest in its protection and support of Macau following the assassination of Governor João Ferreria do Amaral. This new demonstration of Portuguese involvement apparently was accepted by the Chinese, who were then becoming more concerned with a growing series of feudal conflicts.

It was about this time that Macau became a place of refuge, a situation which continued through the rest of the nineteenth and twentieth centuries. From the 1850s, the purpose of the Portas do Cerco was reversed: It would thereafter be used to prevent the Chinese from escaping to Macau rather than for its original intent of keeping foreigners from entering China.[5]

Another change with long-term implications and benefits occurred in the early 1850s through the instigation of Governor Isidoro Francisco Guimarães, who succeeded João Ferreira do Amaral in 1851. Guimarães, wrestling with the continuing problem of boosting the territory's economy, decided to introduce licensed gambling, which is now one of the best-known attractions of Macau and one which appeals to the Chinese passion for gambling.[6] It is also the most lucrative in terms of revenue. Governor Guimarães shrewdly determined that a fundamental and consistent source of income could be obtained through the licensing of gambling houses, and the policy was a financial success for Macau from the start.[7]

Life in Macau was somewhat less controversial during Guimarães' governorship, which continued until 1863. Differences with the Chinese even subsided, especially after 1854 when the Portuguese played a major role in combating piracy in the South China Sea near the port city of Ningbo. Daily life also became more and more pleasant during the 1850s. William C. Hunter, living in Macau as a senior representative of a large Philadelphia firm named Russell and Company, wrote in his recollections published in 1855: "Foreign visitors to the ancient Portuguese city of Macao, founded during the first half of the 16th century, are delighted with its calm quiet life, its brilliant atmosphere and lovely climate."[8]

Macau's historic Dom Pedro V Theatre, dating from the 1850s and recognized as the oldest European theater in Asia, was completely restored in the 1990s.

In addition to increased business interests, several foreign diplomatic agencies opened offices in Macau during the 1850s and 1860s, all anticipating greater involvement and activity in dealing with mainland China. The presence of these businesses and agencies, often located along the beautiful Praia Grande, brought renewed prestige to Macau, along with new and enhanced status for its society and culture.[9] Business interests also included an influx of wealthy merchants and industrial leaders from the Chinese mainland, who added a flavor of "official" acceptability to Macau's growth and development.

Guimarães also played a prominent role in strengthening Portugal's possession and rights regarding Macau. Portugal named Guimarães as an ambassador to China with instructions to negotiate an agreement between the two countries on Macau. These negotiations led to the initialing of the Treaty of Tientsin (Tianjin) in August 1862, "giving full recognition of Macau as a Portuguese colony."[10] The agreement became effective in 1873 and continued in force until 1919, when Portugal and China agreed to a revision of their 1887 Luso-Chinese Treaty of Trade and Friendship (sometimes called the Treaty of Beijing or the Lisbon Agreement). Basically, the 1887 accord had affirmed the "perpetual occupation and government of Macau and its dependencies by Portugal as any other Portuguese possession."[11]

Visible improvements continued during the governorship of Coelho do Amaral, who succeeded Isidoro Francisco Guimarães in 1863. One of the most noticeable changes was the construction of the Guia Lighthouse in 1865. Designed by a Macanese architect named Carlos Vicenta da Rocha, it was the first lighthouse on the South China coast, standing 44 feet high on the top of 262-foot-high Guia Hill. Coelho also instigated the extensive planting of trees along the Praia Grande, construction of the São Francisco Fort, and conversion of the former Jesuit monastery into the military Moorish Barracks.

Portugal's efforts to increase its support and protection for Macau, which had begun in earnest with the arrival of Governor João Ferreira do Amaral in 1846, reached a higher level in 1867 when the legal system of Macau (and other Portuguese colonies) became responsible to the Portuguese Civil Code. In the early 1870s, the Association for the Promotion of the Instruction of the Macanese (APIM) was established on behalf of "the effort and goodwill of those born in Macau."[12] This was followed in 1878 by the APIM Business School, supervised by four instructors. The business school flourished through 1910 in conjunction with the São José Seminary.

One of Southeast Asia's greatest natural disasters in the nineteenth century occurred in 1874 when a tremendous typhoon struck Macau, Hong Kong, and southern China's Guangdong Province. In Hong Kong, the typhoon caused the sinking of thirty-five ships in Victoria Harbor and the deaths of an estimated 2,000 people. Damage in Macau was extremely costly, and was made worse by a fire which may have been started by looters. Among other things, the typhoon uprooted most of the newly planted trees along the Praia Grande, damaged the recently converted Moorish Barracks, and partially destroyed Macau's new lighthouse on Guia Hill.

The typhoon also disrupted Macau's efforts to increase its small manufacturing industry and played a role in reducing the territory's attraction as a storage location for transshipments of cargo between other ports and Hong Kong. The commerce of transshipments for Macau virtually ended with the introduction of steamships in the late nineteenth century. There was no longer any need to store cargo at Macau because the new steam vessels could go directly to and from Hong Kong without having to rely on the changing winds of the monsoon seasons.

By the conclusion of the nineteenth century, cargo ships were almost rare in the ports of Macau, which was focusing on the fishing industry as a prime source of income. With the newfound reliance on the fishing industry, Macau "now gave the impression of being a Portuguese fishing village which had somehow become inhabited by Chinese."[13]

Macau's leadership in the late nineteenth century showed a flash of foresight in considering a project to develop an artificial harbor which would be deep enough to service the new large steamships. The first plans, which focused on the Inner Harbor, were drawn up in 1884 by an engineer named Adolfo

Laureiro. This project, which might have secured a bright long-term financial future for Macau, was never carried out but remained "enmeshed in procrastination and uncertainties."[14]

A modest move to heavy industry occurred in 1886, when Green Island (Ilha Verde, now adjoined to Macau through land reclamation) was chosen as the site for the location of the Green Island Cement Company. Much of the clay for the cement was derived from reclamation work in the harbor. Limestone from quarries north of Guangzhou was transported downriver and unloaded on a specially constructed wharf on the island. This project, a steady source of jobs for the next five decades, provided cement to Macau, Hong Kong, Japan, and elsewhere in East Asia.

One of the current visible reminders of the cement production venture is a company mansion constructed for the Macau manager and his family on a hillside near the factory. The magnificent stone mansion surrounded by a large garden, had a wide colonnaded balcony and ornately decorated rooms and became a center of the social life in Macau.[15]

Sun Yat-sen and Macau

Dr. Sun Yat-sen, the founder of the Chinese Republic, was born in 1866 in Zhongshan County, a part of Guangdong Province which included Macau and the surrounding region. His father had been a tailor who had worked near Macau for a time. Sun studied medicine for one year in Guangzhou and then for five years in Hong Kong, graduating in 1892 from the College of Medicine for Chinese. This institution operated by the British offered courses taught in the English language by British instructors, many of them internationally recognized scientists.[16]

During his years of study in Hong Kong, Sun distinguished himself by achieving the highest possible grades and was one of only two of the college's original students to complete the required courses for graduation successfully. Because of differences between the school's curriculum and British standards, however, the Hong Kong General Medical Council declined to recognize Sun's diploma, formally titled "Licentiate in Medicine and Surgery of the College of Medicine for Chinese, Hong Kong." The diploma did not enable Sun to legally issue certificates for births and deaths, and it also gave him no legal protection in medical disputes. His legal status, therefore, was the same as that of a Chinese herbalist, who did not require a medical diploma.[17]

Sun accepted his legal position gracefully, moving to Macau and opening the "Chinese-Western Apothecary," which primarily dispensed both modern drugs and traditional herbal remedies.[18] He also supplied drugs to the Ching-hu (Chinese) Hospital in Macau and assisted (without charging fees) in treating its patients, even performing surgical operations. Because of his

The Macau home of Sun Yat-sen

medical training in Hong Kong, Sun is regarded as the first Chinese to uti-
lize Western medicine techniques in Macau.[19]

Sun's combined practice of dispensing drugs and treating patients soon
came to the attention of local authorities in Macau, who directed that he be
restricted from treating Portuguese patients. The same order was later
expanded to prohibit pharmacies in Macau from filling any prescriptions written by foreign doctors.[20] Sun's practice as a herbalist was not prohibited by
Macau authorities, but he subsequently closed his Chinese-Western Apothecary and moved to Guangzhou in 1893, where he opened the East-West
Apothecary.

While in Guangzhou, Sun also edited (anonymously) a Chinese section
of a Portuguese weekly newspaper published in Macau in which he promulgated revolutionary political arguments directed against the prevailing divi-
sive ruling factions in southeast China.[21] The newspaper was circulated widely
among overseas Chinese. He also conducted regular meetings of discussion
groups to review efforts to bring about political change in China. All of this
finally culminated in 1910 in his leadership in overthrowing the Ch'ing
Dynasty rulers and his founding of the Chinese Republic. Sun was chosen as
the first president of the Chinese Republic and served in that capacity until
his death in 1925.

Chinese Refugees Flee to Safety of Macau

Life in Macau generally proceeded at a subdued pace as the Portuguese territory entered the twentieth century. In 1899, its population totaled 63,991, including 3,780 Portuguese and 154 other foreigners.[22] By the early 1900s, its total population was estimated at 75,000. This number soon increased, however, as political unrest and related governing problems developed in China. By 1920, for example, refugees from the mainland swelled Macau's population to nearly 84,000, of whom less than 4,000 were Portuguese. By the early 1930s, Macau's population had climbed to about 150,000.

Some of Macau's changes in the early years of the twentieth century were domestic in nature, often involving "insensitive restoration and repainting of historic buildings."[23] One outspoken critic of the disregard for preserving Macau's historic past with dignity was Manuel da Silva Mendes, a transplanted Portuguese who also took an active role in preserving the rights of the Macanese (the multirace citizens whose presence continued to influence Macau's political activities into the 1990s).

Silva Mendes noted that the territory's Public Works Department had spent thousands of patacas (Macau's currency) to improve the city's appearance between 1905 and 1915. He acknowledged there had been some degree of improvement but said "a stroll through the city streets reveals a complete absence of artistic feeling, both in private works and in those of the state."[24]

Other aspects of Macau's glorious past have also diminished through the decades, and particularly so since the beginning of the twentieth century. There is little local folk music, and the traditional costume for women known as the "do" is no longer seen. There was a time when the Cantonese "pai-lou" ornaments and ceremonial dragon boats were important during special occasions, but that is no longer true.

There are still a few people attempting to keep alive the *lingua de Macau*, the Macanese mixture of Portuguese, Indian, and Asian language. And there is still a Portuguese-Cantonese blend of traditional activities associated with births, weddings, and funerals. Most of all, as one author suggests, "Macau would not be Macau without its lion dances, the constant explosion of red firecrackers (to ward off evil spirits), its Portuguese wines and Latin melodies."[25]

There were several political crises in Portugal during the early years of the twentieth century, but they had little lasting effect in Macau. During the *dictadura*, for example, João Franco ruled Portugal from May 1906 until King Carlos I and Crown Prince Luis Filipe were assassinated in February 1908. Portugal's parliament, the Cortes, proclaimed a younger son of Carlos, Manoel II, as king, but he was subsequently overthrown in the Portuguese revolution of October 1910. Following the 1910 revolution, the monarchy was abandoned and

The Lou Lim Iok Garden in Macau is modeled after the famed Chinese classical gardens in Suzhou, an ancient town located on the Grand Canal near Lake Tai, west of Shanghai.

the Republic of Portugal was established, although revolts and governmental changes continued in Portugal until the late 1970s, when a democratic government was installed.

Education was always a priority in Macau, whether developed by the Portuguese government, the Jesuits, or the Chinese. A relaxation of repression against religious orders encouraged the Jesuits to begin returning to Macau's São José Seminary in 1862. Attendance at the seminary by that time had declined to a handful of children learning to read and a few part-time students pursuing Latin. By 1864, however, the number of seminary students had climbed to 216 and by 1870 to 377.[26]

By 1929, there were 124 schools in Macau and on the islands of Taipa and Coloane, with a total enrollment of 9,147. These included a government school, 6 government-subsidized schools, 12 council schools, 4 missionary schools, and 101 privately operated Chinese schools.[27]

The demand for opium, which was a major factor in the two Opium Wars in the nineteenth century, continued to be a convenient and steady source of income for many Macau citizens in the twentieth century. Much of this activity was both monitored and controlled by the Macau government, which in 1935 had licensed 27 retail opium shops and 69 smoking dens in the territory.[28] Anyone walking around Macau's waterfront and streets during the 1950s could hardly fail to become aware of the opium smoke, which floated like incense from boats and homes.[29]

The Lisbon Agreement

One of the most significant political events in the early years of the twentieth century occurred in 1928, when the Lisbon Agreement (the Luso-Chinese Treaty of Friendship and Trade) was renewed between Portugal and China. There was one unresolved aspect of the 1887 agreement that was still not resolved in the 1928 renewal. That was the question of border delineation. Portugal had originally maintained that the borders of the Macau territory should include the tiny peninsula and four adjacent islands. The Chinese insisted, however, that the territory under Portugal's administration include only the peninsula and the islands of Taipa and Coloane.

The question was never resolved and was quietly evaded during negotiations for the 1928 renewal of the agreement.[30] Basically, the agreement confirmed the "perpetual occupation and government of Macau and its dependencies by Portugal as any other Portuguese possession," but stipulated that Portugal should not take action to "alienate Macau and its dependencies without agreement with China."[31] Thus, even though Macau had been a Portuguese possession since 1557, it remained, at least symbolically, under control of China.

Chapter 9
World War II in Macau

In novels, Macau is the capital of intrigue where beautiful Eurasian
women get mixed up with sinister drug dealers or smugglers who use
this territory's ancient trading connections with mainland China,
Hong Kong and Europe to move valuable pieces of Chinese art. —
PAMELA G. HOLLIE[1]

An overwhelming influx of refugees began entering Macau when the
Japanese invaded China in 1937, particularly after the fall of Shanghai. The
population of the little Portuguese enclave increased to about 350,000 by 1940,
and the flood of refugees continued throughout World War II, raising Macau's
population to 600,000 by 1945. Following the surrender and occupation of
Hong Kong in December 1941, the Japanese decided against formally occupying the territory of Macau, perhaps because of its direct link to neutral Portugal. Japanese soldiers went in and out of Macau at will, but Portuguese,
American, and British flags continued to be displayed in Macau without any
interference.[2]

Japanese influence in Macau increased somewhat after August 1943, following an incident in which the Japanese military seized a British steamer (the
Sian) off the coast of Macau and killed twenty guards during the attack. A few
weeks later, apparently concerned about possible repercussions, Japan ordered
Macau to accept Japanese "advisers" as an alternative to full occupation.[3] In a
spiritual bid for protection against the wartime pressures of 1943, a prayer was
scratched on the wall of a Macau cathedral on May 13, the day of Our Lady
of Fátima, which read: "Rainha do Munco: Mae de Portugal, Amparai Maca"
(Queen of the World: Mother of Portugal, Guard Macau." This bit of religious literary graffiti was allowed to remain.[4]

During the course of World War II, the Japanese became more aggressive in dealing with Macau, demanding that the Portuguese formally recognize the puppet government of neighboring Zhongshan County in Guangdong
Province. In addition, the Japanese ordered Portuguese military troops to leave
their posts on Lappa Island, adjacent to Macau. And the Japanese also insisted
on being allowed to make house-to-house searches in Macau.[5]

One of the most interesting of World War II events in Macau centered around a decision by Bishop Ronald Hall, a Hong Kong representative of the Catholic church who had taken a strong interest in Asian affairs. Among other things, Hall's book *China and Britain* demonstrated his insight into Chinese life. In 1944, Bishop Hall decided to ordain Deaconess Florence Lei Tim-Oi of Macau as a priest, so that she could give communion to her congregation of 150 Christians. He issued the order because the war had effectively prevented priests from traveling to Macau each week. In making the decision, Hall argued that the needs of a congregation had priority over the church's position that women should not be priests and stated that the ordaining a woman was better than permitting an unordained person to give communion. [6]

The decision, regardless of its possible virtue, was thoroughly criticized in church circles. London's *Church Times* characterized the ordination by Hall as "outrageous." It was "deplored" by Archbishop Temple, and it was called "uncanonical" by the Chinese House of Bishops.[7] Bishop Hall remained steadfast behind his decision, however, and Florence Lei was eventually honored for her service by Archbishop Runcie.[8]

After the war, Bishop Hall was instrumental in establishing several social programs in Hong Kong, including the Children's Meals Society, the Hong Kong Social Welfare Council, the Street Sleepers Society, and an orphanage. Controversy continued to plague Bishop Hall later in the 1940s, however, when he criticized the actions of the Kuomintang party in China and then openly supported the Communist victors in China's Civil War in 1949.[9]

Most of the Chinese who had fled from China into Macau during World War II returned to their homes, but many from China's Swatow region returned to Macau when a severe drought in 1946 left them starving and desperate. Once in Macau, despite the lack of suitable land, they began developing rice paddies and small vegetable gardens.

Macau and the UN Embargo Against China

Macau managed to survive the ravages of World War II only to deal with thousands of Chinese refugees seeking relief from a devastating mainland drought and then thousands more escaping from the Chinese Civil War. Its precarious existence worsened during the Korean War, when the United States prohibited the export of strategic goods to China in 1950. The embargo was further strengthened in 1951 by the United Nations.

Most of the world had known Macau as a place of nonstop sin and exotic pleasures, with its wondrous array of opium, gambling, smuggling, and women along the Rua da Felicidade (Street of Happiness). The smuggling itself was a burgeoning industry, utilizing a significant percentage of the thousands of fishing junks which plied the waters between Macau and Hong Kong. These

The Palace Santa Sancha in the wooded hills above Praia Grande Bay was originally constructed in 1846 by famed architect Jose de Aquino. In 1937 it began serving as the official residence of Macau's governors.

fishing junks had a design peculiar to the Hong Kong–Macau region according to writer Christopher Rand:

> Their sterns are high and straight, their bows low, their masts cocked forward. Their sails are ribbed and have an odd shape recalling a fan, a leaf, a bat's wing, or perhaps a dorsal fin. Most of their sails are rust-colored or burnt sienna. But they are kept with Chinese thrift, and in time they are patched over and over again, till they become masses of rectangles, like Paul Klee paintings. Sometimes an off-white will be patched in with the burnt sienna. Sometimes other combinations will appear: pink, white and olive green; black, tattletale gray and lavender. A seascape here is apt to have scores of junks in it.... On a quiet sea they look like silhouettes or pop-ups, and they give a sense of perspective, in which they are helped by the countless little islands that dot these waters.[10]

Junks with engines were most suited for the daily routine of smuggling because they could easily transport gasoline and fuel oil from Hong Kong to Macau, after which it would be sold to buyers from mainland China. This roundabout "oil pipeline" was essential for the Chinese because Hong Kong had formally agreed to ban sales of fuel to China during the course of the

Korean War. Patrols of Hong Kong authorities attempted to prevent the smuggling of fuel, but the massive numbers of junks made such monitoring almost impossible. Besides, operators of the junks always maintained they had gone to Hong Kong to gas up and "do a little fishing" on their way back to Macau. Whenever possible, of course, the junks used their sails on the short voyage to Macau, emptied their fuel tanks through hoses into oil drums, and returned again to Hong Kong for another "fishing trip." Despite restrictions of the United Nations embargo against China, the filled oil drums stored in Macau eventually were transported by barge to mainland China.

In a strange set of circumstances, the United Nations embargo against Communist China "forced" Macau to become a busy gold exchange center. Open trading of gold was allowed in Macau because its parent country, Portugal, had remained neutral during World War II and didn't participate in such postwar conventions as the International Monetary Fund. This led to a very busy and very lucrative gold exchange business.

Seaplanes would land at Macau two or three times a week, bringing gold from other Asian cities, usually from Bangkok, Thailand. "It arrived in big bars, and in Macau it was made into little ones for retail sale. Very few of the little bars stayed there."[11] Much of the "customized" gold had initially gone to buyers in China, but pressure from the Chinese Communists forced the sellers in Macau to find purchasers in other countries. The quickest and most convenient way of supplying gold to other countries was through Hong Kong. Under Hong Kong laws, gold could be exported but not imported. Individuals found a variety of ingenious methods of smuggling gold into Hong Kong, where authorities made a small effort to prevent its entry but ignored its possession within the British territory. From Hong Kong, the gold could legally be transported by airplane and ship to other locations in Southeast Asia. One popular destination was Saigon.

Many fortunes were made in the Macau gold market, especially by shrewd businessmen from Hong Kong. According to historian Dick Wilson:

> Every few days in those early post-war years, a plane-load of gold in big bars would land at Macau, officially exported from Bangkok or other Southeast Asian cities. Macau would process this gold into smaller bars, which would then be dispatched to Hong Kong for onward consignment to private customers in the region at much higher prices. At this point it became illegal, because Hong Kong officially regulated the trade in gold, and its officials were supposed to stop it [from] entering. In practice, there was sympathy for Macau in those early years, because Macau's neutrality had enabled many British or Chinese escaped prisoners or refugees from the Japanese to take refuge, and Macau had provided some cloak for Sino-British intelligence activities. Macau was tiny and had no other important means of earning a living, so no one in Hong Kong wanted to stop or spoil its gold trade. But the export of gold from Hong Kong remained legal. Roger Lobo, a wealthy Hong Kong businessman, operated a fleet of Catalina flying boats between Kai Tak [Airport] and the Macau Outer Harbor, as well as coastal ships to ferry bullion on to Southeast Asian destinations, especially Saigon.[12]

The Macau Post Office, located on Leal Senado Square, has helped shape Macau's image over the years through its special stamp issues.

China's tolerance for the Portuguese administration of Macau diminished in the early 1950s, after the Communist victors of the Chinese Revolution began pressuring for control. A series of clashes occurred in 1952 along the narrow border between Macau and mainland China, leading to a month-long disruption of needed firewood and food supplies for the little Portuguese territory.

However, despite a few threatening statements from leading Chinese officials, the People's Republic of China was not yet prepared to order the Portuguese to give up their administration of Macau. In 1955, Macau announced plans for an elaborate celebration to commemorate the 400th anniversary of the Portuguese settlement. This drew strong protests and criticism from Chinese officials, as noted in a statement published in the *People's Daily*: "Macau is Chinese territory. The Chinese people have never forgotten that they have the right to demand the recovery of this territory from the hands of Portugal. The fact that Macau has not yet been returned to China does not mean that the Chinese people can tolerate long continuation of the occupation of Macau."[13] As a result, the festival was cancelled. Macau officials said the territory's financial situation was not good enough to support the celebration in a worthwhile manner.

Meanwhile, refugees from Communist China continued to flow into Macau, reaching an estimated three hundred a month by the late 1950s. Many of the Chinese refugees claimed to be seeking relief from large-scale food shortages on the mainland, while others acknowledged they were escaping from an "intolerable" life and repressive "impersonal discipline" under the Communists.[14] Some were even more specific, saying they fled Communist China to avoid being punished as "Rightist opportunists."[15] They said the "anti-Rightist" campaign in their region "had become so severe that they were willing to risk being shot in attempting escape rather than endure its menacing sweep any longer."[16]

According to a newspaper report filed in Macau by *New York Times* writer Greg MacGregor:

> The degree of opposition to the regime of Red China and the extreme poverty and degradation the Chinese here are willing to accept in its stead can be seen in the faces and daily lives of the people. In daytime, the narrow musty streets are crowded with barefooted, ragged men, women and children begging for coins, occasionally huddled in exhaustion and snatching bits of food or cigarette stubs wherever they can be found. During the misty nights, overhung by the leaden winter skies of the South China Sea, family groups struggle for warmth in the shelter of rotting doorways. Newspapers are snatched and treasured as insulation against the wet and cold.[17]

Macau's total population had climbed from 190,000 in 1955 to an estimated 250,000 in 1959, of which 98 percent were Chinese and the remaining 2 percent were European or Macanese (mixed Portuguese and Indian/Asian descent).

The Beauty of Macau

The people who lived in Macau during the 1950s were for the most part comfortable and content with their lives and life-styles. Some dreamed of one day going on to Hong Kong to make their fortunes, but most made the best of their circumstances. Macau was a place of pleasant sunrises, cool breezes during hot summers, and glorious sunsets reflecting off the unique mix of Chinese and Portuguese architecture.

Historian Austin Coates describes a warm early autumn Macau day in the 1950s:

> The first signs of autumn were in the air, but it being midday the weather was hot and all the high narrow windows, continental and different from anything else on the China coast, were wide open.... I strolled up through the old streets and stairways to the top of one of the low hills on which Macau is built. A glorious sunset was gradually arraying itself and in its clear light, delineating every shadow, the little peninsula of Macau lay below me like an architect's model. The low classical towers of its churches, the battlements of its gently decaying forts, lay with on the one side the Chinese hill of Lappa, separated from them by a muddy branch of the river, and on the other the broad Pearl River estuary dotted far into the distance with the dark sails of several hundred fishing junks.... The streetlamps were being turned on below and the lights of a river steamer could be seen entering the outer harbor from Hong Kong.[18]

Chapter 10

Rioting Breaks Out in Macau

Macau, as [Ian] Fleming recognized, is a wonderful setting for melo-drama, and there was plenty of it this week.—CHARLES MOHR[1]

The Star Ferry Riots in Hong Kong in the summer of 1966, although "attributed by a public inquiry to locally organized hooliganism," reflected a "new mood of restless violence sweeping through the youth culture of the mainland."[2] The uprising in Hong Kong also was a prelude to rioting in Macau during December 1966 and January 1967. In addition, the incidents in Macau and Hong Kong were directly linked to the effects of radical changes occurring on the mainland from China's Great Proletarian Cultural Revolution, which had begun in the spring of 1966.[3]

The Macau rioting originated from an incident on Tuesday, November 15, 1966, when Portuguese policemen were dispatched to prevent construction of a new addition to a pro–Communist school on Taipa Island because the project had not yet been approved by the Macau government. A small clash occurred at the time, causing injuries to both workmen and policemen wielding rubber truncheons. The government, instead of making an official investigation, ignored the incident.

Official Chinese radio from Beijing called attention to the school site confrontation, accusing the Portuguese authorities of "premeditated fascist atrocities against Chinese nationals."[4] After two weeks passed, students, construction workers, and their Communist supporters began regular visits to Government House, the residence of Macau's governor, protesting the lack of action by Portuguese authorities and shouting slogans based on the collected thoughts of Mao Zedong from the familiar little red book *Quotations from Chairman Mao Tse-tung.*

Relevant phrases from *Quotations* included: "Who are our enemies? Who are our friends?"[5] "After the enemies with guns have been wiped out, there will still be enemies without guns."[6] "Fight, fail, fight again, fail again, fight again—till their victory; that is the logic of the people."[7] "As far as our own desire is concerned, we don't want to fight even for a single day. But if circumstances force us to fight, we can fight to the finish."[8] "People of the world, be courageous, dare to fight, defy difficulties and advance wave upon wave."[9] "We must be prepared. Being prepared, we shall be able to deal properly with all kinds of complicated situations."[10] "The richest source of power to wage war lies in the masses of the people."[11] "One can get a grip on something only when it is grasped firmly, without the slightest slackening."[12] "The masses are the real heroes."[13] "Be resolute, fear no sacrifice and surmount every difficulty to win victory."[14] One of the most frequently heard phrases shouted by the rioters was: "Kill the foreign devils!"[15]

Finally, on December 3, 1966, Portuguese policemen were again sent to the school site and ordered to destroy the unfinished building annex. Another confrontation developed, and students of the school claimed they had been beaten by the Portuguese police. The incident escalated on December 4, when hundreds of students and members of the Macau Federation of Trade Unions joined together in organizing street demonstrations which quickly developed into bloody rioting. Swarms of fast-moving rioters surged through Macau for five hours, hitting government officials and battling with policemen. Injuries reportedly involved at least 63 rioters and 20 policemen.[16]

News accounts reported that one Chinese youth had been killed on December 4 by gunfire from Macau policemen, while three young people had been killed late on the night of December 3 when police fired upon curfew breakers.[17] In addition, according to an Associated Press report: "Informants with contacts in Communist China said orders for the anti-Portuguese demonstrations and rioting had been transmitted from the southern Chinese city of Canton [Guangzhou] to Communist leaders in Macau."[18]

At the Macau City Hall, policemen were unable to prevent the rioters from entering offices and removing books, government records, and portraits of former Portuguese governors, which they piled in the street outside and set on fire. Numerous automobiles were wrecked during the rioting, and statues of Portuguese heroes were knocked over and smashed. Police attempted to use tear gas to subdue the rioting, but brisk winds carried the irritating chemical smoke away from the area and over the adjacent harbor. The rioting on Sunday finally came to an end after nightfall, following a radio broadcast appearance by wealthy businessman Ho Yin, Macau's unofficial liaison with China, who said Portuguese authorities had yielded to Chinese demands (which he did not describe during his radio report).[19]

Renewed rioting on December 5 resulted in more gunfire from Portuguese troops on Macau's main street along the waterfront. Two pro–Beijing Chinese died in the violence, and the bloodstained street was blocked off by Portuguese military tanks in an effort to prevent further bloodshed at that location.[20] Groups of militant young Chinese roamed the streets of Macau for two days, intimidating and chasing Europeans whenever they could and sometimes beating them.[21] At least one Portuguese home near the waterfront was broken into and ransacked by the prowling mobs.[22] The total casualties from November 15 through December 5 included 8 people killed from shots fired by the policemen and 212 people injured in the clashes, along with 61 arrests.[23] Adding to the tension were seven Chinese gunboats cruising Macau's harbor areas that frequently moved very close to shore. In response, local authorities issued another all-night curfew order for the entire city of Macau which was enforced by Portuguese military patrols armed with machine guns. The order included a warning that anyone violating the curfew would be fired on.[24]

It was a sudden and tragic explosion of unrest, followed immediately by demands from student leaders for compensation on behalf of the wounded victims and severe penalties to be assessed against the police chief, Octavio Figuiredo, and the Portuguese army commander in charge, Carlos Armando da Mota Cerveira.

Mainland Chinese officials supported the demands, while calling specifically for restrictions on police authority in Macau, closure of the China-Macau border to refugees from the mainland, and the permanent suppression of Nationalist Kuomintang influence from the Republic of China in Taiwan. More specifically, they demanded that "seven agents of the Chiang Kai-shek gang," whose whereabouts were supposedly known to the Portuguese, be turned over to mainland China for "disposition."[25] The seven, originally accused of conducting guerilla raids on the mainland, had been taken into custody in waters off the China coast by the Portuguese in June of 1963.

Macau's governor, Brigadier Nobre de Carvalho, who had arrived in the territory only a week before, realized the futility of trying to fight the demands and quickly agreed to sign a series of pledges based on the demands made by the demonstrators and supported by the Chinese leadership in Beijing. Even more humiliating, the signing process was conducted under a large portrait of Mao Zedong in an office at the Chinese Chamber of Commerce in Macau. From that moment, it was clear to all sides that China was in full control of activities in Macau, despite any Portuguese efforts to claim otherwise.

British Problems in Macau

Chinese Communist-inspired unrest in Macau erupted into a serious diplomatic crisis between Great Britain and China on a Saturday afternoon in May 1967. The British consulate in Macau was stormed by demonstrators who cornered British Consul Norman Ions for nearly two hours in a travel document office. Similar uprisings targeting the British were occurring around the same time in Hong Kong, Shanghai, and Beijing. The Portuguese police, directed to stay out of the crisis in Macau to avoid upsetting the leadership in mainland China, made no attempt to provide protection for the British consulate and its officials.

The 48-year-old Ions, a staunch and stocky gray-haired Briton from Yorkshire, was later confronted on the grounds outside of the consulate. Ions was
not harmed, although the tires on his car were slashed. Meanwhile, demonstrators numbering in the hundreds gathered outside the consulate, chanting
Mao Zedong phrases over and over. Posters were pasted on the outside consulate walls which included such intimidating phrases as "Blood debt must be
paid by blood," "Down with British imperialism," and "Death to all running
dogs."[26] Another poster called for Hong Kong's governor, David Trench, to
"get out of Hong Kong."[27] In addition, on the main door of the consulate, the
demonstrators painted a turtle, symbolizing one of the most serious of Chinese insults.[28]

Two days later, Ions and his vice-consul, John Kemble, moved from the
British consulate to the Estoril Hotel, apparently hoping to put some distance
between themselves and the chanting Chinese demonstrators. In a telephone
conversation with *London Times* correspondent David Bonavia, Ions said, "My
house is plastered all over the place with paint up the steps and so on. We have
told our amahs [local servants] to go away for their own safety. It is a protest
against what is allegedly happening in Hong Kong." Ions said he had not been
harmed personally but had moved to the hotel as a precautionary measure. The
next day, to meet demands of Chinese demonstrators, the Macau bus company
scheduled two new routes, one to the British consulate and the other to the
British travel permit office, about a half-mile from the consulate. Despite the
demonstrations, Ions and his two vice-consuls, John Kemble and Edward Pollard, were attempting to maintain operations at their offices in Macau. The
travel permit office, in particular, was important for anyone wishing to travel
the forty miles by ferry across the Pearl River estuary to Hong Kong since
Macau had no other formal means of issuing such permits.

Finally, in a humiliating experience three days later, Ions and Kemble
were forced to stand in the hot sun for six hours outside the British consulate
while attempting to respond to the challenges and arguments of the Chinese
demonstrators. By then, paint and posters virtually covered the consulate building, and Kemble's automobile had been painted solid black.

Three days later an estimated 50,000 demonstrators gathered for a three-
hour late afternoon rally in Macau, including one hour in front of the British
consulate, in a continued organized protest against the British presence in the
Portuguese territory. Again, Ions stood his ground, meeting the group near the
entrance gate of the consulate "while Communist groups taunted him with
denunciations, slogans, quotations from Mao Zedong and Communist songs."[29]
He also accepted a petition containing grievances and complaints against the
British from the leaders of the demonstration. There was at least one bright
message among all the communications directed to Ions during the days of
demonstrations. It originated among the regulars at the Shortlands Tavern,
Ions' favorite pub in Kent, England, and said simply: "We are all behind you."

Meanwhile, the Communist leadership was also attempting to extend its influence among Macau's 300,000 Chinese population by pressuring local Catholic schools to present the thoughts of Mao Zedong in their classes and assign both teachers and students to participate in the demonstrations. Many of the non-Catholic schools already had begun offering classroom information relating to Mao Zedong and the Communist methodology. In an open form of intimidation towards this end, Communist representatives made regular visits to the Catholic classrooms to monitor the activities of teachers and students and to "take notes on their attitudes and views."[30] Pro–China newspapers in Macau also published stories directed specifically to Catholic young people, encouraging them to purchase Chairman Mao's book of quotations and other literature at Communist bookstores in Macau.

The unrest escalated on May 25, when British consul Norman Ions was again forced to stand outside in the sun, this time for seven hours, confronting demonstrators waving large banners, chanting anti-British slogans and handing him petitions. One observer said that by noon Ions was looking "as red as a boiled lobster, sunburned and exhausted."[31] On May 26, Ions and his vice-consuls Kemble and Pollard went to Hong Kong to discuss possible closure of the British consulate and travel permit office in Macau. Ions acknowledged that he stood outside in the sun for seven hours arguing with the demonstrators as a precaution against potential harm to the local employees of the consulate. While the question of retaining the British consulate in Macau was being debated, a decision was made by the British government to close down its consulate in Shanghai because of the demonstrations there. On Monday, May 29, the British announced the "temporary" closure of the Macau consulate and its travel permit office. Ions and his vice-consuls returned to London "on leave."

The British weren't the only focus of the Communist demonstrators in Macau. Americans were placed on notice that they were also targets of the unrest. Chinese sympathetic to the Communist unrest were urged to boycott American-made products, particularly movies, music recordings, soft drinks, and cigarettes. The United States Department of State issued an advisory dated May 26 urging the 110 Americans living in Macau to leave because of possible danger related to the anti–British demonstrations. In the advisory, Edward E. Rice, the United States consul general in Hong Kong, said: "Macau is not a safe place of residence for Americans and your continued residency there would be at your own risk."[32]

The Influence of Ho Yin

One of the most influential residents of Macau during the 1960s was Ho Yin, a wealthy businessman who enjoyed considerable respect from authorities in Macau, Portugal, and China. Ho, whose financial success was derived largely from his well-organized trading of gold, was characterized variously as a "Communist capitalist" or a "capitalist Communist."[33] One of his most important positions was that of representing the Chinese Chamber of Commerce of Macau on Macau's Legislative Council, the governmental body responsible for developing legislation in Macau. He also was a member of the Executive Council, which advised the governor of the Portuguese enclave on governmental matters, and he was a member of China's National People's Congress. Thus Ho was a key figure in virtually every major decision affecting Macau, whether instigated by Portugal or China, or by Macau itself. His influence helped Macau to deal with the rioting crisis in late 1966 and early 1967, at a time when Portugal and China had no formal relations.

Until the rioting crisis, refugees fleeing Communist China were able to move easily into Macau, some choosing to remain permanently in Macau and others living there while arranging to move on to Hong Kong. The flow of refugees in the early 1960s rose to more than 250 per day, causing concern in the enclave about problems of overcrowding, health care, and adequate food supplies (much of Macau's food was actually provided by mainland China).

For example, Portuguese authorities estimated that 42,475 "permanent" immigrants from mainland China settled in Macau between September 1, 1961, and March 1, 1962.[34] This was particularly significant in relation to Macau's population of 200,000 to 250,000 at that time. An additional 50,000 Chinese passed through Macau during the same period en route to Hong Kong.[35] Thousands more crossed into Macau from neighboring Guangdong province on a regular basis to purchase food and other personal items, which they transported back to their homes.

Many of the Chinese settling in Macau held legal exit permits issued by authorities in Communist China. A large percentage of the exit permits were given, however, to "the aged, sick and blind, in a drive to reduce population pressure in congested areas such as Canton [Guangzhou]."[36] The demand for exit permits from China also led to the proliferation of specialized "travel agencies." As explained by journalist Robert Trumbull:

> The prospective client, on entering the "travel agency," finds no one there but a boy or a watchman. He is told to come back another time. When he leaves he is followed and approached. Payment is agreed upon: It may range from less than a hundred dollars to several thousand. Eventually a relative or friend in some far-off Chinese city suddenly receives a long-awaited exit permit. And some Communist Chinese official has a fatter purse. Once through the centuries-old Barrier Gate that separates Chinese from Portuguese territory at the Macau city limits, the new arrival need only report to the local police to receive an identification card. After a year, this can be exchanged for a certificate of residence. Then, as a legal resident of Macau, the refugee can proceed to Hong Kong openly. Many choose not to wait a year, for opportunities in Macau are far fewer than in Hong Kong's rapidly expanding retail and manufacturing enterprises and

service industries. Another kind of "travel agency" will arrange secret transportation to Hong Kong in the hold of a junk.[37]

By mid–1962, officials in Macau were openly receiving refugees from mainland China, including those without entry papers. In a formal announcement reported by United Press International, the Macau government said: "Macau authorities have always authorized entry for people who possess documentation. It is also a tradition to receive those who do not have any documents."[38] At the same time, officials cautioned against abuse of the situation, warning "unnamed countries" not "to use the plight of the refugees for propaganda purposes or political advantage."[39] By explanation, UPI said the cautionary warning "appeared to be directed mainly against the Chinese Nationalists on Taiwan" to avert their contention that the "stream of refugees" was "proof" that the Communist regime was "on the point of collapse."[40]

Chapter 11

China and Portugal Sign Secret Agreements on Macau

To most Macau residents, Communist China's influence is nothing new because we have long been closely associated with the mainland.—MOK LAI MENG, director, News and Public Affairs, Teledifusão de Macau[1]

China's position on Macau and its administration by Portugal seemed considerably smoother entering the 1970s, and for good reason. Chinese and Portuguese officials had signed a secret agreement in 1967 providing for reasonable cooperation in connection with Macau and assuring Portugal that it could continue administering the affairs of Macau, at least for the time being. By 1969, for instance, a local Communist group known as the "Macau Struggle Committee" had changed its name to the "All Circles Compatriots" and showed a willingness to become less combative and more cooperative with local authorities. Another example of the relaxed pressure involved Radio Vila Verde, a broadcasting outlet that had been taken over by Communist leaders during the 1966 riots and then returned to its previous owners in June 1969. At the same time, Chinese Communist organizations and supporters were allowed complete freedom in Macau to publish newspapers, participate in trade unions, and operate schools and hospitals.[2]

China and Portugal negotiated a second secret agreement in 1979 which, after more than 400 years of de facto existence and limited treaty agreements, fully affirmed Macau's status as a Chinese territory under Portuguese administration. The secret agreement followed the enactment by Portugal in 1976 of the "Organic Statute for Macau" (Estatuto Organico de Macau, or EOM). The Organic Statute was intended to reflect two principles in Portugal's new 1976 constitution which stated: (1) Macau is not part of Portuguese territory and (2) under Portuguese administration, Macau shall be governed by a statute in keeping with her special situation. Under terms of the Organic Statute, the governor of Macau was still appointed by the Portuguese president but would be subject to a nonconfidence vote by Macau legislators (by a two-thirds majority), after which Lisbon could decide whether the governor should be retained or replaced. At the same time, the governor (if dissatisfied with legislative actions or inaction) could request that Portugal's president dissolve the Macau Legislative Assembly and order new elections. In either case, the final decision was entirely the responsibility of the Portuguese president.

Candidates of the conservative Association for the Defense of the Interests of Macau (ADIM) political party won 55 percent of the ballots in the July 1976 elections to capture four of the six directly elected seats in Macau's Legislative Assembly. The turnout was 78 percent, or 2,846 of the 3,649 registered voters. Following challenges and rechecking of the voting results, 2,728 ballots were declared to be valid. Critics complained that, despite participation in the election process by growing numbers of young people, most residents of Macau were simply not interested in choosing their leadership. One obvious deterrent was China's nonrecognition of elections, while another was a concern that registering to vote might lead to repercussions at a later time. Still another was a "traditional Confucian subservience to authority."[3]

Meanwhile, during the rush to resolve state responsibilities during the Portuguese Revolution in 1974, the powerful Armed Forces Movement proposed returning Macau to the People's Republic of China. A contingent of Portuguese officials went to Macau to present their plan personally, but they were directed to return to Lisbon by Ho Yin, China's unofficial representative in the region. According to historian Tom Gallagher: "The Beijing authorities were unwilling to incorporate this speck of the Chinese mainland, since Macau was an excellent source of foreign exchange and, through it, they were able quietly to import precious metals and other goods from countries which officially they had nothing to do with."[4]

China Claims Macau and Hong Kong

Both Macau and Hong Kong were named by China in a 1972 letter to the United Nations requesting their removal from consideration as "colonies." The letter by Huang Hua, China's top representative to the United Nations, was submitted to Salim A. Salim of Tanzania, chairman of the United Nations Special Committee on Colonialism, on March 10, 1972, and stated:

> The questions of Hong Kong and Macau belong to the category of questions resulting from the series of unequal treaties which the imperialists imposed on China. Hong Kong and Macau are part of Chinese territory occupied by the British and Portuguese authorities. The settlement of the questions of Hong Kong and Macau is entirely within China's sovereign right and does not at all fall under the ordinary category of colonial territories. Consequently they should not

The ancient art of dragon dancing highlights the celebration of Chinese New Year in Macau's Leal Senado Square.

be included in the list of colonial territories covered by the declaration of the granting of independence to colonial countries and people. With regard to the questions of Hong Kong and Macau, the Chinese government has consistently held that they should be settled in an appropriate way when conditions are ripe.[5]

Portugal's efforts to assist its former possessions in the early 1970s were noted publicly by Salim, who issued a formal statement in December 1974 praising the Portuguese government for its "positive and concrete steps" and its steady movement towards an "era of consultation and cooperation" with the United Nations.[6] At a news conference at the United Nations in New York, Dr. Antonio de Almeida Santos, Portugal's minister of decolonization (minister of interterritorial coordination) acknowledged the existence of a "tacit agreement" between Beijing and Lisbon providing for no immediate change in the administration of Macau. At the same time, he stressed that Macau was no longer regarded as a colony of Portugal. "We have no political problems in Macau," Almeida said. "As soon as we re-establish normal relations with China, we will talk about Macau."[7]

Portugal established diplomatic relations with China in January 1975 and in February severed its relations with the Republic of China in Taiwan, agreeing to recognize the People's Republic of China as the only legitimate government of China. Following up on these actions, Portugal dispatched Colonel José Eduardo Garcia Leandro to Macau in June 1975 to close down the Portuguese military garrison in Macau and to request the return of Macau to

China. As before, Ho Yin rejected the moves and reiterated that the Chinese leadership in Beijing was not yet ready to permit any change in Portugal's administration of Macau. When queried about China's refusal to accept the immediate return of Macau, officials in Lisbon denied making the proposal in the first place, calling attention instead to a policy statement issued earlier in 1975 which said Macau's future "could be negotiated at the proper time between the two governments."[8]

Tourism Rises to New Levels in Macau

The attraction of Macau for foreign visitors began improving in the late 1960s and soared to new heights in the 1970s. The increased interest, heightened by construction of new casinos, a dog racing track, and a jai alai stadium, led to expansion of ferry services and the introduction of fast-moving hydrofoils between Macau and Hong Kong. In 1972, construction of a bridge linking Macau with Taipa Island, located just south of the tiny peninsula, opened up new recreational areas for tourists. The announcement of plans for the new bridge was made in January 1970 by Macau's governor, Nobre de Carvalho, during his first formal press conference since his appointment in 1966. The new bridge was to be financed mainly by a loan from the Portuguese government.

Officials also began openly discussing ambitious plans for construction of an international airport on Taipa Island, development of a deep-water port on Coloane Island, and development of new recreational attractions, including a fashionable resort, on Macau's second island, Coloane, already linked to Taipa by a causeway. Investment confidence in the area was boosted in 1970 when the Macau Textile Manufacturers opened a modern new textile mill capable of producing 8,000 to 10,000 yards of cotton cloth per day. Later in the 1970s and 1980s, Macau experienced considerable investment in emerging modern industries focusing on electronics, toys, fireworks, plastic items, artificial flowers, porcelain, and garment manufacturing. Fireworks production is concentrated on Taipa Island, and the fireworks are marketed worldwide for celebrations such as the Fourth of July in the United States, Guy Fawkes Day in Great Britain and Australia, and traditional Chinese and other Oriental observances throughout Asia. Much of the new investment in Macau manufacturing and production has been financed by companies based in Hong Kong.

Governor Nobre de Carvalho contributed to the new investment and growth in Macau by announcing in 1970 that foreign banks would be permitted to operate in the territory. The new banking legislation finally became effective in 1972, providing for an influx of new investment capital. The first new banking licenses were granted to the Hong Kong-based Hongkong and Shanghai Banking Corporation and Nam Tung Bank, a division of the mainland's

Bank of China. Six other local commercial banks opened in 1973. Previously, only the Banco Nacional Ultramarino of Portugal had been allowed to provide banking services in Macau.

In addition, the governor promised to relax foreign exchange controls on exports of Macau products and approved pay raises up to 25 percent for Macau's civil servants. The improved investment climate brought almost immediate results that were reflected in a building boom which included construction of more than 50 new buildings in Macau during the first nine months of 1970, compared with 32 buildings constructed during all of 1969. In 1973, the number of completed new buildings totaled 120, and Macau experienced dramatic increases in land prices and rental fees. The burst of construction in 1970 included the opening of 150 new factories, representing a 15 percent increase in the number of industries in Macau, plus development of a multi-million-dollar casino-hotel and an upscale plush resort on Coloane Island.

The growth of Macau's textile industry was disrupted in 1972 when the Portuguese government ordered a ban on establishment of new textile companies because of the imposition of textile quotas announced in August 1971 by the United States government. Hong Kong firms had hoped they could continue to flourish and grow by opening new factories in Macau. The Portuguese ban on new textile companies was intended to protect Macau's already booming textile industry, which by 1972 accounted for about 60 percent of the territory's exports.

According to the Macau Tourist Information Bureau, nearly 2 million people arrived at Macau by ferry and hydrofoil in 1970, of whom 90 percent were weekend gamblers from Hong Kong. Only about 200,000 were characterized as tourists, and they came mostly from Japan, Great Britain, and the United States. Gambling had been a source of revenue for Macau since it was first introduced in 1851 by Governor Isidoro Francisco Guimaraes. For local residents of Macau, gambling represented a freedom to engage in an appealing activity which ranged from the noisy banging and rattling of mah-jongg tiles to the numerous lotteries with their ceremonious drawings and the several backstreet, multilevel fantan houses. According to historian Christopher Rand:

> Fantan is the only game I know that is normally three stories high. There is a long table on the ground floor and, above this, in the ceiling, is a hole of roughly the same dimensions. Above that, in the next ceiling, is another, slightly smaller, hole. There are railings round the holes, and players are seated at them, their bets being lowered and their winnings raised in baskets, on strings, that are the size of deep fingerbowls. Fantan as a game is almost shamefully simple—pure gambling without alleviating frills. The dealer has a pile of small counters, fundamentally beans, but in Macau at that time usually white bone buttons. He cuts out a mass of these by putting a bell-shaped brass instrument down on them. After the betting, he raises the bell and draws the buttons away four at a time, with a wand. The betting is on whether there will be one, two, three or four buttons left at the end.[9]

A spectacular fireworks display over Macau's Praia Grande Bay illuminates the Hotel Lisboa, the city's largest casino-hotel.

In August 1971, tourism was significantly disrupted when Typhoon Rose moved through Hong Kong, seriously damaging shipping links between Macau and Hong Kong. The typhoon damaged nine of eleven hydrofoils which traversed the Pearl River estuary between Macau and Hong Kong, setting back operations of the largest hydrofoil fleet in the world.[10] In addition, one ferryboat was sunk and another damaged among the four ferries providing sea transportation between the two areas. Macau's tourist industry was

adversely affected for several weeks, though most of the hydrofoils were operating again in time for the annual Macau Grand Prix in November.[11]

Tourism to Macau increased considerably through the early 1970s,
exceeding 2 million visitors in 1973 (up 100,000 from 1972). The hydrofoil fleet
was increased in number to 20, a new ferryboat was added, and plans were
made to add two jumbo hydrofoils in early 1974.[12] In addition, two commercial jetfoils, each able to carry 284 passengers, were set to begin operating
between Hong Kong and Macau in late 1974.[13]

The 150th birthday of British artist George Chinnery, who lived in Macau
from 1825 until his death in 1852, was especially commemorated in 1974. As
described by author Robin Hutcheon: "The ceremony consisted of a short ecu-
menical service at the Chapel in the Old Protestant Cemetery where Chinnery is buried, the mounting and unveiling of a plaque on Chinnery's monument by the Governor of Macau, General Nobre de Carvalho, the opening of
an exhibition of Chinnery's works at the Museum Luís de Camões, with a cat-
alogue in Portuguese and Chinese prepared by Luís Gonzaga Gomes, and the
renaming of a street after the artist."[14] In addition, the Macau government
issued a special commemorative postage stamp in late 1974, that featured a self-
portrait of Chinnery painted in 1840.

Macau Restrains Illegal Immigrants from Mainland China

Thousands of mainland Chinese found ways to enter Macau illegally
during the late 1970s, most of them hoping to continue on to Hong Kong,
where they might be able to live and earn money undetected by local authorities. As Hong Kong officials increased their efforts to locate and deport illegal immigrants, however, many realized they were confined to Macau and
began returning to China on their own. Unofficial estimates suggested that
more than 120,000 Chinese had illegally entered Macau from 1978 to 1980,
raising Macau's population to more than 400,000.[15]

One common method of going the 40 miles by sea from Macau to Hong
Kong was on a "snakeboat," a small, fast-moving fishing vessel that offered
refugees a forged identity card as part of its package. The cost of snakeboat
passage by October 1980 had increased to US$4,000—up about 40 percent
from the going rate a year earlier. Although the snakeboat business continued
to be brisk and lucrative, patrol boats around the British territory began to
reduce the numbers of people attempting to enter Hong Kong illegally.
Authorities reported fewer than 600 arrests in Hong Kong waters through the
first nine months of 1980, compared with 2,150 during all of 1979.[16]

Macau finally had to take action of its own because of overcrowding in
the Portuguese territory, which was made worse by a high birth rate and a
shortage of available housing. In August 1979, authorities began identifying

the illegal immigrants and placing them in trucks to be returned to China through the Portas do Cerca. Within a month of Macau's stepped-up enforcement, an estimated 4,000 Chinese had been transported back to the mainland.[17]

Chapter 12

Talks with China on the Future of Macau

Deng Xiaoping, the Chinese Communist Party deputy chairman and elder statesman, yesterday described the future of Macau as "no problem."—MARY LEE[1]

Residents of Macau, nervously monitoring China's talks with Great Britain during the early 1980s on the future of Hong Kong, realized that their future would soon include the end of Portuguese administration and the assimilation of the little territory into China. After two years of discussion, Great Britain and China signed an agreement outlining the terms of the July 1, 1997, handover of Hong Kong to Chinese rule. Officials of Portugal and China announced in 1985 that negotiations on Macau would begin in 1986, suggesting that its reversion to Chinese rule would probably follow similar guidelines as the accord on Hong Kong.

As I noted in a previous book on Hong Kong:

> The Joint Declaration for Hong Kong defined a number of basic changes effective when the British lease expires July 1, 1997. One significant change was the designation of Hong Kong as a "Special Administrative Region" within China, with retention of its status as a free port and international financial center. Laws already in force would remain unchanged, and local government authorities would maintain public order. The agreement pledged continuation of Hong Kong's social and economic systems and "lifestyle" until the year 2047, including the right to strike and freedom of speech, assembly, travel, press, correspondence, occupation, association and religion. Residents of Hong Kong would not be taxed by China. In addition, the agreement provided for establishment of the Sino-British Joint Liaison Group (to ensure the "smooth transfer" of government in 1997), consideration of Hong Kong land leases extending beyond 1997 and development of the Basic Law, a constitution-like document defining rights and policies of post-1997 Hong Kong.[2]

Governor Expands Voting Base in Macau

Macau's governor, Vasco Almeida e Costa, introduced in February 1984, expanded voting for seats in the Legislative Assembly, with twenty-one candidates campaigning for six available legislative seats. More than 51,000 residents of Macau's estimated 400,000 population were registered to vote under the new laws, which provided equal voting rights to all residents, regardless of how long they had lived in the enclave.

In announcing his voter expansion plans, the governor said: "We're not forcing them to participate, but opening the doors for participation." (Strict voter qualification requirements had limited registration in the 1980 and 1976 elections to fewer than 4,000.) Besides the six directly elected members, the Legislative Assembly would include six indirectly elected members (chosen by large professional and social organizations) and five members to be appointed by the governor.

Despite the increased number of registered voters for the August 1984 elections, most observers expected a very low turnout, mainly because of traditional political apathy among the Chinese. They were pleasantly surprised, however, when more than 29,000 ballots were cast, representing about 56 percent of the 51,000 registered voters.[3] Governor Vasco Almeida e Costa expressed satisfaction about the election and its outcome, stressing that "its importance was that it had removed the link between Portuguese domestic politics and the Macau assembly."[4]

One of the first formal discussions about Macau's future occurred in February 1985, when Governor Vasco de Almeida e Costa visited Beijing, Shanghai, and Guangzhou for a week-long series of talks on expanding economic cooperation between the Portuguese enclave and China. The official announcement, issued in Beijing by Xinhua (China's official news agency), said the governor and Chinese leaders would also discuss "other matters of mutual interest."[5] Another series of talks occurred in May 1985, when the Portuguese president, Antonio Ramalho Eanes, made a formal visit to Beijing. During that visit, according to Xinhua, the future of Macau was discussed by Portugal's foreign minister, Jaime Gama, and China's foreign minister, Wu Xueqian, who characterized the two and one-half hours of talks as "constructive and useful."[6]

A joint announcement by President Eanes and Prime Minister Zhao Ziyang said the two countries had "agreed to hold talks in the near future on resolving the question of Macau."[7] The announcement, referring specifically to the secret agreement signed in February 1979 between China and Portugal which designated Macau as a Chinese territory administered by the Portuguese, acknowledged "the good cooperation between the two governments in dealing with the affairs of Macau on the basis of that understanding."

In a news conference before leaving Beijing, President Eanes declined to specify when Macau would actually be returned to China, saying only that it would occur "when we [Portugal and China] both feel it is the right moment."[8] Eanes also noted that the issue of Macau's future had not been part of the official agenda for his visit to Beijing but was raised during the talks by Chinese officials.[9] He also said Portugal and China had a "common objective" in maintaining the prosperity and stability of Macau.[10] Eanes followed up his visit to Beijing with a one-day stopover in Macau on his return to Lisbon, urging politicians and others to work towards cooperation in connection with Macau's future and announcing that negotiations between China and Portugal on Macau would begin in 1986.

One of the most influential residents of Macau, wealthy businessman Ho Yin, was instrumental in maintaining communications between Portugal and China before the two countries established formal diplomatic relations in 1979. Ho, an official representative of the mainland Chinese government, was a prominent figure in Macau's society and politics from the 1960s until his death in 1983. He was generally accepted in Macau by both the Portuguese administration and the Chinese community.[11]

Ho's business interests included hotels, restaurants, banking and land transportation (taxis and buses). In addition, he was a leading member and sometimes officer of Macau's Chinese General Chamber of Commerce, Macau's Legislative Assembly, several public utility companies serving Macau and the Standing Committee of the Chinese National People's Congress.

Tourism Rises in Macau

Nearly five million tourists visited Macau in 1981, of whom 75 percent were residents of Hong Kong who were attracted by the gambling casinos and racetracks featuring both horses and dogs. Another attraction was the jai alai stadium where viewers could watch and wager on jai alai, a fast-moving sport originating with the Spanish Basques in which players with long wicker claws compete by slinging balls against the walls of a three-sided court. Most of the nearly three dozen professional jai alai players in Macau are from the Basque region of Spain.

Gambling in Macau, established in the 1850s through licensing permitted by Governor Isidoro Francisco Guimaraes, became more of a business in 1934 when the Macau government granted exclusive rights to the Tai Xing Company for control of casino-style gaming in the territory. Tai Xing opened its first casino in the Central Hotel, located near the Loyal Senate. The growth of casino gambling in Macau under Tai Xing was given a dramatic boost after the Chinese Communists were successful in driving out the Chinese Nationalists in 1949 and banned gambling in mainland China.

Tai Xing's monopoly continued until January 1962, when the Macau government awarded the lucrative exclusive contract to the Macau Tourism and

Entertainment Company (Sociedade de Turismo e Diversoes de Macau, or STDM), headed by wealthy businessman Stanley Ho. STDM added popular European and American games, such as baccarat and roulette, and improved winning odds for gamblers. In addition, STDM began operating fast jetfoils and hovercraft ferries to speed transportation of gamblers from Hong Kong.

By the end of 1985, there were 5 gambling casinos in Macau with some 130 tables offering games of blackjack, craps, roulette, and baccarat, plus 625 slot machines.[12] In addition, betting centers around Macau began offering instant lotteries in 1984, from which revenues helped finance social welfare programs in the territory. Most of the gambling in Macau is conducted in the casinos, however. In 1985, for instance, 25 billion patacas (about U.S. $3.2 billion) was bet in the casinos, compared with 500 million patacas in all other forms of wagering.[13]

A Portuguese army general, Nuno Melo Egidio, assumed the governorship of Macau in February 1979, succeeding Colonel Garcia Leandro. His arrival coincided with the long-awaited establishment of formal diplomatic relations between China and Portugal. Egidio spent his first year studying Macau's precarious situation as a Portuguese-administered territory under virtual domination by the People's Republic of China. In one of his first significant actions as governor, Egidio brought in eighty senior policemen from Portugal in late 1979 to help strengthen security in the territory and to reduce corruption within Macau's police force, which was sometimes characterized as "the foreign legion of the Far East."[14]

Portugal's new diplomatic relations with China were an important factor in Governor Egidio's official visit to Beijing, the first ever by a governor of Macau. While meeting with Chinese leaders, Egidio secured approval for two major territory projects—a new airport on reclaimed land and a bridge linking the island of Taipa with the Macau peninsula. He also received guarantees for additional electricity and water supplies from the Chinese mainland, which were vital to successful development of future projects in Macau. In addition, he was assured by Chinese leaders of their support for continued Portuguese administration of Macau, at least for the time being.

Egidio, who stepped down as governor in February 1981 to become chief of the general staff of the Portuguese armed forces, was succeeded in June 1981 by Vasco de Almeida e Costa, a Portuguese naval commander. Almeida e Costa was sworn in as the 116th governor of Macau by President Antonio Eanes of Portugal during an elaborate formal ceremony at Lisbon's Belem Palace. One of his major challenges as governor was to oversee revision of Macau's 1979 constitution, which is known as the Organic Statute. He also continued working towards development of a new airport, a new deep-water port, land reclamation, offshore banking, increased trade with China, and the establishment of satellite towns on the islands of Taipa and Coloane. In addition, although Macau already enjoyed considerable investment from sources in Hong Kong, the new governor took an aggressive interest in attracting new investment interest from other countries, making several business trips in 1982 to such places as Lisbon, Paris, Singapore, and Malaysia. In July 1982, President Eanes of Portugal announced that Almeida e Costa would continue as governor of Macau for a full three-year term.

One of Governor Almeida e Costa's most significant actions occurred in February 1984, when President Eanes approved his recommendation to dissolve Macau's Legislative Assembly and order the election of a new legislature within 180 days that would be chosen under voting rights granted to all Chinese residents in Macau. Previously, voting had been limited to a few thousand residents, mostly Portuguese and Macanese (locally born Eurasians), comprising about two percent of the estimated 450,000 people living in Macau.

Chapter 13

Portugal and China Agree on the Future of Macau

From our point of view, we were very glad that Portugal accepted a rather easy process for the handing over of Macau to Chinese sovereignty.—DENG XIAOPING[1]

Formal negotiations between China and Portugal on the future of Macau began in Beijing with a two-day session on June 30 and July 1, 1986. The Chinese team was headed by Zhou Nan, China's deputy foreign minister, while the Portuguese negotiators were led by Dr. Rui Barbosa Medina, Portugal's ambassador to the United Nations. Zhou had been China's chief representative in the 1982–84 negotiations for the Hong Kong agreement with Great Britain.

The talks, although confidential, were characterized by Chinese officials as consistent with applying Deng Xiaoping's stated policy of "one country, two systems" to the territory of Macau. That policy, suggesting a workable combination of Communism and capitalism under jurisdiction of the People's Republic of China, was first promoted prior to the 1982–84 negotiations between China and Great Britain which led to the 1984 agreement for the reversion of Hong Kong to China in 1997.

After the 1949 Chinese Communist victory in China's Civil War, there was an increasing pressure by the Chinese leadership to regain control over all of China's territory, including the British colony of Hong Kong, the Portuguese colony of Macau and the island of Taiwan, now home to the Nationalist Republic of China. This renewed hope was reflected in *The Rise of Modern China* (3d edition) in which historian Immanuel Hsu wrote: "In its 4,000 years of recorded history, China has been divided and reunited countless times. If history is any guide, and if politics is the art of expecting the unexpected, then we need not lose heart over the present difficulties. The genius of the Chinese people will find a way to make China one again."[2]

The second round of talks between China and Portugal was held on September 8 and 9, 1986, also in Beijing. Following the third round of negotiations on October 21 and 22, a joint communiqué announced "broad agreement" on the planned transition of Macau from Portuguese administration to Chinese rule. In a general phrase characterizing the talks that was intended to placate citizens of Macau, the communiqué said: "The two sides continued in-depth discussions of the sensitive items of the agenda in a friendly and harmonious atmosphere, and reached a broad agreement."[3]

One of the most debated issues of the agreement was the actual date on which Macau would be returned to China. Negotiators for Lisbon had wanted the transition to occur in the year 2007 to commemorate 450 years of Portuguese administration of Macau. China insisted that the handover occur before the end of the twentieth century. After four rounds of negotiations spread over nine months, the governments of Portugal and China agreed in March 1987 that Macau would revert to Chinese rule on December 20, 1999. The negotiations and agreement on the accord raised, at least briefly, new recognition for the Portuguese-administered territory of Macau, which had been virtually ignored during the twentieth century despite its long historical significance.

The Joint Declaration for Macau, initialed in Beijing on March 26, 1987, was formally signed on April 13, 1987 in the Great Hall of the People in Beijing by Portugal's prime minister, Anibal Cavaco Silva, and China's premier, Zhao Ziyang. Among those witnessing the signing of the historic agreement were China's supreme leader, Deng Xiaoping, and its president, Li Xiannian. The Joint Declaration provided for the designation of Macau as a "special administrative region," with a guarantee of fifty years of autonomy beyond 1999 and continuation of its social, economic, and political systems. After the signing, Cavaco Silva said: "Portugal will do everything in order to maintain the stability and to promote the economic development of the territory and of its population."[4]

Zhou Nan, who headed China's negotiating team, earlier described the agreement as "the resolution of a long-standing question left over by history."[5] At the initialing ceremony in March, Zhou commented that the Sino-Portuguese Joint Declaration marked "yet another important step of the Chinese people in striving for the realization of the grand goal of the reunification of the motherland in this century."[6]

The agreement was similar to one negotiated during 1982-84 for Hong Kong, with a major difference—the ethnic Chinese citizens of Macau and their descendants after 1999 would be granted full citizenship rights by the Portuguese government. This meant that a large percentage of Macau's citizens could live in Portugal, rather than China, if they so chose. These citizens would even have the right to live and work in any of the European Union countries, including England, because Portugal was a member of the EU.

At a news conference in Macau on April 18, 1987, Governor Cavaco Silva said: "Whoever is Portuguese now or becomes Portuguese before 1999 will have the right to remain Portuguese in the future, and so will their children

View of Macau from the verandah of the elegant Bela Vista, built in the nineteenth century and newly remodeled in the 1990s.

and grandchildren."[7] Thus, according to Portuguese law, nationality would be based on bloodline rather than by place of birth. Although China had earlier issued a statement opposing the granting of Portuguese nationality to a large number of ethnic Chinese citizens of Macau, the Chinese leadership soon conceded the issue, which was estimated to affect some 90,000 citizens of Macau, or about one-fifth of the total population of the territory.

The Hong Kong agreement provided for possible resettlement in England before 1997 of only about 8.3 percent of the territory's six million residents. The Macau agreement allowed for possible resettlement before 1999 of nearly 100,000 of its citizens, or more than twenty percent of its population.

Another difference between the Macau and Hong Kong agreements concerned the makeup and selection of legislators and chief executives. In Macau, under terms of Annex I of the Joint Declaration: "The legislature shall be composed of local inhabitants and the majority of its members shall be elected ... and its chief executive shall be appointed by the Central Government on the basis of the results of elections or consultations held in Macau." This seemed to allow for the appointment of at least some members of Macau's Legislative Assembly. According to the Hong Kong accord, however, "The legislature of the Hong Kong Special Administrative Region shall be constituted by elections."

Much of the cautious but equitable relationship between China and Macau during the 1980s was largely the result of behind-the-scenes efforts of wealthy Chinese businessmen with close ties to Beijing. One example was Ma Man-kee, a multimillionaire real estate and banking executive who conducted his business activities from an office above an antique shop located at the promenade of the Praia Grande. Visitors to Ma's office were immediately made aware of his political priorities after seeing two framed photographs on a wall—a very large photo of China's supreme leader Deng Xiaoping and a small photo of Antonio Ramalho Eanes, the former president of Portugal.[8]

Preparation for Macau's transition from Portuguese administration to Chinese rule began in earnest following the April 1987 signing of the Sino-Portuguese Joint Declaration on Macau. One of the most determined efforts would be to establish ethnic Chinese citizens in upper level government positions, which had previously been held primarily by Portuguese or Macanese individuals. Most of these Chinese were unable to converse or communicate in Portuguese, which was perceived as a major problem in preparing for the smooth transition of Macau in 1999. Therefore, as part of the preparation, hundreds of middle-rank civil servants were enrolled in courses to improve their fluency in both Chinese and Portuguese. In late 1987, forty Chinese individuals were selected to take an intensive one-year course in Lisbon on public administration and the Portuguese language. Another fifty were chosen for the course in 1988. Under the conditions for their selection to take the courses, these individuals agreed to return to Macau and work for the Macau government for at least three years.

Another transition development occurred in 1988, when China's Premier Li Peng proposed establishment of a Macau Basic Law Drafting Committee (BLDC). This committee was to be responsible for drawing up a constitution-like document that would govern Macau after 1999. The proposal was duly approved by China's National People's Congress, and Chinese officials announced in September 1988 the appointment of 48 representatives to the BLDC, primarily legal experts, leading mainland officials, and noted personalities. Nineteen appointed representatives of the group were from Macau, including casino magnate Stanley Ho and businessman Dr. Ma Man-kee, who were already looked upon favorably by the Chinese leadership.

In still another positive move towards the pending reversion of Macau, the Legislative Assembly voted in February 1989 to make Chinese an official language, along with Portuguese. Legislators directed that all official documents in Macau be written in both Mandarin Chinese and Portuguese by the end of 1989. In April 1989, the transition process gained strength when the 19 Macau representatives of the BLDC approved the appointment of 88 members to the Basic Law Consultative Committee (BLCC). This group included a cross-section of people in Macau, such as bankers, traders, business executives, senior civil servants, and trade unionists.

For many residents of Macau, the pending transition to China rule was perhaps not so fearful as was the situation in Hong Kong. Under terms of a memorandum in the Sino-Portuguese agreement, full Portuguese citizenship had been granted to anyone born in Macau before October 3, 1981, and, in January 1989, Portugal began issuing burgundy-colored European Community passports to more than 100,000 Macau residents, nearly one-quarter of the estimated 450,000 residents of the enclave.

These passports, unlike those issued in Hong Kong, would be valid beyond the 1999 handover to China and would transfer Portuguese nationality to children of the document holders. In addition, the passports qualified holders to live and work in Portugal or anywhere in the European Community (now European Union), whereas the new British passports in Hong Kong were mainly travel documents, holders of these British passports would subsequently require permits to live and work in Great Britain.

Macau's relationship with China seemed to be hardly affected by the June 4, 1989, forceful suppression of pro-democratic demonstrators in Beijing's Tiananmen Square by the Chinese military. A scheduled meeting of Chinese and Portuguese officials developing Macau's Basic Law was held as planned, and the Macau government announced that the events in Beijing would not interfere with plans to build an international airport on Taipa Island. Without apparent encouragement by local protest leaders, however, more than 50,000 demonstrators gathered in central Macau to show concern about the Tiananmen massacre.

Expanded Voting for Elections in Macau

Under the terms of Macau's new electoral law, which was enacted in 1984, all Macau residents were qualified to vote for directly elected seats in the Legislative Assembly and the two municipal bodies, the Loyal Senate (Leal Senado) and the Municipal Council of the Islands (Camara Municipal das Ilhas). Before 1984, voting was limited only to Portuguese and Macanese (mixed Portuguese-Asian or Portuguese-Malaccan descent), plus Chinese citizens residing in Macau for five years or longer.

Some 56 percent of Macau's registered voters cast ballots for directly elected seats in the legislature and municipal councils in the 1984 elections, suggesting significant voter interest which officials had hoped would continue in future elections. However, possibly because of little public encouragement from the Macau government, the turnout on October 9, 1988, was much worse than expected, with fewer than 30 percent of the 67,492 registered voters in Macau casting ballots.

Three of the six directly elected legislators were pro–Beijing candidates, while the other three were independent liberal candidates, without support from mainland China. Among the remaining legislators in the 17-member Legislative Assembly, six were indirectly elected as representatives of business and social groups, and five were appointed by the governor of Macau. The Legislative Assembly, as Macau's leading governmental body, had responsibility over development of the budget of the Macau government, acted on regulations related to civil servants, and could approve or reject laws proposed by the Macau administration.

Macau's 1984 electoral law increased membership in the Loyal Senate from eight to fifteen, of which six were directly elected, six were indirectly elected (as representatives of social and business organizations), and three were appointed by the Macau governor. The Loyal Senate had jurisdiction over the Macau peninsula, while the Municipal Council of the Islands was responsible for matters concerning Macau's two islands, Taipa and Coloane. Among the eleven members of the Municipal Council, four were directly elected, four indirectly elected, and three appointed by the governor. Before 1984, all but two members of the Loyal Senate were either appointed by the governor or chosen by Portuguese residents in a high tax bracket, while all members of the Municipal Council of the Islands were similarly appointed or chosen.

Macau Governor Vasco de Almeida e Costa, who had been appointed to his position by President Antonio Ramalho Eanes of Portugal in 1981, resigned the governorship in January 1986 to coincide with the end of Eanes' term of office. Eanes was succeeded as president of Portugal by Mario Soares, who subsequently appointed 55-year-old Dr. Joaquim Pinto Machado, a surgeon from Oporto and one of Soares' top advisers, as the new governor of Macau.

Pinto Machado arrived in Macau in May 1986, just weeks before the opening of talks between China and Portugal on the future of Macau. The appointment marked the first time the governorship of Macau was held by a non-military official. Although there had been rumors and speculation about problems between the governor and some members of his administration, Dr. Pinto Machado surprised leaders in both Macau and Lisbon by abruptly resigning his post in late May 1987, saying he was upset by the degree of corruption in Macau. He claimed the corruption included "financial irregularities" in tourism, gambling and broadcasting, plus widespread prostitution.[9] Pinto Machado said he decided to resign "for reasons of institutional dignity which I have not forsaken, reasons which are of such importance to me personally that I should lose my self-respect were I not to continue to value them."[10]

To replace Pinto Machado, Portugal's President Mario Soares named 60-year-old Carlos Melancia, one of his closest associates and an electronics engineer, as the new governor of Macau. Soares presided over swearing-in ceremonies for Melancia in Lisbon on July 9, 1987. Melancia arrived in Macau during the first week of August 1987 and immediately promised to work towards development of an airport and deep-water port for Macau.

The Influence of Stanley Ho

From the 1970s into the 1990s, one of the most influential residents of Macau was billionaire businessman Stanley Ho Hung-sun, head of the Macau Tourism and Entertainment Company (Sociedade de Turismo e Diversões de Macau, or STDM), which in 1962 was granted the exclusive franchise to operate all of Macau's casinos. By the 1990s, STDM was providing half of the revenue income for the Macau government and had developed much of the territory's tourist needs, such as hotels and transportation. Ho also maintained gambling interests in other countries and owned Shun Tak Shipping, which operates the ferries, hydrofoils, and jetfoils linking Macau to Hong Kong across the estuary of the Pearl River Delta between the two enclaves. His net worth was estimated in 1992 at U.S.$1.1 billion.[11]

Macau's Legislative Assembly voted in September 1986 to extend until the year 2001 STDM's license to continue operating its five casinos. The approval also included permission for STDM to offer shares on the Hong Kong stock market and participate in several major construction projects designed to improve housing and transportation in Macau.

Under the terms of the renewed license, STDM would pay the government a minimum of 250 million patacas (U.S.$18.9 million) or 26 percent of its annual income, whichever amount was higher. The arrangement with STDM was important to the continued growth and financial security of Macau, as it had been since it was first negotiated and granted in 1962. To demonstrate the value of the agreement, STDM paid the Macau government 430 million patacas in taxes in 1985, which amounted to 40 percent of the government's revenue for that year.[12] Most of this money was derived from the estimated 4.1 million people who visited Macau during 1985, more than 80 percent of whom came from Hong Kong on weekends to try their luck in the casinos.[13]

The gambling season in Macau officially opens with the Chinese New Year in late January or February. The annual ritual, little changed through the 1980s and 1990s, begins on New Year's Eve with elaborate ceremonies at the Casino Lisboa, one of the most prominent landmarks in Macau. For this event, thousands of people gather at the Casino Lisboa to witness the arrival of a black Mercedes-Benz, with the governor of Macau, and a dark green Rolls-Royce, bringing Stanley Ho, the head of STDM and the controlling force behind the casinos of Macau.

In one of the most significant moments of the annual tradition, these two gentlemen place the first bets of the new gambling season at a roulette table, amidst applause by surrounding dignitaries elegantly dressed in fur coats, lavish evening gowns, and tuxedos. Ho himself, unlike his customers, is known for avoiding gambling, other than the once-a-year ceremony on the eve of the Lunar New Year. "I don't like gambling," Ho once said. "I don't have the patience for it."[14]

Casino gambling is Macau's most popular attraction and a prime reason for the millions of people who visit the territory each year.

Stanley Ho was born in Hong Kong into a family of considerable affluence. While Stanley was a boy, however, his father's financial fortunes suffered extensive reversal, sending him into bankruptcy and causing him to abandon his family in disgrace and resettle in Vietnam. Despite his new life of near-poverty, Ho managed to obtain a scholarship to attend Hong Kong University, and then, upon the invasion of Hong Kong by the Japanese, he fled to Macau to live with an uncle.

The *Santa Maria* is one of several jetfoils carrying passengers on the 40-mile sea-journey between Macau and Hong Kong.

Young Stanley later acknowledged the business expertise he learned from his uncle, which he applied during the war by selling wood oil to the Japanese in return for food and textiles needed by Western refugees in Macau.[15] During the war years, he expanded his trading to include selling precious metals and airplanes to China, and during the Korean War embargo he used his Macau connections to sell corrugated iron, rubber tires, and other goods to China.[16] As a result, Ho was a millionaire by age 24 and used his wealth to purchase property and bid for Macau's exclusive casino franchise. He played a crucial role in the late 1970s in helping China and Portugal to resolve the administrative and diplomatic crisis over Macau, which eventually led to the formal agreement in the 1980s outlining the return of Macau to China in 1999.

During the 1980s, Stanley Ho personally owned 20 percent of STDM, which was responsible for managing the five casinos then operating in Macau, along with operating five hotels, ferries, hydrofoils, and jetfoils between Macau and Hong Kong, plus Macau's greyhound racing track and jai alai stadium. STDM also operated during this period 40 tugboats and dredges which removed silt from the harbors of Macau. More than 50,000 of the estimated 420,000 people living in Macau during the late 1980s were employed by

Macau's Museu de Vinho (Wine Museum) reflects the role of Portuguese wine in the long colonial history of Macau, including an exhibition of wine-making equipment, photographs and a tasting room.

STDM.[17] Besides developing his business interests, Ho has maintained a high public profile in both Macau and Hong Kong, where his home at 1 Repulse Bay is one of Hong Kong's most prestigious addresses. He regularly donates large amounts of money for sports and cultural activities in Macau and Hong Kong, frequently accepting invitations to judge beauty pageants, and can be counted on to purchase the most expensive or desirable item offered at Macau's yearly charity auction.

Following the successful completion of negotiations in early 1987 between China and Portugal regarding Macau's 1999 transition to Chinese rule, Stanley Ho predicted the agreement would be "favorable for business" in Macau.[18] Ho made his comments while in Lisbon to sign a contract giving his Macau Tourism and Entertainment Company a controlling 51.9 percent interest in the Estoril-Sol Group, which operated several five-star hotels in Portugal and the Estoril gambling casino outside Lisbon. "We saw the same influx of foreign money in Hong Kong after the agreement with Great Britain," he said. "Before the agreement between Portugal and China, the future was uncertain. Now the future is settled. We are assured fifty years of [a] capitalist system—one country, two systems."[19]

The increasing numbers of visitors to Macau in 1987 prompted an upswing of interest in building new hotels, adding seagoing transportation from

Two men playing Chinese chess (and a third person watching) in the Camões Garden.

Taiwan, improving highways from Macau into China, planning a new bridge to link the Macau peninsula with Taipa Island, developing a new deepwater harbor, and planning for an international airport. Dredging work began in June 1988 for a deepwater port at Ka Ho Harbor on Coloane Island that was intended to significantly benefit trading prospects for Macau. Upon completion of the project in 1991, oceangoing vessels up to 10,000 tons could dock at Macau, compared with previous limits of 2,000-ton ships. The port was also designed to handle up to 10,800 containers per month, opening new and profitable prospects for the lucrative business of transshipments.

An estimated 2.3 million people visited Macau during the first six months of 1987, and the number of visitors rose by 15 percent during the first six months of 1988. More than 80 percent of those visitors were residents of Hong Kong who were attracted to Macau on weekends to gamble at the casinos or bet on horse racing, dog racing, and jai alai.

Macau Grand Prix

The Macau Grand Prix, a glitzy, noisy, fast-paced car-racing event seen on television each November by more than 500 million people in 75 countries, was first proposed in the early 1950s by Portuguese telecommunications engineer

Racing cars move into position at the start of the annual Macau Grand Prix, Asia's premier motor-racing event, held each November.

Fernando de Macedo Pinto, who dreamed up plans for a motorized "treasure hunt" conducted on the city's cobbled streets.[20] He sought advice from the Hong Kong Motor Sports Club, whose president, Paul du Toit, suggested the event should be a full-fledged road race.[21] By the 1970s, the Grand Prix in Macau was internationally known and a favorite event for the world's leading race-car drivers, often compared to the Monaco Grand Prix. In the early 1990s, writer Nury Vittachi described the Macau Grand Prix as "a carnival of primal human experiences: money, fame, love and death."[22] To commemorate the prestige of the event, the Macau Grand Prix Museum was opened in 1993, and it attracted some 20,000 visitors in its first year.

The number of visitors from Taiwan during the first six months of 1988 totaled 51,930, or an overwhelming 1,500 percent increase from the same period in 1987. The increase was the result mainly of the establishment of a regular ferry between Macau and Kaohsiung in southern Taiwan that was operated by Stanley Ho's Macau Tourism and Entertainment Company. Meanwhile, Hong Kong developer Gordon Wu proposed construction of a 24-mile highway linking Macau with Hong Kong, which he said would cut in half the travel time between the two enclaves (then one hour by sea).

Two men preparing decorations for a weekend festival in Macau.

The influence of China became considerably more visible in Macau after the April 1987 signing of the Sino-Portuguese Joint Declaration. China's official news agency, Xinhua, opened an office in Macau on September 21, 1987, replacing the trading firm of Nam Kwong Company as Beijing's main representative in Macau. The first director of Macau's new Xinhua office was

Zhou Ding, who was formerly a deputy Communist party general of the Shenzhen Special Economic Zone. Zhou said his reports to China would focus on changes in Macau's economic and political matters, along with efforts to determine "the wishes of its people."[23]

The 1987 Sino-Portuguese Joint Declaration on Macau, which was similar to the 1984 Sino-British Joint Declaration on Hong Kong, promised establishment of Macau as a "special administrative region" (SAR) in 1999 under the name "Macau, China" and guaranteed that its social, legal, and economic systems would remain unchanged through the year 2049. The Macau SAR would maintain its executive, legislative, and judicial authority, but the People's Republic of China would assume control over its defense and foreign matters. The Joint Declaration on Macau was formally signed in a small ceremony on April 13, 1987, in Beijing by Prime Minister Anibal Cavaco Silva of Portugal and Premier Zhao Ziyang of China.

Chapter 14

Macau in the 1990s—
Growth and Optimism

*Compared with Hong Kong, Macau is viewed by many as an example
of a smooth transition from colonial to Chinese rule.* —MICHAEL
WESTLAKE, editor, *Far Eastern Economic Review*[1]

Business in Macau began booming in the early 1990s, stimulated in part
by Taiwanese investors speculating in the development of luxury housing projects. Investors from Hong Kong also played a major role in boosting Macau's
economy, particularly on the island of Taipa, the location of Macau's new
international airport. Macau's transition from Portuguese administration to
Chinese rule seemed to be moving along quite smoothly. It appeared that it
would be a solid example of Deng Xiaoping's "one country, two systems" vision
to unify China.

One of the elements affecting potential investment in Macau was the
looming 1997 handover of Hong Kong from British administration to Chinese
rule. To attract wealthy Hong Kong investors who were seeking to leave before
1997 and to provide a boost to its residential property market, the Macau
Legislative Assembly approved the Investment and Immigration Act of 1995
that permitted foreign investors purchasing property in Macau valued at more
than U.S.$256,000 to become permanent residents of the enclave. Most agreed
that the legislation was essentially a temporary alternative for investors, since
Macau would be reverting to China in 1999. They also agreed, however, that
it would indeed bring considerable improvement to Macau's property market.

Tourism continued to rise in the 1990s, exceeding 7.8 million in 1994,
aided by a new terminal to service the regular sea crossings from Hong Kong
of ferries, jetfoils, and hydrofoils, plus daily helicopter service begun in November 1990 by East Asia Airlines. The eight-passenger helicopters made the 40-
mile flight from Hong Kong in twenty minutes, less than half the time required
for the fastest jetfoil.[2] Arrivals from Hong Kong alone were exceeding 6 million by the early 1990s, mostly attracted by the gambling casinos, whose number had increased to nine by the mid–1990s.

The Macau Ferry Terminal, opened in 1994, was designed to handle up to 30 million visitors a year making the 40-mile sea-crossing from Hong Kong by jetfoil, hydrofoil or high-speed ferry. In addition, a helipad is located on the roof.

As the result of recent extensive land reclamation, even the land area of Macau had grown by 1995 to 9 square miles, nearly twice the 1912 figure of 4.9 square miles for Macau and the islands of Taipa and Coloane.[3] Adelino Frias dos Santos, director of Macau's Land Registry and Map Department, said planned reclamation between the islands of Taipa and Coloane would raise to nearly 10.8 square miles the total land area of Macau by the year 2000.[4] One major project developed on reclaimed land at Macau's Outer Harbor was the U.S.$50 million Cultural Centre next to the Mandarin Oriental Hotel. The building, scheduled to open in 1997, is designed to house the Camões Museum, two auditoriums, landscaped gardens, restaurants, and lounges.

Much of Macau's activity in the early 1990s was devoted to construction of its new U.S.$1 billion international airport, which was developed on reclaimed land connected to Taipa Island. Testing of navigational systems at the new airport began in June 1995 to verify that the facility would meet international standards for landing and takeoff procedures for commercial airliners.

One of Macau's major construction projects in the early 1990s was the 1,434-foot-long bridge linking the Macau peninsula and Taipa Island, the site of the new airport. A main access road from the bridge connected to a new

Macau's Friendship Bridge, linking Macau and Taipa Island, opened in the mid–1990s to serve as the main access highway from the Macau International Airport to mainland China.

border crossing into the Zhuhai Economic Zone of mainland China (replacing the former Portas do Cerco, which became a commemorative monument in a small park). The U.S.$75 million Friendship Bridge (Ponte da Amizade) was formally opened in April 1994 by Prime Minister Anibal Cavaco Silva of Portugal.

The official airport opening in December 1995 included an appearance by President Mario Soares of Portugal. Antonio Diogo Pinto, chairman of the Macau International Airport Company (CAM), said the new airport, with a potential passenger capacity of 6 million passengers per year, would be able to achieve success by attracting as little as 10 percent of "an exploding regional market."[5] He predicted that the new airport, offering 24-hour service and easy access to Hong Kong and mainland China, would be profitable by the year 2002. Stanley Ho, whose STDM is a major party in the airport project, was instrumental in negotiating twice-weekly flights by the supersonic Concorde from London and Paris to Macau.

By 1991, Macau's exports were becoming substantial. Exports of garments and textiles, for instance, totaled U.S.$1.24 billion in 1991. Other exports, and their values in American dollars, in 1991 included toys ($172.4 million), artificial flowers ($31.4 million), footwear ($18.1 million); electronic products

Macau's new international airport, shown here in an artist's impression, opened in December 1995, constructed almost entirely on reclaimed land for US$1 billion.

($12.3 million), luggage ($13.4 million), optical goods ($10.3 million), and ceramics ($7.33 million).[6] Gambling, of course, remained the number one source of income for Macau, totaling 3.6 billion patacas (U.S.$450 million) in 1992, about one-third higher than in 1991,[7] with expectations of 5.5 billion patacas (U.S.$786 million) in 1996.[8]

By 1993, more than 200 Chinese companies were established in Macau, with total assets valued at more than U.S.$5.1 billion.[9] Even more significantly, the Macau-Chinese Enterprises Association reported in October 1993 that Chinese companies held 50 percent of Macau's financial and banking businesses, 45 percent of its tourist industry (excluding gambling), 40 percent of its real estate and construction area, and 25 percent of its trading and commerce activity.[10] Even the United Nations University added its support in 1991 to the growing optimism about the future of the enclave by opening its International Institute for Software Technology in Macau, which is designed to provide research, development, and advanced training needs for developing countries.

General Rocha Vieira Named Governor of Macau

Macau's governor, Carlos Melancia, who had succeeded Pinto Machado in 1987, resigned his post in September 1990, complaining that he was unable to gain control over corruption and administrative problems in the territory. Melancia's possible resignation had been rumored for months in newspaper stories in both Macau and Lisbon. Prior to his resignation, Melancia also accused officials appointed by Portugal's prime minister, Anibal Cavaco Silva, of "giving in to Chinese pressure" and harming the long-term interests of Portugal by allowing the Chinese too much input in preparing for the 1997 handover of Macau to China.[11]

Melancia had also criticized the Chinese government for interfering in the affairs of Macau. In May 1990, for instance, he was especially critical of Lu Ping, head of China's Hong Kong and Macau Affairs Office, claiming Lu was wrong in admonishing the Macau government for "sluggish preparations" towards the 1999 reversion of the territory to Chinese rule.[12] Melancia said he was also upset that Lu had demanded the removal of the Taipei Trade and Tourism Office in Macau and the removal of a well-known local landmark, the statue of João Ferreira do Amaral, the nineteenth-century governor of Macau who was assassinated after making substantial reforms that strengthened Portugal's administration of the enclave, such as expelling the *Hoppos* (Chinese customs officials), requiring Chinese fishermen to pay taxes, and building new roads on the little peninsula. Lu Ping had characterized the statue of Ferreira do Amaral as a symbol of colonialism.[13]

President Mario Soares of Portugal, in an effort to demonstrate his concern for the people of Macau, made a personal visit to the territory in November 1990 after attending ceremonies in Japan to mark the enthronement of Emperor Akihito. Soares had already appointed Francisco Nabo, previously a deputy to Melancia, to serve as acting governor of Macau until after Portugal's presidential elections on January 13, 1991. After his reelection as president of Portugal in January 1991, Soares announced that Portuguese General Vasco Rocha Vieira of Portugal would become Macau's new governor, succeeding Carlos Melancia. Rocha Vieira had previously been a minister in Soares' government, with special responsibility for the Azores Islands.

General Rocha Vieira was sworn in as Macau's governor in Lisbon on April 23, 1990. He pledged to maintain control over Macau's financial situation and to continue working for future development, specifically citing construction of an international airport on Taipa Island. He also began taking action against corruption in Macau, which had been one of the reasons Melancia had given for his resignation. On July 10, 1990, Governor Rocha Vieira said he would appoint a high commissionerto deal with corruption and administrative illegality, saying "the fight against corruption has already started, named through the fight against bureaucracy, holding civil servants responsible for what they do."[14] Macau's Legislative Assembly had approved creation of the anticorruption official, who would have extensive powers to investigate alleged irregularities and complaints of corruption regarding government officials, legislators, government agencies, banks, and franchised companies.

Outdoor patio of the 23-room deluxe Pousada de São Tiago, built on the site of Macau's historic fortress of São Tiago da Barra (Barra Fort).

In addition, Governor Rocha Vieira had helped smooth relations with China by suggesting that all major issues regarding Macau should be fully considered by both Lisbon and Beijing. He said the problems of Macau before the 1999 reversion to Chinese rule had "outgrown the decision-making capacity of the Macau government."[15] His efforts to bring together officials from

Macau's international airport, opened in December 1995, was built on 473 acres of reclaimed land and is capable of handling 2,000 passengers per hour.

Portugal and China to help resolve Macau's problems were met with a positive response from all sides. One of his successful priorities was to encourage negotiations towards development of the international airport for Macau. In 1992, the governor and the Chinese premier, Li Peng, met in Lisbon; after their meeting Rocha Vieira said he had been assured that Macau would have "great autonomy" after its reversion to Chinese rule in 1999. Li also commented after the meeting, saying: "Macau will have its own laws, its market economy, with all the rights that are guaranteed today."[16]

Earlier, in 1990, the Macau Legislative Assembly approved an increase in the number of its legislators from 17 to 33. Selection of the legislators would continue under a formula of 35 percent directly elected, 35 percent indirectly elected as representatives of functional constituencies such as lawyers, educators, and labor unions, and 30 percent appointed by the governor.

The Ghost of Macau

The Seminary of São José was closed in 1966, but it has been watched over by Father Manuel Teixeira, who was ordained there in 1934. Father Teixeira, a prolific writer who has published more than 100 books about Macau, has often been referred to as "The Ghost of Macau" because of his flowing white robes and long white beard. Interviewed at age 80 in 1992 by *Travel/Holiday* writer

Lucretia Stewart, the priest said his responsibilities during Macau's transition period to 1999 included caring for several large paintings depicting sacred subjects that had been intended for a seminary museum of religious art. "In my kingdom I am all alone," he said, but he noted that five Chinese priests also reside at the seminary.[17] Following a brief tour of the seminary, Father Teixeira invited the journalist to a small modern kitchen for "tea" and conversation about changes in Macau. There were three kinds of tea, Stewart said: "Scottish tea [whisky], Portuguese tea [port] and 'lion's tea,' which turned out to be some kind of terrifying Chinese spirits."[18]

What does the future hold for Macau? Writer Jonathan Porter believes it is "debatable" whether the 1999 handover "will bring sudden changes to the city."[19] According to Porter, Macau's rapid development of the 1990s has transformed it "almost beyond any resemblance to its former character as a rather somnolent and picturesque artifact of Portuguese colonialism." Porter says that "much of the fascination with Macau ... rested on its unique preservation of the vestiges of Western interaction with China over the span of more than four centuries," adding that its transformation amounts to "a significant departure from its previous conditions of isolation and political and economic inconsequence that contributed to its special charm." In Porter's opinion, "Macau has so long existed in the shadow of the economic power of neighboring Hong Kong that it has been all too easy to dismiss it as either irrelevant or insignificant in its own right or to ignore it entirely."[20] His conclusion is that "At the very least, the transformation of Macau, rivaling that of Hong Kong, will affect the economic balance with its neighbors and will itself become a significant attraction for investment and industrial and capital development."[21]

Other writers have different visions, focusing on the run-up to the 1999 reversion. Rone Tempest of the *Los Angeles Times* says the booming mainland Chinese economy in the 1990s has caused the Portuguese to engage in "a frantic effort to cement cultural, linguistic and economic ties" with the little enclave.[22] She also quotes Gary Ngai Mei-cheong, vice president of the Cultural Institute of Macau, as voicing concern about Macau being swallowed up by the booming neighboring Chinese city of Zhuhai: "The only way out for Macau in 1999 is to develop our sense of cultural identity as a strong Latin culture with a different way of living, what makes up the uniqueness of Macau. We can be a window into Latin countries for China and a gateway into China for Europe and Latin America. This is the only way we can survive that is different from Hong Kong and different from Zhuhai."[23]

Macau's mayor, José Luís de Sale Marques, agrees: "Our biggest concern is that Macau might not be able to develop itself and have a sense of place in its own right in the region. The biggest concern is that we might not be able to differentiate ourselves from our neighbors."[24]

Appendix A

Sino-Portuguese Joint Declaration

of the Government of the People's Republic of China and the Governor of the Republic of Portugal on the Question of Macau

The Government of the People's Republic of China and the Government of the Republic of Portugal have reviewed with satisfaction the development of the friendly relations between the two governments and peoples since the establishment of diplomatic relations between the two countries and agreed that a proper negotiated settlement by the two governments of the question of Macau, which is left over from the past, is conducive to the economic growth and social stability of Macau and to the further strengthening of the friendly relations and cooperation between the two countries. To this end, they have, after talks between the delegations of the two governments, agreed to declare as follows:

1. The Government of the People's Republic of China and the Government of the Republic of Portugal declare that the Macau area (including the Macau Peninsula, Taipa Island and Coloane Island, hereinafter referred to as Macau) is Chinese territory, and that the Government of the People's Republic of China will resume the exercise of sovereignty over Macau with effect from December 20, 1999.

2. The Government of the People's Republic of China declares that in line with the principle of "one country, two systems," the People's Republic of China will pursue the following basic policies regarding Macau:

(1) In accordance with the provisions of Article 31 of the Constitution of the People's Republic of China, the People's Republic of China will establish a Macau Special Administrative Region of the People's Republic of China upon resuming the exercise of sovereignty over Macau.

(2) The Macau Special Administrative Region will be directly under the authority of the Central People's Government of the People's Republic of China, and will enjoy a high degree of autonomy, except in foreign and defense affairs, which are the responsibilities of the Central People's Government. The Macau Special Administrative Region will be vested with executive, legislative and independent judicial power, including that of final adjudication.

129

(3) Both the government and the legislature of the Macau Special Administrative Region will be composed of local inhabitants. The Chief Executive will be appointed by the Central People's Government on the basis of the results of elections or consultations to be held in Macau. Officials holding principal posts will be nominated by the Chief Executive of the Macau Special Administrative Region for appointment by the Central People's Government. Public servants (including police) of Chinese nationality and Portuguese and other foreign nationalities previously serving in Macau may remain in employment. Portuguese and other foreign nationals may be appointed or employed to hold certain public posts in the Macau Special Administrative Region.

(4) The current social and economic systems in Macau will remain unchanged, and so will the lifestyle. The laws currently in force in Macau will remain basically unchanged. All rights and freedoms of the inhabitants and other persons in Macau, including those of the person, of speech, of the press, of assembly, of association, of travel and movement, of strike, of choice of occupation, of academic research, of religion and belief, of communication and the ownership of property will be ensured by law in the Macau Special Administrative Region.

(5) The Macau Special Administrative Region will, on its own, decide policies in the fields of culture, education, science and technology, and protect cultural relics in Macau according to Law.

In addition to Chinese, Portuguese may also be used in organs of government and in the legislature and the courts in the Macau Special Administrative Region.

(6) The Macau Special Administrative Region may establish mutually beneficial economic relations with Portugal and other countries. Due regard will be given to the economic interests of Portugal and other countries in Macau. The interests of the inhabitants of Portuguese descent in Macau will be protected by law.

(7) Using the name "Macau, China," the Macau Special Administrative Region may, on its own, maintain and develop economic and cultural relations, and in this context conclude agreements with states, regions and relevant international organizations.

The Macau Special Administrative Region Government may, on its own, issue travel documents for entry into and exit from Macau.

(8) The Macau Special Administrative Region will remain a free port and a separate customs territory in order to develop its economic activities. There will be free flow of capital. The Macau pataca, as the legal tender of the Macau Special Administrative Region, will continue to circulate and remain freely convertible.

(9) The Macau Special Administrative Region will continue to have independent finances. The Central People's Government will not levy taxes on the Macau Special Administrative Region.

(10) The maintenance of public order in the Macau Special Administrative Region will be the responsibility of the Macau Special Administrative Region Government.

(11) Apart from displaying the national flag and national emblem of the People's Republic of China, the Macau Special Administrative Region may use a regional flag and emblem of its own.

(12) The above-stated basic policies and the elaboration of them in Annex I to this Joint Declaration will be stipulated in a Basic Law of the Macau Special Administrative Region of the People's Republic of China by the National People's Congress of the People's Republic of China, and they will remain unchanged for 50 years.

3. The government of the People's Republic of China and the Government of the Republic of Portugal declare that, during the transitional period between the date of the entry into force of this Joint Declaration and December 19, 1999, the Government of the Republic of Portugal will be responsible for the administration of Macau. The Government of the Republic of Portugal will continue to promote the economic growth of Macau and maintain its social stability, and the Government of the People's Republic of China will give its cooperation in this connection.

4. The Government of the People's Republic of China and the Government of the Republic of Portugal declare that, in order to ensure the effective implementation of this Joint Declaration and create appropriate conditions for the transfer of government in 1999, a Sino-Portuguese Joint Liaison Group will be set up when this Joint Declaration enters into force, and that it will be established and will function in accordance with the relevant provisions of Annex II to this Joint Declaration.

5. The Government of the People's Republic of China and the Government of the Republic of Portugal declare that land leases in Macau and other related matters will be dealt with in accordance with the relevant provisions of the Annexes to this Joint Declaration.

6. The Government of the People's Republic of China and the Government of the Republic of Portugal agree to implement all the preceding declarations and the Annexes which are a component part of the Joint Declaration.

7. This Joint Declaration and its Annexes shall enter into force on the date of the exchange of instruments of ratification, which shall take place in Beijing. This Joint Declaration and its Annexes shall be equally binding.

Done in duplicate at Beijing on April 13, 1987 in the Chinese and Portuguese languages, both texts being equally authentic.

(*Signed*) Zhao Ziyang, Prime Minister
For the Government of the People's Republic of China.

(*Signed*) Anibal Cavaco Silva, Prime Minister
For the Government of the Republic of Portugal.

Annex I: Elaboration by the Government of the People's Republic of China of its Basic Policies Regarding Macau

The Government of the People's Republic elaborates the basic policies of the People's Republic of China regarding Macau as set out in Paragraph 2 of the Joint

Declaration of the Government of the People's Republic of China and the Government of the Republic of Portugal on the Question of Macau as follows:

I

The Constitution of the People's Republic of China stipulates in Article 31 that "the state may establish Special Administrative Regions when necessary. The systems to be instituted in Special Administrative Regions shall be prescribed by laws enacted by the National People's Congress in the light of the specific conditions."

In accordance with this Article, the People's Republic of China shall, upon the resumption of the exercise of sovereignty over Macau on December 20, 1999, establish the Macau Special Administrative Region of the People's Republic of China.

The National People's Congress of the People's Republic of China shall enact and promulgate a Basic Law of the Macau Special Administrative Region of the People's Republic of China (hereinafter referred to as the Basic Law) in accordance with the Constitution of the People's Republic of China, stipulating that, after the establishment of the Macau Special Administrative Region, the socialist system and socialist policies shall not be practiced in Macau Special Administrative Region and that the current social and economic systems and lifestyle in Macau shall remain unchanged for 50 years.

The Macau Special Administrative Region shall be directly under the authority of the Central People's Government of the People's Republic of China, and shall enjoy a high degree of autonomy, except in foreign and defense affairs, which are the responsibilities of the Central People's Government. The Macau Special Administrative Region shall be vested with executive, legislative and independent judicial power, including that of final adjudication. The Central People's Government shall authorize the Macau Special Administrative Region to conduct, on its own, those external affairs specific in Section VIII of this Annex.

II

The executive power of the Macau Special Administrative Region shall be vested in the government of the Macau Special Administrative Region. The government of the Macau Special Administrative Region shall be composed of local inhabitants.

The Chief Executive of the Macau Special Administrative Region shall be appointed by the Central People's Government on the basis of the results of elections or consultations to be held in Macau. Officials holding principal posts (equivalent to assistant-secretaries, procurator-general and principal officer of the police service) shall be nominated by the Chief Executive of the Macau Special Administrative Region for appointment by the Central People's Government.

The executive authorities shall abide by the law and shall be accountable to the legislature.

III

The legislative power of the Macau Special Administrative Region shall be vested in the legislature of the Macau Special Administrative Region. The legislature shall be composed of local inhabitants, and the majority of its members shall be elected.

After the establishment of the Macau Special Administrative Region, the laws, decrees, administrative regulations and other normative acts previously in force in Macau shall be maintained, save for whatever therein may contravene the Basic Law or subject to any amendment by the Macau Special Administrative Region legislature.

The legislature of the Macau Special Administrative Region may enact laws in accordance with the provisions of the Basic Law and legal procedures, and such laws shall be reported to the Standing Committee of the National People's Congress of the People's Republic of China for the record. Laws enacted by the legislature of the Macau Special Administrative Region which are in accordance with the Basic Law and legal procedures shall be regarded as valid.

The legal system of the Macau Special Administrative Region shall consist of the Basic Law, the laws previously in force in Macau and the laws enacted by the Macau Special Administrative Region as above.

IV

Judicial power in the Macau Special Administrative Region shall be vested in the courts of the Macau Special Administrative Region. The power of final adjudication shall be exercised by the Court of Final Appeal in the Macau Special Administrative Region. The courts shall exercise judicial power independently and free from any interference, and shall be subordinated only to the law. The judges shall enjoy the immunities appropriate to the performance of their functions.

Judges of the Macau Special Administrative Region courts shall be appointed by the Chief Executive of the Macau Special Administrative Region acting in accordance with the recommendation of the independent commission composed of local judges, lawyers and noted public figures. Judges shall be chosen by reference to their professional qualifications. Qualified judges of foreign nationalities may also be invited to serve as judges in the Macau Special Administrative Region.

A judge may only be removed for inability to discharge the functions of his office, or for behavior incompatible with the post he holds, by the Chief Executive acting in accordance with the recommendation of a tribunal appointed by the president of the Court of Final Appeal, consisting of no fewer than three local judges.

The removal of judges of the Court of Final Appeal shall be decided upon by the Chief Executive in accordance with the recommendation of a review committee consisting of members of the Macau Special Administrative Region legislature. The appointment and removal of judges of the Court of Final Appeal shall be reported to the Standing Committee of the National People's Congress for the record.

The prosecuting authority of the Macau Special Administrative Region shall exercise procuratorial functions as vested by law, independently and free from any interference.

The system previously in force in Macau for appointment and removal of supporting members of the judiciary shall be maintained.

On the basis of the system previously operating in Macau, the Macau Special Administrative Region Government shall make provisions for local lawyers and lawyers from outside Macau to practice in the Macau Special Administrative Region.

The Central People's Government shall assist or authorize the Macau Special Administrative Region Government to make appropriate arrangements for reciprocal juridical assistance with foreign states.

V

The Macau Special Administrative Region shall, according to law, ensure the rights and freedoms of the inhabitants and other persons in Macau as provided for by the laws previously in Macau, including freedom of the person, of speech, of the press, of assembly, of demonstration, of association (*e.g.*, to form and join non-official associations), to form and join trade unions, of travel and movement, of choice of occupation and work, of strike, of religion and belief, of education and academic research; inviolability of the home and of communications, and the right to have access to law and court; rights concerning the ownership of private property and of enterprises and their transfer and inheritance, and to obtain appropriate compensation for lawful deprivation paid without undue delay; freedom to marry and the right to form and raise a family freely.

The inhabitants and other persons in the Macau Special Administrative Region shall all be equal before the law, and shall be free from discrimination, irrespective of nationality, descent, sex, race, language, religion, political or ideological belief, educational level, economic status or social conditions.

The Macau Special Administrative Region shall protect, according to law, the interests of residents of Portuguese descent in Macau and shall respect their customs and cultural traditions.

Religious organizations and believers in the Macau Special Administrative Region may carry out activities as before for religious purposes and within the limits as prescribed by law, and may maintain relations with religious organizations and believers outside Macau. Schools, hospitals and charitable institutions attached to religious organizations may continue to operate as before. The relationship between religious organizations in the Macau Special Administrative Region and those in other parts of the People's Republic of China shall be based on the principles of non-subordination, non-interference and mutual respect.

VI

After the establishment of the Macau Special Administrative Region, public servants (including police) of Chinese nationality and Portuguese and other foreign nationalities previously serving in Macau may all remain in employment and continue their service with pay, allowances and benefits no less favorable than before. Those of the above-mentioned public servants who have retired after the establishment of the Macau Special Administrative Region shall, in accordance with regulations currently in force, be entitled to pensions and allowances on terms no less favorable than before, and irrespective of their nationality or place of residence.

The Macau Special Administrative Region may appoint Portuguese and other foreign nationals previously serving in the public service in Macau or currently holding Permanent Identity Cards of the Macau Special Administrative Region to public posts (except certain principal official posts). The Macau Special Administrative Region may also invite Portuguese and other foreign nationals to serve as advisers or hold professional and technical posts. The Portuguese and other foreign nationals holding public posts in the Macau Special Administrative Region shall be employed only in their individual capacities and shall be responsible exclusively to the Macau Special Administrative Region.

The appointment and promotion of public servants shall be on the basis of qualifications, experience and ability. Macau's previous system of employment, discipline, promotion and normal rise in rank for the public service shall remain basically unchanged.

VII

The Macau Special Administrative Region shall, on its own, decide policies in the fields of culture, education, science and technology, such as policies regarding the languages of instruction (including Portuguese) and the system of academic qualifications and the recognition of academic degrees. All educational institutions may remain in operation and retain their autonomy. They may continue to recruit teaching and administrative staff and use teaching materials from outside Macau. Students shall enjoy freedom to pursue their education outside the Macau Special Administrative Region. The Macau Special Administrative Region shall protect cultural relics in Macau according to law.

VIII

Subject to the principle that foreign affairs are the responsibility of the Central People's Government, the Macau Special Administrative Region may, on its own, using the name "Macau, China," maintain and develop relations and conclude and implement agreements with states, regions and relevant international or regional organizations in the appropriate fields, such as the economy, trade, finance, shipping, communications, tourism, culture, science and technology and sports.

Representatives of the Macau Special Administrative Region Government may participate, as members of the delegations of the Government of the People's Republic of China, in international organizations or conferences in appropriate fields limited to states and affecting the Macau Special Administrative Region, or may attend in such other capacity as may be permitted by the Central People's

Government and the organization or conference concerned, and may express their views in the name of "Macau, China." The Macau Special Administrative Region may, using the name "Macau, China," participate in international organizations and conferences not limited to states.

Representatives of the Macau Special Administrative Region Government may participate, as members of delegations of the Government of the People's Republic of China, in negotiations conducted by the Central People's Government at the diplomatic level directly affecting the Macau Special Administrative Region.

The application to the Macau Special Administrative Region of international agreements to which the People's Republic of China is or becomes a party shall be decided by the Central People's Government, in accordance with the circumstances of each case and the needs of the Macau Special Administrative Region and after seeking the views of the Macau Special Administrative Region. International agreements to which the People's Republic of China is not a party but which are implemented in Macau may remain implemented in the Macau Special Administrative Region. The Central People's Government shall, according to the circumstances and the needs, authorize or assist the Macau Special Administrative Region Government to make appropriate arrangements for the application to the Macau Special Administrative Region of other relevant international agreements.

The Central People's Government shall, in accordance with the circumstances of each case and the needs of the Macau Special Administrative Region, take steps to ensure that the Macau Special Administrative Region shall continue to retain its status in an appropriate capacity in those international organizations of which the People's Republic of China is a member and in which Macau participates in one capacity or another. The Central People's Government shall, according to the circumstances and the needs, facilitate the continued participation of the Macau Special Administrative Region in an appropriate capacity in those international organizations in which Macau is a participant in one capacity or another, but of which the People's Republic of China is not a member.

Foreign consular and other official or semi-official missions may be established in the Macau Special Administrative Region with the approval of the Central People's Government. Consular and other official missions established in Macau by states which have established formal diplomatic relations with the People's Republic of China may be maintained. According to the circumstances of each case, consular and other official missions in Macau of states having no formal diplomatic relations with the People's Republic of China may either be maintained or changed to semi-official missions. States not recognized by the People's Republic of China can only establish non-governmental institutions.

The Republic of Portugal may establish a Consulate-General in the Macau Special Administrative Region.

IX

The following categories of persons shall have the right of abode in the Macau Special Administrative Region and be qualified to obtain Permanent Identity Cards of the Macau Special Administrative Region:

—the Chinese Nationals who were born or who have ordinarily resided in Macau before or after the establishment of the Macau Special Administrative Region for a continuous period of 7 years or more, and persons of Chinese nationality born outside Macau of such Chinese nationals;

—the Portuguese who were born in Macau or who have ordinarily resided in Macau before or after the establishment of the Macau Special Administrative Region for a continuous period of 7 years or more and who, in either case, have taken Macau as their place of permanent residence: and

—the other persons who have ordinarily resided in Macau for a continuous period of 7 years or more and have taken Macau as their place of permanent residence before or after the establishment of the Macau Special Administrative Region, and persons under 18 years of age who were born of such persons in Macau before or after the establishment of the Macau Special Administrative Region.

The Central People's Government shall authorize the Macau Special Administrative Region Government to issue, in accordance with the law, passports of the Macau Special Administrative Region of the People's Republic of China to all Chinese nationals who hold Permanent Identity Cards of the Macau Special Administrative Region, and other travel documents of the Macau Special Administrative Region of the People's Republic of China to all other persons lawfully residing in the Macau Special Administrative Region.

The above passports and travel documents of the Macau Special Administrative Region shall be valid for all states and regions and shall record the holder's right to return to the Macau Special Administrative Region.

For the purpose of traveling to and from the Macau Special Administrative Region, inhabitants of the Macau Special Administrative Region may use travel documents issued by the Macau Special Administrative Region Government, or by other competent authorities of the People's Republic of China, or of other states. Holders of Permanent Identity Cards of the Macau Special Administrative Region may have this fact stated in their travel documents as evidence that the holders have the right of abode in the Macau Special Administrative Region.

Entry into the Macau Special Administrative Region by inhabitants of other parts of China shall be regulated in an appropriate way.

The Macau Special Administrative Region may apply immigration controls on entry into, stay in and departure from the Macau Special Administrative Region by persons from foreign states and regions.

Unless restrained by law, holders of valid travel documents shall be free to leave the Macau Special Administrative Region without special authorization.

The Central People's Government shall assist or authorize the Macau Special Administrative Region Government to negotiate and conclude visa abolition agreements with the states and regions concerned.

X

The Macau Special Administrative Region shall decide its economic and trade policies on its own. As a free port and a separate customs territory, it shall maintain and develop economic and trade relations with all states and regions and continue to participate in relevant international organizations and international trade agreements, such as the General Agreement on Tariffs and Trade and agreements regarding international trade in textiles. Export quotas, tariff preferences and other similar arrangements obtained by the Macau Special Administrative Region shall be enjoyed exclusively by the Macau Special Administrative Region. The Macau Special Administrative Region shall have authority to issue its own certificates of origin for products manufactured locally, in accordance with prevailing rules of origin.

The Macau Special Administrative Region shall protect foreign investments in accordance with the law.

The Macau Special Administrative Region may, as necessary, establish official and semi-official economic and trade missions in foreign countries, reporting the establishment of such missions to the Central People's Government for the record.

XI

After the establishment of the Macau Special Administrative Region, the monetary and financial systems previously practiced in Macau shall remain basically unchanged. The Macau Special Administrative Region shall decide its monetary and financial policies on its own. It shall safeguard the free operation of the financial institutions and the free flow of capital within, into and out of the Macau Special Administrative Region. No exchange control policy shall be applied in the Macau Special Administrative Region.

The Macau pataca, as the legal tender of the Macau Special Administrative Region, shall continue to circulate and remain freely convertible. The authority to issue Macau currency shall be vested in the Macau Special Administrative Region Government. The Macau Special Administrative Region Government may authorize designated banks to perform or continue to perform the functions of its agents in the issuance of Macau currency. Macau currency bearing references inappropriate to the status of Macau as a Special Administrative Region of the People's Republic of China shall be progressively replaced and withdrawn from circulation.

XII

The Macau Special Administrative Region shall draw up, on its own, its budget and taxation policy. The Macau Special Administrative Region shall report its budgets and final accounts to the Central People's Government for the record. The Macau Special Administrative Region shall use its financial revenues exclusively for its own purposes and they shall not be handed over to the Central People's Government. The Central People's Government shall not levy taxes on the Macau Special Administrative Region.

XIII

The Central People's Government shall be responsible for the defense of the Macau Special Administrative Region.

The maintenance of public order in the Macau Special Administrative Region shall be the responsibility of the Macau Special Administrative Region.

XIV

Legal leases of land granted or decided upon before the establishment of the Macau Special Administrative Region and extending beyond December 19, 1999, and all rights in relation to such leases, shall be recognized and protected according to law by the Macau Special Administrative Region. Land leases approved or renewed after the establishment of the Macau Special Administrative Region shall be dealt with in accordance with the relevant land laws and policies of the Macau Special Administrative Region.

Annex II: Arrangements for the Transitional Period

In order to ensure the effective implementation of the Joint Declaration of the Government of the People's Republic of China and the Government of the Republic of Portugal on the Question of Macau and create appropriate conditions for the transfer of government of Macau, the Government of the People's Republic of China and the Government of the Republic of Portugal have agreed to continue their friendly cooperation during the transitional period between the date of entry into force of the Joint Declaration and December 19, 1999.

For this purpose, the Government of the People's Republic of China and the Government of the Republic of Portugal have agreed to set up a Sino-Portuguese Joint Liaison Group and a Sino-Portuguese Land Group in accordance with the provisions of Paragraphs 3, 4 and 5 of the Joint Declaration.

I. Sino-Portuguese Joint Liaison Group

1. The Joint Liaison Group shall be an organ for liaison, consultation and exchange of information between the two governments. It shall not interfere in the administration of Macau, nor shall it have any supervisory role over that administration.

2. The functions of the Joint Liaison Group shall be:

    (a) to conduct consultations on the implementation of the Joint Declaration and its Annexes;

    (b) to exchange information and conduct consultations on matters relating to the transfer of government of Macau in 1999;

    (c) to conduct consultations on actions to be taken by the two governments to enable the Macau Special Administrative Region to maintain and develop external economic, cultural and other relations;

    (d) to exchange information and conduct consultations on other subjects as may be agreed by the two sides.

Matters on which there is disagreement in the Joint Liaison Group shall be referred to the two governments for solution through consultations.

3. Each side shall designate a leader of ambassadorial rank and four other members of the group. Each side may also designate experts and supporting staff as required, whose number shall be determined through consultations.

4. The Joint Liaison Group shall be established on the entry into force of the Joint Declaration and shall start work within three months after its establishment. It shall meet in Beijing, Lisbon and Macau alternately in the first year of work. Thereafter, it shall have its principal base in Macau. The Joint Liaison Group shall continue its work until January 1, 2000.

5. Members, experts and supporting staff of the Joint Liaison Group shall enjoy diplomatic privileges and immunities or such privileges and immunities as are compatible with their status.

6. The working and organizational procedures of the Joint Liaison Group shall be agreed between the two sides through consultations within the guidelines laid down in this Annex. The work of the Joint Liaison Group shall remain confidential unless otherwise agreed.

II. Sino-Portuguese Land Group

1. The two governments have agreed that, with effect from the entry into force of the Joint Declaration, land leases in Macau and related matters shall be dealt with in accordance with the following provisions:

(a) Leases of land granted previously by the Portuguese Macau government that expire before December 19, 1999, except temporary leases and leases for special purposes, may, in accordance with the relevant laws and regulations currently in force, be extended for a period expiring not later than December 19, 2049, with a premium to be collected.

(b) From the entry into force of the Joint Declaration until December 19, 1999, and in accordance with the relevant laws and regulations currently in force, new leases of land may be granted by the Portuguese Macau government for terms expiring not later than December 19, 2049, with a premium to be collected.

(c) The total amount of new land, including fields reclaimed from the sea and undeveloped land, to be granted under Section II, Paragraph 1(b) of this Annex, shall be limited to 20 hectares a year. The Land Group may, on the basis of the proposals of the Portuguese Macau government, examine any change in the above-mentioned quota and make decisions accordingly.

(d) From the entry into force of the Joint Declaration until December 19, 1999, all incomes obtained by the Portuguese Macau government from granting new leases and renewing leases shall, after deduction of the average cost of land production, be shared equally between the Portuguese Macau government and the future government of the Macau Special Administrative Region. All the income so obtained from land by the Portuguese Macau government, including the amount of the above-mentioned deduction, shall be used for financing land development and public works in Macau. The Macau Special Administrative Region Government's share of land income shall serve as a reserve fund of the government of the Macau Special Administrative Region and shall be deposited in banks incorporated in Macau and, if necessary, may be used by the Portuguese Macau government for land development and public works in Macau during the transition period with the endorsement of the Chinese side.

2. The Sino-Portuguese Land Group shall be an organ for handling land leases in Macau and related matters on behalf of the two governments.

3. The functions of the Land Group shall be:

(a) to conduct consultations on the implementation of Section II of this Annex;

(b) to monitor the amount and terms of land granted, and division and use of income from land granted in accordance with the provisions of Section II, Paragraph 1 of this Annex;

(c) to examine proposals of the Portuguese Macau government for drawing on the Macau Special Administrative Region Government's share of income from land and to make recommendations to the Chinese side for decision. Matters on which there is disagreement in the Land Group shall be referred to the two governments for solution through consultations.

4. Each side shall designate three members of the Land Group. Each side may also designate experts and supporting staff as required, whose number shall be determined through consultations.

5. Upon the entry into force of the Joint Declaration, the Land Group shall be established and shall have its principal base in Macau. The Land Group shall continue its work until December 19, 1999.

6. Members, experts and supporting staff of the Land Group shall enjoy diplomatic privileges and immunities or other privileges and immunities as are compatible with their status.

7. The working and organizational procedures of the Land Group shall be agreed between the two sides through consultations within the guidelines laid down in this Annex.

Memoranda

(TO BE EXCHANGED BETWEEN THE TWO SIDES)

Memorandum

In connection with the Joint Declaration with the Joint Declaration of the Government of the people's Republic of China and the Government of the Republic of Portugal on the Question of Macau signed this day, the Government of the People's Republic of China declares:

The inhabitants in Macau who come under the provisions of the Nationality Law of the People's Republic of China, whether they are holders of the Portuguese travel or identity documents or not, have Chinese citizenship. Taking account of the historical background of Macau and its realities, the competent authorities of the Government of the People's Republic of China will permit Chinese nationals in Macau previously holding Portuguese travel documents to continue to use these documents for traveling to other states and regions after the establishment of the Macau Special Administrative Region. The above-mentioned Chinese nationals will not be entitled to Portuguese consular protection in the Macau Special Administrative Region and other parts of the People's Republic of China.

Memorandum

In connection with the Joint Declaration of the Government of the Republic of Portugal and the Government of the People's Republic of China on the Question of Macau signed this day, the Government of the Republic of Portugal declares:

In conformity with the Portuguese legislation, the inhabitants in Macau who, having Portuguese citizenship, are holders of a Portuguese passport on December 19, 1999, may continue to use it after this date. No person may acquire Portuguese citizenship as from December 20, 1999, by virtue of his or her connection with Macau.

Appendix B

The Basic Law
of the Macau Special
Administrative Region of
the People's Republic of China

Adopted at the First Session of the Eighth National People's Congress on March 31, 1993.

Preamble

Macau, including the Macau Peninsula, Taipa Island and Coloane Island, has been part of the territory of China since ancient times; it was gradually occupied by Portugal after the mid-16th century. On 13 April 1987, the Chinese and Portuguese Governments signed the Joint Declaration on the Question of Macau, affirming that the Government of the People's Republic of China will resume the exercise of sovereignty over Macau with effect from 20 December 1999, thus fulfilling the long-cherished common aspiration of the Chinese people for the recovery of Macau.

Upholding national unity and territorial integrity, contributing to social stability and economic development, and taking account of its history and realities, the People's Republic of China has decided that upon China's resumption of the exercise of sovereignty over Macau, a Macau Special Administrative Region will be established in accordance with the provisions of Article 31 of the Constitution of the People's Republic of China, and that under the principle of "one country, two systems," the socialist system and policies of the People's Republic of China regarding Macau have been elaborated by the Chinese Government in the Sino-Portuguese Joint Declaration.

In accordance with the Constitution of the People's Republic of China, the National People's Congress hereby enacts the Basic Law of the Macau Special Administrative Region of the People's Republic of China, prescribing the systems to be practised in the Macau Special Administrative Region, in order to ensure the implementation of the basic policies of the People's Republic of China regarding Macau.

Chapter I: General Principles

Article 1   The Macau Special Administrative Region is an inalienable part of the People's Republic of China.

Article 2   The National People's Congress authorizes the Macau Special Administrative Region to exercise a high degree of autonomy and enjoy executive, legislative and independent judicial power, including that of final adjudication, in accordance with the provisions of this law.

Article 3   The executive authorities and legislature of the Macau Special Administrative Region shall be composed of permanent residents of Macau in accordance with the relevant provisions of this Law.

Article 4   The Macau Special Administrative Region shall safeguard the rights and freedoms of the residents of the Macau Special Administrative Region and of other persons in the Region in accordance with law.

Article 5   The socialist system and policies shall not be practised in the Macau Special Administrative Region, and the previous capitalist system and way of life shall remain unchanged for 50 years.

Article 6   The Macau Special Administrative Region shall protect the right of private ownership of property in accordance with law.

Article 7   The land and natural resources within the Macau Special Administrative Region shall be State property, except for the private land recognised as such according to the laws in force before the establishment of the Macau Special Administrative Region. The Government of the Macau Special Administrative Region shall be responsible for their management, use and development and for their lease or grant to individuals or legal persons for use or development. The revenues derived therefrom shall be exclusively at the disposal of the government of the Region.

Article 8   The laws, decrees, administrative regulations and other normative acts previously in force in Macau shall be maintained, except for any that contravenes this Law, or subject to any amendment by the legislature or other relevant organs of the Macau Special Administrative Region in accordance with legal procedures.

Article 9   In addition to the Chinese language, Portuguese may also be used as an official language by the executive authorities, legislature and judiciary of the Macau Special Administrative Region.

Article 10   Apart from displaying the national flag and national emblem of the People's Republic of China, the Macau Special Administrative Region may also use a regional flag and regional emblem.

The regional flag of the Macau Special Administrative Region is a green flag with five stars, lotus flower, bridge and sea water.

The regional emblem of the Macau Special Administrative Region is composed of five stars, lotus flower, bridge and sea water encircled by the words "Macau Special Administrative Region of the People's Republic of China" in Chinese and "MACAU" in Portuguese.

Article 11   In accordance with Article 31 of the Constitution of the People's Republic of China, the systems and policies practised in the Macau Special Administrative Region, including the social and economic systems, the system for safeguarding the fundamental rights and freedoms of its residents, the executive, legislative and judicial systems, and the relevant policies, shall be based on the provisions of this Law.

No law, decree, administrative regulations and normative acts of the Macau Special Administrative Region shall contravene this Law.

Chapter II: Relationship Between the Central Authorities and the Macau Special Administrative Region.

Article 12 The Macau Special Administrative Region shall be a local administrative region of the People's Republic of China, which shall enjoy a high degree of autonomy and come directly under the Central People's Government.

Article 13 The Central People's Government shall be responsible for the foreign affairs relating to the Macau Special Administrative Region.

The Ministry of Foreign Affairs of the People's Republic of China shall establish an office in Macau to deal with foreign affairs.

The Central People's Government authorizes the Macau Special Administrative Region to conduct relevant external affairs on its own in accordance with this Law.

Article 14 The Central People's Government shall be responsible for the defence of the Macau Special Administrative Region.

The Government of the Macau Special Administrative Region shall be responsible for the maintenance of public order in the Region.

Article 15 The Central People's Government shall appoint or remove the Chief Executive, the principal officials of the government and the Procurator-General of the Macau Special Administrative Region in accordance with the relevant provisions of this Law.

Article 16 The Macau Special Administrative Region shall be vested with executive power. It shall, on its own, conduct the administrative affairs of the Region in accordance with the relevant provisions of this Law.

Article 17 The Macau Special Administrative Region shall be vested with legislative power.

Laws enacted by the legislature of the Macau Special Administrative Region must be reported to the Standing Committee of the National People's Congress for the record. The reporting for record shall not affect the entry into force of such laws.

If the Standing Committee of the National People's Congress, after consulting the Committee for the Basic Law of the Macau Special Administrative Region under it, considers that any law enacted by the legislature of the Region is not in conformity with the provisions of this Law regarding affairs within the responsibility of the Central Authorities or regarding the relationship between the Central Authorities and the Region, the Standing Committee may return the law in question but shall not amend it. Any law returned by the Standing Committee of the National People's Congress shall immediately be invalidated. This invalidation shall not have retroactive effect, unless otherwise provided for in the laws of the Region.

Article 18 The laws in force in the Macau Special Administrative Region shall be this Law, the laws previously in force in Macau as provided for in Article 8 of this Law, and the laws enacted by the legislature of the Region.

National laws shall not be applied in the Macau Special Administrative Region except for those listed in Annex III to this Law. The laws listed therein shall be applied locally by way of promulgation or legislation by the Region.

The Standing Committee of the National People's Congress may add to or delete from the list of laws in Annex III after consulting its Committee for the Basic Law of the Macau Special Administrative Region and the government of the Region. Laws listed in Annex III to this Law shall be confined to those relating to defence and foreign affairs as well as other matters outside the limits of the autonomy of the Region as specified by this Law.

In the event that the Standing Committee of the National People's Congress decides to declare a state of war or, by reason of turmoil within the Macau Special Administrative Region which endangers national unity and is beyond the control of the government of the Region, decides that the Region is in a state of emergency, the Central People's Government may issue an order applying the relevant national laws in the Region.

Article 19 The Macau Special Administrative Region shall be vested with independent judicial power, including that of final adjudication.

The courts of the Macau Special Administrative Region shall have jurisdiction over all cases in the Region, except that the restrictions on their jurisdiction imposed by the legal system and principles previously in force in Macau shall be maintained.

The courts of the Macau Special Administrative Region shall have no jurisdiction over acts of state such as defence and foreign affairs. The courts of the Region shall obtain a certificate from the Chief Executive on questions of fact concerning acts of state such as defence and foreign affairs whenever such questions arise in the adjudication of cases. This certificate shall be binding on the courts. Before issuing such a certificate, the Chief Executive shall obtain a certifying document from the Central People's Government.

Article 20 The Macau Special Administrative Region may enjoy other powers granted to it by the National People's Congress, the Standing Committee of the National People's Congress or the Central People's Government.

Article 21 Chinese citizens who are residents of the Macau Special Administrative Region shall be entitled to participate in the management of state affairs according to law.

In accordance with the assigned number of seats and the selection method specified by the National People's Congress, the Chinese citizens among the residents of the Macau Special Administrative Region shall locally elect deputies of the Region to the National People's Congress to participate in the work of the highest organ of state power.

Article 22 No department of the Central People's Government and no province, autonomous region, or municipality directly under the Central Government may interfere in the affairs which the Macau Special Administrative Region administers on its own in accordance with this Law.

If there is a need for departments of the Central Government, or for provinces, autonomous regions, or municipalities directly under the Central Government to set up offices in the Macau Special Administrative Region, they must obtain the consent of the government of the Region and the approval of the Central People's Government.

All offices set up in the Macau Special Administrative Region by departments of the Central Government, or by provinces, autonomous regions, or municipalities directly under the Central Government, and the personnel of these offices shall abide by the laws of the Region.

For entry into the Macau Special Administrative Region, people from other provinces, autonomous regions or municipalities directly under the Central Government must apply for approval. Among them, the number of persons who enter the Region for the purpose of settlement shall be determined by the competent authorities of the Central People's Government after consulting the government of the Region.

The Macau Special Administrative Region may establish an office in Beijing.

Article 23 The Macau Special Administrative Region shall enact laws on its own to prohibit any act of treason, secession, sedition, subversion against the Central people's Government, or theft of state secrets, to prohibit foreign political organizations or bodies from conducting political activities in the Region, and to prohibit political activities in the Region, and to prohibit political organizations or bodies of the Region from establishing ties with foreign political organizations or bodies.

Chapter III: Fundamental Rights and Duties of the Residents

Article 24 Residents of the Macau Special Administrative Region ("Macau residents") shall include permanent residents and non-permanent residents.

The permanent residents of the Macau Special Administrative Region shall be:

(1) Chinese citizens born in Macau before or after the establishment of the Macau Special Administrative Region and their children of Chinese nationality born outside Macau;

(2) Chinese citizens who have ordinarily resided in Macau for a continuous period of not less than seven years before or after the establishment of the Macau Special Administrative Region and their children of Chinese nationality born outside Macau after they have become permanent residents;

(3) The Portuguese who were born in Macau and have taken Macau as their place of permanent residence before or after the establishment of the Macau Special Administrative Region;

(4) The Portuguese who have ordinarily resided in Macau for a continuous period of not less than seven years and have taken Macau as their place of permanent residence before or after the establishment of the Macau Special Administrative Region;

(5) Other persons who have ordinarily resided in Macau for a continuous period of not less than seven years and have taken Macau as their place of permanent residence before or after the establishment of the Macau Special Administrative Region;

(6) Persons under 18 years of age born in Macau of those residents listed in category (5) before or after the establishment of the Macau Special Administrative Region.

The above-mentioned residents shall have the right of abode in the Macau Special Administrative Region and shall be qualified to obtain permanent identity cards.

The non-permanent residents of the Macau Special Administrative Region shall be persons who are qualified to obtain Macau identity cards in accordance with the laws of the Region but have no right of abode.

Article 25   All Macau residents shall be equal before the law, and shall be free from discrimination, irrespective of their nationality, descent, sex, race, language, religion, political persuasion or ideological belief, educational level, economic status or social conditions.

Article 26   Permanent residents of the Macau Special Administrative Region shall have the right to vote and the right to stand for election in accordance with law.

Article 27   Macau residents shall have freedom of speech, of the press and of publication; freedom of association, of assembly, of procession and of demonstration; and the right and freedom to form and join trade unions, and to strike.

Article 28   The freedom of the person of Macau residents shall be inviolable.

No Macau resident shall be subjected to arbitrary or unlawful arrest, detention or imprisonment. In case of arbitrary or unlawful detention or imprisonment, Macau residents have the right to apply to the court for the issuance of a writ of *habeas corpus.*

Unlawful search of the body of any resident or deprivation or restriction of the freedom of the person shall be prohibited.

Torture or inhuman treatment of any resident shall be prohibited.

Article 29   Macau residents shall not be punished by law, unless their acts constitute a crime and they shall be punished for it as expressly prescribed by law at the time.

When charged with criminal offences, Macau residents shall enjoy the right to an early court trial and shall be presumed innocent before convicted.

Article 30   The human dignity of Macau residents shall be inviolable. Humiliation, slander and false accusation against residents in any form shall be prohibited.

Macau residents shall enjoy the right to personal reputation and the privacy of their private and family life.

Article 31   The homes and other premises of Macau residents shall be inviolable. Arbitrary or unlawful search of, or intrusion into, a resident's home or other premises shall be prohibited.

Article 32   The freedom and privacy of communication of Macau residents shall be protected by law. No department or individual may, on any grounds, infringe upon the freedom and privacy of communication of residents except that the relevant authorities may inspect communication in accordance with the provisions of the law to meet the needs of public security or of investigation into criminal offences.

Article 33   Macau residents shall have freedom of movement within the Macau Special Administrative Region and freedom of emigration to other countries and regions. They shall have freedom to travel and to enter or leave the Region and shall have the right to obtain travel documents in accordance with law. Unless restrained by law, holders of valid travel documents shall be free to leave the Region without special authorization.

Article 34   Macau residents shall have freedom of conscience.

Macau residents shall have freedom of religious belief and freedom to preach and to conduct and participate in religious activities in public.

Article 35   Macau residents shall have freedom of choice of occupation and work.

Article 36   Macau residents shall have the right to resort to law and to have access to the courts, to lawyers' help for protection of their lawful rights and interests, and to judicial remedies.

Macau residents shall have the right to institute legal proceedings in the courts against the acts of the executive authorities and their personnel.

Article 37   Macau residents shall have freedom to engage in education, academic research, literary and artistic creation, and other cultural activities.

Article 38   The freedom of marriage of Macau residents and their right to form and raise a family freely shall be protected by law.

The legitimate rights and interests of women shall be protected by the Macau Special Administrative Region.

The minors, the aged and the disabled shall be taken care of and protected by the Macau Special Administrative Region.

Article 39   Macau residents shall have the right to social welfare in accordance with law. The welfare benefits and retirement security of the labour force shall be protected by law.

Article 40   The provisions of the International Covenant on Civil and Political Rights, International Covenant on Economic, Social and Cultural Rights, and international labour conventions as applied to Macau shall remain in force and shall be implemented through the laws of the Macau Special Administrative Region.

The rights and freedoms enjoyed by Macau residents shall not be restricted unless as prescribed by law. Such restrictions shall not contravene the provisions of the first paragraph of this Article.

Article 41   Macau residents shall enjoy the other rights and freedoms safeguarded by the laws of the Macau Special Administrative Region.

Article 42   The interests of the residents of Portuguese descent in Macau shall be protected by the Macau Special Administrative Region in accordance with law, and their customs and cultural traditions shall be respected.

Article 43   Persons in the Macau Special Administrative Region other than Macau residents shall, in accordance with law, enjoy the rights and freedoms of Macau residents prescribed in this Chapter.

Article 44   Macau residents and other persons in Macau shall have the obligation to abide by the laws in force in the Macau Special Administrative Region.

Chapter IV: Political Structure

Section 1: The Chief Executive

Article 45   The Chief Executive of the Macau Special Administrative Region shall be the head of the Macau Special Administrative Region and shall represent the Region.

The Chief Executive of the Macau Special Administrative Region shall be accountable to the Central People's Government and the Macau Special Administrative Region in accordance with the provision of this Law.

Article 46   The Chief Executive of the Macau Special Administrative Region shall be a Chinese citizen of not less than 40 years of age who is a permanent resident of the Region and has ordinarily resided in Macau for a continuous period of not less than 20 years.

Article 47   The Chief Executive of the Macau Special Administrative Region shall be selected by election or through consultations held locally and be appointed by the Central People's Government.

The specific method for selecting the Chief Executive is prescribed in Annex I: "Method for the Selection of the Chief Executive of the Macau Special Administrative Region."

Article 48   The term of office of the Chief Executive of the Macau Special Administrative Region shall be five years. He or she may serve for not more than two consecutive terms.

Article 49   The Chief Executive of the Macau Special Administrative Region, during his or her term of office, shall have no right of abode in any foreign country and shall not engage in any activities for his or her personal gains. The Chief Executive, on assuming office, shall declare his or her assets to the President of the Court of Final Appeal of the Macau Special Administrative Region. This declaration shall be put on record.

Article 50   The Chief Executive of the Macau Special Administrative Region shall exercise the following powers and functions:

(1) To lead the government of the Region;

(2) To be responsible for the implementation of this law and other laws which, in accordance with this Law, apply in the Macau Special Administrative Region;

(3) To sign bills passed by the Legislative Council and to promulgate laws;

To sign budgets passed by the Legislative Council and report the budgets and final accounts to the Central People's Government for the record:

(4) To decide on government policies and to issue executive orders;

(5) To formulate the administrative regulations and promulgate them for implementation;

(6) To nominate and to report to the Central People's Government for appointment the following principal officials: Secretaries of Departments, Commissioner Against Corruption, Director of Audit, the leading members of the Police and the customs and excise; and to recommend to the Central People's Government the removal of the above-mentioned officials;

(7) To appoint part of the members of the Legislative Council;

(8) To appoint or remove members of the Executive Council;

(9) To appoint or remove presidents and judges of the courts at all levels and procurators in accordance with legal procedures;

(10) To nominate and report to the Central People's Government for appointment of the Procurator-General and recommend to the Central People's Government the removal of the Procurator-General in accordance with legal procedures.

(11) To appoint or remove holders of public office in accordance with legal procedures;

(12) To implement the directives issued by the Central People's Government in respect of the relevant matters provided for in this Law;

(13) To conduct, on behalf of the Government of the Macau Special Administrative Region, external affairs and other affairs as authorized by the Central Authorities;

(14) To approve the introduction of motions regarding revenues or expenditure to the Legislative Council;

(15) To decide, in the light of security and vital public interests, whether government officials or other personnel in charge of government affairs should testify or give evidence before the Legislative Council or its committees;

(16) To confer medals and titles of honour of the Macau Special Administrative Region in accordance with law;

(17) To pardon persons convicted of criminal offences or commute their penalties in accordance with laws; and

(18) To handle petitions and complaints.

Article 51   If the Chief Executive of the Macau Special Administrative Region considers that a bill passed by the Legislative Council is not compatible with the overall interests of the Region, he or she may give his or her reasons in writing and return it to the Legislative Council within 90 days for reconsideration. If the Legislative Council passes the original bill again by not less than a two-thirds majority of all the members, the Chief Executive must sign and promulgate it within 30 days or act in accordance with the provisions of Article 52 of this Law.

Article 52   The Chief Executive of the Macau Special Administrative Region may dissolve the Legislative Council under any of the following circumstances:

(1) The Chief Executive refuses to sign a bill passed the second time by the Legislative Council; and

(2) The Legislative Council refuses to pass a budget introduced by the government or any other bills which he or she considers concern the overall interests of the Region, and after consultations, consensus still cannot be reached.

Before dissolving the Legislative Council, the Chief Executive must consult the Executive Council and he or she shall explain the reason for it to the public.

The Chief Executive may dissolve the Legislative Council only once in each term of his or her office.

Article 53 If the Legislative Council of the Macau Special Administrative Region fails to pass the budget introduced by the government, the Chief Executive may approve provisional short-term appropriations according to the level of expenditure of the previous fiscal year.

Article 54 The Chief Executive of the Macau Special Administrative Region must resign under any of the following circumstances:

(1) When he or she loses the ability to discharge his or her duties as a result of serious illness or other reasons;

(2) When, after the Legislative Council is dissolved because he or she twice refuses to sign a bill passed by it, the new Legislative Council again passes by a two-thirds majority of all the members the original bill in dispute, but he or she still refuses to sign it within 30 days; and

(3) When, after the Legislative Council is dissolved because it refuses to pass a budget or any other bill concerning the overall interests of the Macau Special Administrative Region, the newly elected Legislative Council still refuses to pass the original bill in dispute.

Article 55 If the Chief Executive of the Macau Special Administrative Region is not able to discharge his or her duties for a short period, such duties shall temporarily be assumed by the secretaries of the departments in the order of precedence, which shall be stipulated by law.

In the event that the office of Chief Executive becomes vacant, a new Chief Executive shall be selected within 120 days in accordance with the provisions of Article 47 of this Law. During the period of vacancy, his or her duties shall be assumed according to the provisions of paragraph 1 of this Article and the choice of the acting Chief Executive shall be reported to the Central People's Government for approval. The acting Chief Executive shall abide by the provisions of Article 49 of this Law.

Article 56 The Executive Council of the Macau Special Administrative Region shall be an organ for assisting the Chief Executive in policy-making.

Article 57 Members of the Executive Council of the Macau Special Administrative Region shall be appointed by the Chief Executive from among the principal officials of the executive authorities, members of the Legislative Council and public figures. Their appointment or removal shall be decided by the Chief Executive. The term of office of members of the Executive Council shall not extend beyond the expiry of the term of office of the Chief Executive who appoints them. Members of the original Executive Council shall remain in office until the new Chief Executive is selected.

Members of the Executive Council of the Macau Special Administrative Region shall be Chinese citizens who are permanent residents of the Region.

The Executive Council shall be composed of seven to eleven persons. The Chief Executive may, as he or she deems necessary, invite other persons concerned to sit in on meetings of the Council.

Article 58 The Executive Council of the Macau Special Administrative Region shall be presided over by the Chief Executive. The meeting of the Executive Council shall be held at least once each month. Except for appointment, removal and disciplining of officials and the adoption of measures in emergencies, the Chief Executive shall consult the Executive Council before making important policy decisions, introducing bills to the Legislative Council, formulating administrative regulations, or dissolving the Legislative Council.

If the Chief Executive does not accept a majority opinion of the Executive Council, he or she shall put the specific reasons on record.

Article 59   A Commission Against Corruption shall be established in the Macau Special Administrative Region. It shall function independently and its Commissioner shall be accountable to the Chief Executive.

Article 60   A Commission of Audit shall be established in the Macau Special Administrative Region. It shall function independently and its Director shall be accountable to the Chief Executive.

Section 2: The Executive Authorities

Article 61   The Government of the Macau Special Administrative Region shall be the executive authorities of the Region.

Article 62   The head of the Government of the Macau Special Administrative Region shall be the Chief Executive of the Region. General secretariats, directorates of services, departments and divisions shall be established in the Government of the Macau Special Administrative Region.

Article 63   The principal officials of the Macau Special Administrative Region shall be Chinese citizens who are permanent residents of the Region and have ordinarily resided in Macau for a continuous period of not less than 15 years.

The principal officials of the Macau Special Administrative Region, at the time of assuming office, shall declare their property to the President of the Court of Final Appeal of the Macau Special Administrative Region for the record.

Article 64   The Government of the Macau Special Administrative Region shall exercise the following powers and functions:

(1) To formulate and implement policies;

(2) To conduct administrative affairs;

(3) To conduct external affairs as authorized by the Central People's Government under this Law;

(4) To draw up and introduce budgets and final accounts;

(5) To introduce bills and motions and to draft administrative regulations; and

(6) To designate officials to sit in on the meetings of the Legislative Council to hear opinions or speak on behalf of the government.

Article 65   The Government of the Macau Special Administrative Region must abide by the law and be accountable to the Legislative Council of the Region; it shall implement laws passed by the Council and already in force; it shall present regular policy addresses to the Council; and it shall answer questions raised by members of the Council.

Article 66   The Executive authorities of the Macau Special Administrative Region may, when necessary, establish advisory bodies.

Section 3: The Legislature

Article 67　The Legislative Council of the Macau Special Administrative Region shall be the legislature of the Region.

Article 68　The Legislative Council of the Macau Special Administrative Region shall be composed of permanent residents of the Region.

The majority of its members shall be elected.

The method for forming the Legislative Council is prescribed in Annex II: "Method for the Formation of the Legislative Council of the Macau Special Administrative Region."

Members of the Legislative Council, upon assuming office, shall declare their financial situation in accordance with legal procedures.

Article 69　The term of office of the Legislative Council of the Macau Special Administrative Region shall be four years, except for the first term which shall be stipulated otherwise.

Article 70　If the Legislative Council of the Macau Special Administrative Region is dissolved by the Chief Executive in accordance with the provisions of this Law, it must, within 90 days, be reconstituted in accordance with Article 68 of this Law.

Article 71　The Legislative Council of the Macau Special Administrative Region shall exercise the following powers and functions:

(1) To enact, amend, suspend or repeal laws in accordance with the provisions of this Law and legal procedures;

(2) To examine and approve budgets introduced by the government; and examine the report on audit introduced by the government;

(3) To decide on taxation according to government motions and approve debts to be undertaken by the government;

(4) To receive and debate the policy addresses of the Chief Executive;

(5) To debate any issue concerning public interests;

(6) To receive and handle complaints from Macau residents;

(7) If a motion initiated jointly by one-third of all the members of the Legislative Council charges the Chief Executive with serious breach of law or dereliction of duty and if he or she refuses to resign, the Council may, by a resolution, give a mandate to the President of the Court of Final Appeal to form an independent investigation committee to carry out investigation. If the committee considers the evidence sufficient to substantiate such charges, the Council may pass a motion of impeachment by a two-thirds majority of all its members and report it to the Central People's Government for decision; and

(8) To summon, as required when exercising the above-mentioned powers and functions, persons concerned to testify or give evidence.

Article 72　The Legislative Council of the Macau Special Administrative Region shall have a President and a Vice President who shall be elected by and from among the members of the Legislative Council.

The President and Vice President of the Legislative Council shall be Chinese citizens who are permanent residents of the Region and have ordinarily resided in Macau for a continuous period of not less than 15 years.

Article 73   In case of absence of the President of the Legislative Council of the Macau Special Administrative Region, the Vice President shall act as President.

In the event that the office of President or of Vice President of the Legislative Council becomes vacant, a new President or Vice President shall be elected.

Article 74   The President of the Legislative Council of the Macau Special Administrative Region shall exercise the following powers and functions:

(1) To preside over meetings;

(2) To decide on the agenda, giving priority to government bills for inclusion in the agenda upon the request of the Chief Executive;

(3) To decide on the dates of meetings;

(4) To call special sessions during the recess;

(5) To call emergency sessions on his or her own, or upon the request of the Chief Executive; and

(6) To exercise other powers and functions as prescribed in the rules of procedure of the Legislative Council.

Article 75   Members of the Legislative Council of the Macau Special Administrative Region may introduce bills in accordance with the provisions of this Law and legal procedures. Bills which do not relate to public expenditure or political structure or the operation of the government may be introduced individually or jointly by members of the Council. The written consent of the Chief Executive shall be required before bills relating to government policies are introduced.

Article 76   Members of the Legislative Council of the Macau Special Administrative Region shall have the right to raise questions about the government work in accordance with legal procedures.

Article 77   The quorum for the meeting of the Legislative Council of the Macau Special Administrative Region shall be not less than one-half of all its members. Except otherwise prescribed by this Law, bills and motions shall be passed by more than half of all the members of the Council.

The rules of procedure of the Legislative Council shall be made by the Council on its own, provided that they do not contravene this Law.

Article 78   A bill passed by the Legislative Council of the Macau Special Administrative Region may take effect only after it is signed and promulgated by the Chief Executive.

Article 79   Members of the Legislative Council of the Macau Special Administrative Region shall be immune from legal action in respect of their statements and voting at meetings of the Council.

Article 80   Members of the Legislative Council of the Macau Special Administrative Region, excluding active criminals, shall not be subjected to arrest without the permission of the Council.

Article 81   The President of the Legislative Council of the Macau Special Administrative Region shall declare, according to the decision of the Council, that a member of the Council is no longer qualified for the office under any of the following circumstances;

(1) When he or she loses the ability to discharge his or her duties as a result of serious illness or other reasons;

(2) When he or she assumes posts which he or she is not permitted by law to hold concurrently;

(3) When he or she, with no valid reason, is absent from meetings for five consecutive times or for 15 times intermittently without the consent of the President of the Legislative Council;

(4) When he or she breaches his or her oath; and

(5) When he or she is convicted and sentenced to imprisonment for more than 30 days for a criminal offence committed within or outside the Region.

Section 4: The Judiciary

Article 82 The courts of the Macau Special Administrative Region shall exercise the judicial power.

Article 83 The courts of the Macau Special Administrative Region shall exercise judicial power independently. They shall be subordinated to nothing but law and shall not be subject to any interference.

Article 84 The primary courts, intermediate courts and Court of Final Appeal shall be established in the Macau Special Administrative Region.

The power of final adjudication of the Macau Special Administrative Region shall be vested in the Court of Final Appeal of the Region.

The structure, powers and functions as well as operation of courts of the Macau Special Administrative Region shall be prescribed by law.

Article 85 The primary courts of the Macau Special Administrative Region may, when necessary, establish special courts.

The previous system concerning criminal prosecution shall be maintained.

Article 86 An administrative court shall be established in the Macau Special Administrative Region. It is the court which shall have jurisdiction over administrative and tax cases. If a party refuses to accept a judgment by the administrative court, he or she shall have the right to file an appeal with an intermediate court.

Article 87 Judges of the courts of the Macau Special Administrative Region at all levels shall be appointed by the Chief Executive on the recommendation of an independent commission composed of local judges, lawyers and eminent persons. Judges shall be chosen on the basis of their professional qualifications. Qualified judges of foreign nationality may also be employed.

A judge may only be removed for inability to discharge his or her functions, or for behavior incompatible with his or her post, by the Chief Executive on the recommendation of a tribunal appointed by the President of the Court of Final Appeal and consisting of not fewer than three local judges.

The removal of the judges of the Court of Final Appeal shall be decided on by the Chief Executive upon the recommendation of a review committee consisting of members of the Legislative Council of the Macau Special Administrative Region.

The appointment and removal of the judges of the Court of Final Appeal shall be reported to the Standing Committee of the National People's Congress for the record.

Article 88   The presidents of courts of the Macau Special Administrative Region at all levels shall be chosen from among judges and appointed by the Chief Executive.

The President of the Court of Final Appeal of the Macau Special Administrative Region shall be a Chinese citizen who is a permanent resident of the Region.

The appointment and removal of the President of the Court of Final Appeal shall be reported to the Standing Committee of the National People's Congress for the record.

Article 89   The judges of the Macau Special Administrative Region shall exercise judicial power according to law, instead of according to any order or instruction, except in the situation as prescribed in paragraph 3 of Article 19 of this Law.

Judges shall be immune from legal action for discharging his or her judicial functions.

During the term of his or her office, a judge shall not concurrently assume other public or private posts, nor shall he or she assume any post in organizations of a political nature.

Article 90   The procuratorates of the Macau Special Administrative Region shall exercise procuratorial functions as vested by law, independently and free from any interference.

The Procurator-General of the Macau Special Administrative Region shall be a Chinese citizen who is a permanent resident of the Region, shall be nominated by the Chief Executive and appointed by the Central People's Government.

Procurators shall be nominated by the Procurator-General and appointed by the Chief Executive.

The structure, powers and functions as well as operation of the procuratorates shall be prescribed by law.

Article 91   The system previously in force in Macau for appointment and removal of supporting members of the judiciary shall be maintained.

Article 92   On the basis of the system previously operating in Macau, the Government of the Macau Special Administrative Region may make provisions for local lawyers and lawyers from outside Macau to practise in the Region.

Article 93   The Macau Special Administrative Region may, through consultations and in accordance with law, maintain judicial relations with the judicial organs of other parts of the country, and they may render assistance to each other.

Article 94   With the assistance or authorization of the Central People's Government, the Macau Special Administrative Region may make appropriate arrangements with foreign states for reciprocal judicial assistance.

Section 5: Municipal Organs

Article 95   Municipal organizations which are not organs of political power may be established in the Macau Special Administrative Region. Entrusted by the government of the Region, they shall provide services in such fields as culture, recreation and environmental sanitation, and shall be consulted by the government of the Region on the above-mentioned affairs.

Article 96   The functions, powers and structure of the municipal organizations shall be prescribed by law.

Section 6: Public Servants

Article 97   Public servants serving in the Macau Special Administrative Region must be permanent residents of the Region, except for those as prescribed by Articles 98 and 99 of this Law and except for technical personnel of certain professions and junior public servants recruited by the Government of the Macau Special Administrative Region.

Article 98   Upon the establishment of the Macau Special Administrative Region, public servants, including the police and supporting members of the judiciary previously serving in Macau, may all remain in employment, continue service and retain their seniority with pay, allowances, benefits and conditions of service no less favourable than before.

The Government of the Macau Special Administrative Region shall pay to the above-mentioned public servants who are entitled to pensions and allowances under the laws previously in force in Macau and who remain in employment and retire after the establishment of the Macau Special Administrative Region, or to their dependents, all pensions and allowances due to them on terms no less favourable than before, and irrespective of their nationality or place of residence.

Article 99   The Government of the Macau Special Administrative Region may employ Portuguese and other foreign nationals previously serving in the public service in Macau, or those holding permanent identity cards of the Region, to serve as public servants in government departments at all levels, unless otherwise provided by this Law.

The relevant government departments of the Macau Special Administrative Region may also employ Portuguese and other foreign nationals as advisers or to fill professional and technical posts.

These individuals shall be employed only in their individual capacities and shall be responsible to the Government of the Macau Special Administrative Region.

Article 100   The appointment and promotion of public servants shall be on the basis of their qualifications, experience and ability. Macau's previous system of employment, discipline, advanced and regular promotion may basically remain unchanged, but may be improved along with the development of the Macau society.

Section 7: Swearing Allegiance

Article 101   The Chief Executive, principal officials, members of the Executive Council and of the Legislative Council, judges and procurators in the Macau Special Administrative Region must uphold the Basic Law of the Macau Special Administrative Region of the People's Republic of China, devote themselves to their duties, be honest in performing official duties, swear allegiance to the Macau Special Administrative Region and take an oath to this effect in accordance with law.

Article 102   When assuming office, the Chief Executive, principal officials, President of the Court of Final Appeal and Procurator-General of the Macau Special Administrative Region must swear allegiance to the People's Republic of China, apart from taking the oath under Article 101.

Chapter V: Economy

Article 103   The Macau Special Administrative Region shall, in accordance with law, protect the right of individuals and legal persons to the acquisition, use, disposal and inheritance of property and their right to compensation for lawful deprivation of their property.

Such compensation shall correspond to the real value of the property concerned at the time and shall be freely convertible and paid without undue delay.

The ownership of enterprises and the investments from outside the Region shall be protected by law.

Article 104   The Macau Special Administrative Region shall have independent finances.

All the financial revenues of the Macau Special Administrative Region shall be managed and controlled by the Region itself and shall not be handed over to the Central People's Government.

The Central People's Government shall not levy taxes in the Macau Special Administrative Region.

Article 105   The Macau Special Administrative Region shall follow the principle of keeping expenditure within the limits of revenues in drawing up its budget, and strive to achieve a fiscal balance, avoid deficits and keep the budget commensurate with the growth rate of its gross domestic product.

Article 106   The Macau Special Administrative Region shall practise an independent taxation system.

The Macau Special Administrative Region shall, taking the low tax policy previously pursued in Macau as reference, enact laws on its own concerning types of taxes, tax rates, tax reductions, allowances and expenditures, and other matters of taxation. The taxation system for franchised businesses shall be otherwise prescribed by law.

Article 107   The monetary and financial systems of the Macau Special Administrative Region shall be prescribed by law.

The Government of the Macau Special Administrative Region shall, on its own, formulate monetary and financial policies, safeguard the free operation of financial markets and all kinds of financial institutions, and regulate and supervise them in accordance with law.

Article 108   The Macau Pataca, as the legal tender in the Macau Special Administrative Region, shall continue to circulate.

The authority to issue Macau currency shall be vested in the Government of the Macau Special Administrative Region. The issue of Macau currency must be backed by a 100 percent reserve fund. The system regarding the issue of Macau currency and the reserve fund system shall be prescribed by law.

The Government of the Macau Special Administrative Region may authorize designated banks to perform or continue to perform the function of its agents in the issuance of Macau currency.

Article 109 No foreign exchange control policies shall be applied in the Macau Special Administrative Region. The Macau Pataca shall be freely convertible.

The foreign exchange reserve of the Macau Special Administrative Region shall be managed and controlled by the Government of the Macau Special Administrative Region according to law.

The Government of the Macau Special Administrative Region shall safeguard the free flow of capital within, into and out of the Region.

Article 110 The Macau Special Administrative Region shall maintain the status of a free port and shall not impose any tariff unless otherwise prescribed by law.

Article 111 The Macau Special Administrative Region shall pursue the policy of free trade and safeguard the free movement of goods, intangible assets and capital.

Article 112 The Macau Special Administrative Region shall be a separate customs territory.

The Macau Special Administrative Region may, using the name "Macau, China," participate in relevant international organizations and international trade agreements (including preferential trade arrangements), such as the General Agreement on Tariffs and Trade, and arrangements regarding international trade in textiles.

Export quotas, tariff preferences and other similar arrangements, which are obtained or made by the Macau Special Administrative Region or which were obtained or made but remain valid, shall be enjoyed exclusively by the Region.

Article 113 The Macau Special Administrative Region may issue its own certificates of origin for products in accordance with prevailing rules of origin.

Article 114 The Macau Special Administrative Region shall, in accordance with law, protect the free operation of industrial and commercial enterprises and make its own policies on the development of industry and commerce.

The Government of the Macau Special Administrative Region shall improve the economic environment and provide legal guarantees for promoting the development of industry and commerce and for encouraging investments, technological progress and development of new industries and new markets.

Article 115 The Macau Special Administrative Region, in the light of its economic development, shall make labour policy and improve labour law on its own.

The Macau Special Administrative Region shall establish consultative coordination organizations composed of representatives from the government, the employers' organizations and the employees' organizations.

Article 116 The Macau Special Administrative Region shall maintain and improve Macau's previous systems of shipping management and shipping regulation, and make shipping policy on its own.

The Macau Special Administrative Region shall be authorized by the Central

People's Government to maintain a shipping register and issue related certificates under its legislation, using the name "Macau, China."

With the exception of foreign warships, access for which requires the special permission of the Central People's Government, ships shall enjoy access to the ports of the Macau Special Administrative Region in accordance with the laws of the Region.

Private shipping businesses and shipping-related businesses and terminals in the Macau Special Administrative Region may continue to operate freely.

Article 117   The Government of the Macau Special Administrative Region may, with the authorization of the Central People's Government, formulate, on its own, various systems for the civil aviation management.

Article 118   The Macau Special Administrative Region shall, on its own, make policies on tourism and recreation in the light of its overall interests.

Article 119   The Macau Special Administrative Region shall carry out the protection of environment in accordance with law.

Article 120   The Macau Special Administrative Region shall, in accordance with law, recognize and protect all the lawful leases of land granted or decided upon before the establishment of the Macau Special Administrative Region which extend beyond 19 December 1999, and all rights in relation to such leases.

The grant or renewal of land leases after the establishment of the Macau Special Administrative Region shall be dealt with in accordance with the relevant land laws and policies of the Region.

Chapter VI: Cultural and Social Affairs

Article 121   The Government of the Macau Special Administrative Region shall, on its own, formulate policies on education, including policies regarding the educational system and its administration, the language of instruction, the allocation of funds, the examination system, the recognition of educational qualifications and the system of academic awards so as to promote educational development.

The Government of the Macau Special Administrative Region shall, in accordance with law, gradually institute a compulsory education system.

Community organizations and individuals may, in accordance with law, run educational undertakings of various kinds.

Article 122   The existing educational institutions of all kinds in Macau may continue to operate. All educational institutions in the Macau Special Administrative Region shall enjoy their autonomy and teaching and academic freedom in accordance with law.

Educational institutions of all kinds may continue to recruit staff and use teaching materials from outside the Macau Special Administrative Region. Students shall enjoy freedom of choice of educational institutions and freedom to pursue their education outside the Macau Special Administrative Region.

Article 123   The Government of the Macau Special Administrative Region shall, on its own, formulate policies to improve medical and health services and to develop Western and traditional Chinese medicine. Community organizations and individuals may provide various medical and health services in accordance with law.

Article 124 The Government of the Macau Special Administrative Region shall, on its own, formulate policies on science and technology and protect by law achievements in scientific and technological research, patents, discoveries and inventions.

The Government of the Macau Special Administrative Region shall, on its own, decide on the scientific and technological standards and specifications applicable in Macau.

Article 125 The Government of the Macau Special Administrative Region shall, on its own, formulate policies on culture, including literature, art, broadcasting, film and television programmes.

The Government of the Macau Special Administrative Region shall protect by law the achievements and the lawful rights and interests of authors in their literary, artistic and other creation.

The Government of the Macau Special Administrative Region shall protect by law scenic spots, historical sites and other historical relics as well as the lawful rights and interests of the owners of antiques.

Article 126 The Government of the Macau Special Administrative Region shall, on its own, formulate policies on press and publication.

Article 127 The Government of the Macau Special Administrative Region shall, on its own, formulate policies on sports. Non-governmental sports organizations may continue to exist and develop in accordance with law.

Article 128 The Government of the Macau Special Administrative Region, consistent with the principle of religious freedom, shall not interfere in the internal affairs of religious organizations or in the efforts of religious organizations and believers in Macau to maintain and develop relations with their counterparts outside Macau, or restrict religious activities which do not contravene the laws of the Region.

Religious organizations may, in accordance with law, run seminaries and other schools, hospitals and welfare institutions and provide other social services. Schools run by religious organizations may continue to provide religious education, including courses in religion.

Religious organizations shall, in accordance with law, enjoy the rights to acquire, use, dispose of and inherit property and the right to receive donations. Their previous property rights and interests shall be protected by law.

Article 129 The Government of the Macau Special Administrative Region shall, on its own, establish a system concerning the professions and, based on impartiality and rationality, formulate provisions for assessing professional qualifications or qualifications for practise in the various professions and issuing corresponding certificates.

Persons with professional qualifications or qualifications for professional practise obtained prior to the establishment of the Macau Special Administrative Region may retain their previous qualifications in accordance with the relevant regulations of the Macau Special Administrative Region.

The Government of the Macau Special Administrative Region shall, in accordance with the relevant regulations, recognize the professions and the professional organizations recognized prior to the establishment of the Region and may, as required by social development and in consultation with the parties concerned, recognize new professions and professional organizations.

Article 130   On the basis of the previous social welfare system, the Government of the Macau Special Administrative Region shall, on its own, formulate policies on the development and improvement of the social welfare system in the light of the economic conditions and social needs.

Article 131   Local organizations providing social services in the Macau Special Administrative Region may, on their own, decide their forms of service, provided that the law is not contravened.

Article 132   The Government of the Macau Special Administrative Region shall, when necessary and possible, gradually improve the policy previously practised in Macau in respect of subventions for non-governmental organizations in fields such as education, science, technology, culture, sports, recreation, medicine and health, social welfare and social work.

Article 133   The relationship between non-governmental organizations in fields such as education, science, technology, culture, news media, publication, sports, recreation, the professions, medicine and health, labour, women, youth, returned overseas nationals, social welfare and social work, as well as religious organizations in the Macau Special Administrative Region and their counterparts in other parts of the country, shall be based on the principles of non-subordination, non-interference and mutual respect.

Article 134   Non-governmental organizations in fields such as education, science, technology, culture, news media, publication, sports, recreation, the professions, medicine and health, labour, women, youth, returned overseas nationals, social welfare and social work as well as religious organizations in the Macau Special Administrative Region may maintain and develop relations with their counterparts in foreign countries and regions and with relevant international organizations. They may, as required, use the name "Macau, China" in the relevant activities.

Chapter VII: External Affairs

Article 135   Representatives of the Government of the Macau Special Administrative Region may, as members of delegations of the Government of the People's Republic of China, participate in negotiations at the diplomatic level directly affecting the Region conducted by the Central people's Government.

Article 136   The Macau Special Administrative Region may, on its own, using the name "Macau, China," maintain and develop relations and conclude and implement agreements with foreign states and regions and relevant international organizations in the appropriate fields, including the economic, trade, financial and monetary, shipping, communications, tourism, cultural, science and technology, and sports fields.

Article 137 Representatives of the Government of the Macau Special Administrative Region may, as members of delegations of the People's Republic of China, participate in international organizations or conferences in appropriate fields limited to states and affecting the Region, or may attend in such other capacity as may be permitted by the Central People's Government and the international organizations or conferences concerned, and may express their views, using the name "Macau, China."

The Macau Special Administrative Region may, using the name "Macau, China," participate in international organizations and conferences not limited to states.

The Central People's Government shall, in accordance with the circumstances and needs of the Region, take measures to ensure that the Macau Special Administrative Region shall continue to retain its status in an appropriate capacity in those international organizations of which the People's Republic of China is a member and in which Macau participates in one capacity or another.

The Central People's Government shall, in accordance with the circumstances and needs of the Region, facilitate the continued participation of the Macau Special Administrative Region in an appropriate capacity in those international organizations in which Macau is a participant in one capacity or another, but of which the People's Republic of China is not a member.

Article 138 The application to the Macau Special Administrative Region of international agreements to which the People's Republic of China is a member or becomes a party shall be decided by the Central People's Government, in accordance with the circumstances and needs of the Region, and after seeking the views of the government of the Region.

International agreements to which the People's Republic of China is not a party, but which are implemented in Macau, may continue to be implemented in the Macau Special Administrative Region. The Central People's Government shall, as necessary, authorize or assist the government of the Region to make appropriate arrangements for the application to the Region of other relevant international agreements.

Article 139 The Central People's Government shall authorize the Government of the Macau Special Administrative Region to issue, in accordance with law, passports of the Macau Special Administrative Region of the People's Republic of China to all Chinese citizens who hold permanent identity cards of the Region, and travel documents of the Macau Special Administrative Region of the People's Republic of China to all other persons lawfully residing in the Region. The above passports and travel documents shall be valid for all states and regions and shall record the holder's right to return to the Region.

The Government of the Macau Special Administrative Region may apply immigration controls on entry into, stay in and departure from the Region by persons from foreign states or regions.

Article 140 The Central People's Government shall assist or authorize the Government of the Macau Special Administrative Region to negotiate and conclude visa abolition agreements with relevant foreign states or regions.

Article 141 The Macau Special Administrative Region may, as necessary, establish official or semi-official economic and trade missions in foreign countries and shall report the establishment of such missions to the Central people's Government for the record.

Article 142 The establishment of foreign consular and other official or semi-official missions in the Macau Special Administrative Region shall require the approval of the Central People's Government.

Consular and other official missions established in Macau by states which have formal diplomatic relations with the People's Republic of China may be maintained.

According to the circumstances of each case, consular and other official missions established in Macau by states which have no formal diplomatic relations with the People's Republic of China may either remain or change to semi-official missions.

States not recognized by the People's Republic of China may only establish non-governmental institutions in the Region.

Chapter VIII: Interpretation and Amendment of the Basic Law

Article 143 The power of interpretation of this Law shall be vested in the Standing Committee of the National People's Congress. The Standing Committee of the National People's Congress shall authorize the courts of the Macau Special Administrative Region to interpret on their own, in adjudicating cases, the provisions of this Law which are within the limits of the autonomy of the Region.

The courts of the Macau Special Administrative Region may also interpret other provisions of this Law in adjudicating cases. However, if the courts of the Region, in adjudicating cases, need to interpret the provisions of this Law concerning affairs which are the responsibility of the Central People's Government, or concerning the relationship between the Central Authorities and the Region, and if such interpretation will affect the judgments in the cases, the courts of the Region shall, before making their final judgments which are not appealable, seek an interpretation of the relevant provisions from the Standing Committee of the National People's Congress through the Court of Final Appeal of the Region. When the Standing Committee makes an interpretation of the provisions concerned, the courts of the Region, in applying those provisions, shall follow the interpretation of the Standing Committee. However, judgments previously rendered shall not be affected.

The Standing Committee of the National People's Congress shall consult its Committee for the Basic Law of the Macau Special Administrative Region before giving an interpretation of this Law.

Article 144 The power of amendment of this Law shall be vested in the National People's Congress.

The power to propose bills for amendments to this Law shall be vested in the Standing Committee of the National People's Congress, the State Council, and the Macau Special Administrative Region. Amendment bills from the Macau Special Administrative Region shall be submitted to the National People's Congress by the delegation of the Region to the National People's Congress after obtaining the consent of two-thirds of the deputies of the Region to the National People's Congress, two-thirds of all the members of the Legislative Council of the Region, and the Chief Executive of the Region.

Before a bill for amendment to this Law is put on the agenda of the National People's Congress, the Committee for the Basic Law of the Macau Special Administrative Region shall study it and submit its views.

No amendment to this Law shall contravene the established basic policies of the People's Republic of China regarding Macau.

Chapter IX: Supplementary Provisions

Article 145 Upon the establishment of the Macau Special Administrative Region, the laws previously in force in Macau shall be adopted as laws of the Region, except for those which the Standing Committee of the National People's Congress declares to be in contravention of this Law. If any laws are later discovered to be in contravention of this Law, they shall be amended or cease to have force in accordance with the provisions of this Law and legal procedure.

Documents, certificates and contracts valid under the laws previously in force in Macau, and the rights and obligations provided for in such documents, certificates or contracts shall continue to be valid and be recognized and protected by the Macau Special Administrative Region, provided that they do not contravene this Law.

The contracts signed by the Portuguese Macau Government, whose terms of validity extend beyond 19 December 1999, shall continue to be valid, except those which a body authorized by the Central People's Government publicly declares to be inconsistent with the provisions about transitional arrangements contained in the Sino-Portuguese Joint Declaration and which need to be re-examined by the Government of the Macau Special Administrative Region.

Annex I: Method for the Selection of the Chief Executive of the Macau Special Administrative Region

1. The Chief Executive shall be elected by a broadly representative Election Committee in accordance with this Law and appointed by the Central People's Government.

2. The Election Committee shall be composed of 300 members from the following sectors:

Industrial, commercial and financial sectors: 100.

Cultural and educational sectors and other professions: 80.

Labour, social services, religious and other sectors: 80.

Representatives of members of the Legislative Council, representatives of members of the municipal organs, Macau deputies to the National People's Congress, and representatives of Macau members of the National Committee of the Chinese People's Political Consultative Conference: 40.

The term of office of the Election Committee shall be five years.

3. The delimitation of the various sectors, the organizations in each sector eligible to return Election Committee members and the number of such members returned by each of these organizations shall be prescribed by an electoral law enacted by the Macau Special Administrative Region in accordance with the principles of democracy and openness.

Corporate bodies in various sectors shall, on their own, elect members to the Election Committee, in accordance with the number of seats allocated and the election methods as prescribed by the electoral law.

Members of the Election Committee shall vote in their individual capacities.

4. Candidates for the office of Chief Executive may be nominated jointly by not less than 50 members of the Election Committee. Each member may nominate only one candidate.

5. The Election Committee shall, on the basis of the list of the nominees, elect the Chief Executive designate by secret ballot on a one-person one-vote basis. The specific election method shall be prescribed by the electoral law.

6. The first Chief Executive shall be selected in accordance with the "Decision of the National People's Congress of the People's Republic of China on the Method for the Formation of the First Government, the First Legislative Council and the First Judiciary of the Macau Special Administrative Region."

7. If there is a need to amend the method for selecting the Chief Executive for the terms subsequent to the year 2009, such amendments must be made with the endorsement of a two-thirds majority of all the members of the Legislative Council and the consent of the Chief Executive, and they shall be reported to the Standing Committee of the National People's Congress for approval.

Annex II: Method for the Formation of the Legislative Council of the Macau Special Administrative Region

I. In the first term, the Legislative Council shall be formed in accordance with the "Decision of the National People's Congress of the People's Republic of China on the Method for the Formation of the First Government, the First Legislative Council and the First Judiciary of the Macau Special Administrative Region."

The Legislative Council in the second term shall be composed of 27:

Members directly returned: 10.
Members indirectly returned: 10.
Appointed members: 7.

The Legislative Council in the third and subsequent terms shall be composed of 29:

Members directly returned: 12.
Members indirectly returned: 10.
Appointed members: 7.

II. The method for electing members of the Legislative Council shall be specified by an electoral law introduced by the Government of the Macau Special Administrative Region and passed by the Legislative Council.

III. If there is a need to change the method for forming the Legislative Council of the Macau Special Administrative Region in and after 2009, such amendments must be made with the endorsement of a two-thirds majority of all the members of the Council and the consent of the Chief Executive, and they shall be reported to the Standing Committee of the National People's congress for the record.

Annex III: National Laws to Be Applied in the Macau Special Administrative Region

The following national laws shall be applied locally, with effect from 20 December 1999, by way of promulgation or legislation by the Macau Special Administrative Region:

1. Resolution on the Capital, Calendar, National Anthem and National Flag of the People's Republic of China.

2. Resolution on the National Day of the People's Republic of China.

3. Nationality Law of the People's Republic of China.

4. Regulations of the People's Republic of China Concerning Diplomatic Privileges and Immunities.

5. Regulations of the People's Republic of China Concerning Consular Privileges and Immunities.

6. Law on the National Flag of the People's Republic of China.

7. Law on the National Emblem of the People's Republic of China.

8. Law of the People's Republic of China on the Territorial Sea and the Contiguous Zone.

Decision of the National People's Congress on the Method for the Formation of the First Government, the First Legislative Council and the First Judiciary of the Macau Special Administrative Region

Adopted by the Eighth National People's Congress at its First Session on 31 March 1993.

1. The First Government, the First Legislative Council and the First Judiciary shall be formed in accordance with the principles of state sovereignty and smooth transition.

2. The National People's Congress shall establish a Preparatory Committee for the Macau Special Administrative Region, which shall be responsible for preparing the establishment of the Region and shall prescribe the specific method for forming the First Government, the First Legislative Council and the First Judiciary in accordance with this Decision. The Preparatory Committee shall be composed of mainland members and of Macau members who shall constitute not less than 50 percent of its membership. Its Chairman and members shall be appointed by the Standing Committee of the National People's Congress.

3. The Preparatory Committee for the Macau Special Administrative Region shall be responsible for preparing the establishment of the Selection Committee for the First Government of the Macau Special Administrative Region ("the Selection Committee").

The Selection Committee shall be composed entirely of permanent residents of Macau and must be broadly representative. It shall include Macau deputies to the National People's Congress, representatives of Macau members of the National Committee of the Chinese People's Political Consultative Conference, persons with practical experience who have served in Macau's executive, legislative and advisory organs prior to the establishment of the Macau Special Administrative Region, and persons representative of various strata and sectors of society.

The Selection Committee shall be composed of 200 members:

    Industrial, commercial and financial sectors: 60.

    Cultural and educational sectors and other professions: 50.

    Labour, social services, religious and other sectors: 50.

Former political figures, Macau deputies to the National People's Congress, and representatives of the Macau members of the National Committee of the Chinese People's Political Consultative Conference: 40.

4. The Selection Committee shall recommend the candidate for the first Chief Executive through local consultations or through nomination and election after consultation, and report the recommended candidate to the Central People's Government for appointment. The term of office of the first Chief Executive shall be the same as the regular term.

5. The Chief Executive of the Macau Special Administrative Region shall be responsible for preparing the formation of the First Government of the Region in accordance with this Law.

6. The first Legislative Council of the Macau Special Administrative Region shall be composed of 23 members, with 8 members returned through indirect elections, and 7 members appointed by the Chief Executive. If the composition of the last Macau Legislative Council before the establishment of the Macau Special Administrative Region is in conformity with the relevant provisions of this Decision and the Basic Law of the Macau Special Administrative Region, those of the elected members who uphold the Basic Law of the Macau Special Administrative Region of the People's Republic of China and pledge allegiance to the Macau Special Administrative Region of the People's Republic of China, and who meet the requirements set forth in the Basic Law of the Region may, upon confirmation by the Preparatory Committee, become members of the First Legislative Council of the Region. Any vacancy in the First Legislative Council of the Region shall be filled by a decision of the Preparatory Committee.

The term of office of members of the First Legislative Council of the Macau Special Administrative Region shall last until 15 October 2001.

7. The Preparatory Committee of the Macau Special Administrative Region shall be responsible for organizing the Court of the Macau Special Administrative Region in accordance with the Basic Law of the Region.

Proposal by the Drafting Committee for the Basic Law of the Macau Special Administrative Region on the Establishment of the Committee for the Basic Law of the Macau Special Administrative Region under the Standing Committee of the National People's Congress.

1. Name: The Committee for the Basic Law of the Macau Special Administrative Region under the Standing Committee of the National People's Congress.

2. Affiliation: To be a working committee under the Standing Committee of the National People's Congress.

3. Function: To study questions arising from the implementation of Articles 17, 18, 143 and 144 of the Basic Law of the Macau Special Administrative Region and submit its views thereon to the Standing Committee of the National People's Congress.

4. Composition: Ten members, five from the mainland and five from Macau, including persons from the legal profession, appointed by the Standing Committee of the National People's Congress for a term of office of five years. Macau members shall be Chinese citizens who are permanent residents of the Macau Special Administrative Region with no right of abode in any foreign country and shall be nominated jointly by the Chief Executive, President of the Legislative Council and President of the Court of Final Appeal of the Region for appointment by the Standing Committee of the National People's Congress.

Decision by the National People's Congress on the Establishment of the Macau Special Administrative Region of the People's Republic of China

Adopted by the Eighth National People's Congress at its First Session on 31 March 1993.

In accordance with the provisions of Article 31 and sub-paragraph 13 of Article 62 of the Constitution of the People's Republic of China, the Eighth National People's Congress decides at its First Session:

1. That the Macau Special Administrative Region is to be established as of 20 December 1999; and

2. That the area of the Macau Special Administrative Region covers the Macau Peninsula, Taipa Island and Coloane Island. The map of the administrative division of the Macau Special Administrative Region will be published by the State Council separately.

Decision of the National People's Congress on Approving the Proposal by the Drafting Committee for the Basic Law of the Macau Special Administrative Region on the Establishment of the Committee for the Basic Law of the Macau Special Administrative Region under the Standing Committee of the National People's Congress

Adopted by the Eighth National People's Congress at its First Session on 31 March 1993.

The Eighth National People's Congress decides at its First Session:

1. To approve the proposal by the Drafting Committee for the Basic Law of the Macau Special Administrative Region on the establishment of the Committee for the Basic Law of the Macau Special Administrative Region under the Standing Committee of the National People's Congress; and

2. To establish the Committee for the Basic Law of the Macau Special Administrative Region under the Standing Committee of the National People's Congress when the Basic Law of the Macau Special Administrative Region of the People's Republic of China is put into effect.

Decision of the National People's Congress on the Basic Law of the Macau Special Administrative Region of the People's Republic of China

Adopted by the Eighth National People's Congress at its First Session on 31 March 1993.

The Eighth National People's Congress at its First Session adopts the Basic Law of the Macau Special Administrative Region of the People's Republic of China, including Annex I, "Method for the Selection of the Chief Executive of the Macau Special Administrative Region"; Annex II, "Method for the Formation of the Legislative Council of the Macau Special Administrative Region"; Annex III, "National Laws to Be Applied in the Macau Special Administrative Region"; and the designs of the regional flag and regional emblem of the Macau Special Administrative Region. Article 31 of the Constitution of the People's Republic of China provides: "The state may establish special administrative regions when necessary. The systems to be instituted in special administrative regions shall be prescribed by law enacted by the National People's Congress in the light of specific conditions." The Basic Law of the Macau Special Administrative Region is constitutional as it is enacted in accordance with the Constitution of the People's Republic of China in the light of the specific conditions of Macau. The systems, policies and laws to be instituted after the establishment of the Macau Special Administrative Region shall be based on the Basic Law of the Macau Special Administrative Region.

The Basic Law of the Macau Special Administrative Region of the People's Republic of China shall be put into ..effect as of 20 December 1999.

Antonio Fialho Ferreira's Account
of His Journey to Macau with News of the Restoration

*Narrative of the Journey made at His Majesty's orders by Antonio
Fialho Ferreira from this Kingdom to the City of Macao in China,
and of the most joyful proclamation of H.M. The King Our Lord
Dom João IV, whom God preserve in the said City and southern parts.*

SIRE:

I write this letter to Your Majesty from the island of Saint Helena, where it remains in the hope of arriving sooner than I, forwarded on some Portuguese vessel which might stop here, which may well be the case since I am sailing on a Dutch ship which will take longer going by way of Holland. For that reason, and because of what may happen, I deem it best to give an account to Your Majesty of how I performed the mission which was entrusted to me in the remotest land in which Your Majesty has vassals, which, since it is so distant (in comparison with Lisbon) may well be termed another world, and thus I can say that I come from another world.

Your Majesty sent me in the year 1641 to the regions of the Orient with the news of the joyful proclamation of Your Majesty's accession in Portugal. I sailed the Ocean beyond all of India, crossing the Equator thrice and reaching forty degrees of the Austral regions. I passed through all of that archipelago, giving the glad news of Your Majesty's joyous accession to the Kingdom of Portugal and of how Your Majesty is a King given by God. Heaven favored me so highly in this enterprise that not only the Portuguese and native Christians but even the local population and Mohammedans openly acclaimed Your Majesty, giving thanks to Our Lord for seeing themselves delivered from the Castilian yoke and captivity.

I entered the stronghold of Iacatra and City of Batavia, the chief fortress of the Dutch, where I gave an account to that General of the separation of the Kingdom of Portugal from that of Castile and how Your Majesty had sent an Ambassador to Holland, who was well received by the States General of the United

Provinces [Holland] and the Prince of Orange, with promises not only of good friendship but likewise help for the defense of that Kingdom. He found this somewhat hard to believe at first, owing to the news that he had given to the Directors in Holland, promising them that within three years all India would be within control of their fleets. I pressed this matter very earnestly, pledging my personal integrity to the utmost degree should any truth be found wanting, trying to persuade him likewise that the wars should cease in India, an advantage which he recognized.

During this time, some ships arrived from various ports in Holland bringing confirmation of the news, and he was convinced that I had spoken the truth. Thereupon he listened to me in earnest, and after that none of the ships which left that port captured any ship of ours. At my request he forthwith released all the prisoners of war—removing the irons in which they were working on their fortifications—who were numerous and included nobles, gentlemen, captains and soldiers, the majority of whom I shipped to India, there to serve Your Majesty in the fleets of that State. At that time I also sent advisory letters by land and sea, by means of natives to the regions I could not personally visit, such as Solor, Borneo, Iapara, Cambaya, Cochin-China, Funquim, Asiam, Capatane, and especially to the Kingdom of Macassar, where Portuguese merchants are always to be found, in order that advisories from them could be sent to Manila, a Spanish Colony, to forewarn the citizens of Macao who go there annually. This matter was carried through most diligently, purchasing for the purpose a ship at our own cost, by a citizen of Macao going on that ship with my letters, carrying also another missive from the Vicar of the Kingdom of Macassar to the Castilian Governor with the favor and approval of the Mohammedan King, who is a great friend of ours and prizes himself on being a brother in arms of Your Majesty's and shows great hatred towards Spain.

The news reached Manila at an opportune moment since, in the complete absence of all news from Mexico, the Governor was persuaded that the Dutch were about to launch an attack on Macao with thirty warships (the letter containing a report to this effect). He therefore gave an immediate order that the Portuguese should return to defend it with their own personnel and money. Meanwhile, the bearer of the letters secretly handed mine to the Captain-Major from Macao, after which the letters were read to other merchants who believed them and, putting implicit faith in them, fitted out a ship with the utmost dispatch in which they embarked without delay and safely reached Macao (bringing their full financial support). Some remained behind to await another opportunity, in which it seems they were ill advised, since it is certain they will be arrested when any news arrives from Spain.

I embarked for Macau on a ship which the Dutch General placed at my disposal to carry me there. On the eve of my sailing, there arrived from India on another Dutch ship a Portuguese gentleman with a letter from the Viceroy of Goa addressed to the Dutch General, and orders to procure a suspension of arms until the arrival of news of the conclusion of peace from Europe. He carried another letter of Your Majesty's for the City of Macao, together with another one from the Viceroy, which he handed over to me. I reached my destination safely after a successful voyage, landing in the City of Macao in disguise. Although I was speedily recognized, despite my casual garb of Flemish fashion, people thought that I had been pirated by the Dutch and, knowing that I brought with me thirty men of those who had been released in Iacatra, everybody imagined that I had come to ask for ransom money.

While these and other rumors were being circulated, I felt the pulse of public opinion, without openly declaring myself, and spoke with persons of trust. I found that everyone was divided into rival cliques, with the most bitter controversy that ever yet existed among the Portuguese nation concerning judicial matters. By my own industry and through my agents, and with the Divine Favor, I persuaded all government officials of Macao to gather at the Public Council Assembly building—judges, aldermen and the public attorney, plus the Captain of the garrison, who is stationed there with all of his councilors, as well as the Governor of the Bishopric, the Prelates of all the Religious Orders, and some of the nobility of the City of Macao.

When they were all thus assembled, I described to them the events preceding the proclamation of Your Majesty's accession in the Kingdom of Portugal and of subsequent events before my departure from Lisbon. I explained to them how Your Majesty was proclaimed, sworn and obeyed by all the estates of the Nobility, regular and secular clergy, and by all the other classes without any opposition. So effective were my statements, and so moved were their hearts, that without further ado they all rose to their feet, crying with one voice, "LONG LIVE OUR LORD THE KING DOM JOÃO THE FOURTH, LONG LIVE, LONG LIVE THE PRINCE DOM THEODOSIO HIS SON, LONG LIVE"—some gripping their swords, others raising them high in the air, and some even baring their chests, declaring loudly that they would sacrifice their blood, lives and hearts in Your Majesty's service, and for the defense of the Kingdom. The rest of the people in Macao acted in the same way as soon as the news was divulged, while at the same time peals of bells and other instruments of joy were rung. Loyal subjects not content that this recognition should only remain vocal regarding this occasion, demanded that a record be made forthwith in one of the books of the Municipality, to which they would all pledge their subservience and their lives in defense of the King. Furthermore, they demanded that great celebrations should be arranged so that native inhabitants and other foreigners could understand the degree of loyalty that the Portuguese in this remote part of the world rejoiced in the Restoration of the Kingdom, which they had already given up as lost. These celebrations continued for more than two months, both on foot and on horse, by day and night, with such splendor that it equaled the ostentation of any Court in Europe. Nor were the Bishopric and Religious Orders found lacking in thanksgiving processions. A voluminous narrative was made of all this which will shortly be published in that Court, including an account of the act of swearing allegiance to your Majesty and to His Highness, Prince Dom Theodosio, which seemed to be more impressive than that of Lisbon, except for the Royal Presence and the nobility of the Kingdom which assisted at this latter function.

Personal feuds were ended in tearful embraces, with the most long-standing foes consigning their bitter hatreds to oblivion and their weapons to the hearth (as the saying goes). Of the secular clergy, or rather the Religious and other Churchmen, they likewise agreed and swore to withdraw all disputes pending the matters being referred to the relevant tribunals, concerning which papers were forwarded to Portugal by way of India.

When the celebrations were over, I again assembled the Government, to whom I handed a Decree of Your Majesty by which it was granted the Japan voyage for the first four consecutive years, for the purpose of fortifying the City and making it defensible against possible incursion by the Spaniards. This grant could not be realized since trade with Manila has now been disrupted, as I advised Your Majesty in a letter of October 1641, sent by the Dutch. I presented another Decree of Your Majesty's in which the City of Macao was furthermore licensed to undertake a voyage direct to Lisbon, without sailing via India; but this likewise could not be carried out, to the great sorrow of all the citizens. That is because they lacked the large sums of silver bullion which they formerly derived from Japan (which was their principal subsistence) and their capital funds were at a low ebb. Also, they had no ships of sufficient size to make such a lengthy voyage since, with the loss of the Japan trade, they had been dispatched elsewhere.

They showed that they regretted this inability more on account of being thereby deprived of the opportunity of serving Your Majesty rather than because of their own private interests. They possessed two hundred and fifty pieces of admirably cast iron cannons of various calibers, for use both on land and sea; more than fifty bronze cannons, firing missiles of 16 to 25 pounds; over twenty thousand round bullets of cast iron; approximately four hundred thousand pounds of copper which remain in charge of the metal foundry, and which are being used up continually; and a great quantity of powder, many muskets and small-caliber matchlock rifles, which are made there and among the best in the world, although sold very cheaply. Part of all this belongs to Your Majesty's treasury, derived from the profits of the Japan voyages, which were so very profitable during these last years. The citizens of Macao were deeply grieved that they could not send all these instruments of war to Lisbon forthwith, to participate in the wars which they believe Your Majesty must be engaged in.

Seeing that it was thus impossible for me to bring to Your Majesty in a ship (as I had wished) the joyful tidings of this acclamation that I made (resulting in the City of Macao rendering allegiance with the loyalty I have related, as also the merchants who reside throughout the Southern parts), I resolved to buy a small vessel at my own cost (for I spent not a farthing of Your Majesty's treasury in either the outward or homeward voyage). I embarked on that ship with five of my sons and sailed through various regions proclaiming Your Majesty in places where the news had not yet arrived, until I again reached the Dutch stronghold of Batavia. I informed the General of Batavia that the City of Macao had sworn allegiance to Your Majesty and prevented him from sending a fleet which he had assembled for the purpose of taking it. He had been convinced that, owing to its proximity to Spanish territory, Macao would not swear allegiance to the Kingdom of Portugal. Since he had long coveted the City of Macao because of its trade and potential plunder—for, as everyone knows, it is the richest emporium in the world—he apparently regretted this lost opportunity. In order not to lose the expenses he had made to assemble the fleet, he dispatched it against the Castilian fortresses in the Moluccas, to where it sailed at the same time as my departure from Batavia.

At Batavia, I left the ship in which I came from Macao, since it was too small for the rest of the voyage, and asked the Dutch General for passage on another vessel. He granted me passage on a ship of my own choice, in which I am sailing for Holland, unless during the voyage I do not meet with a Portuguese ship to which I can transfer. And even if this should not occur, my going to Holland will serve to inform our Ambassador (if Your Majesty has one there) of certain matters concerning the East which are vital to discuss. From there I will go directly to the Kingdom of Portugal to lay at Your Majesty's feet the papers which narrate how I performed the business on which I was sent, with fuller details than I can present here. I will bring my five sons, who all wear the sword and who dared to make this voyage freely and voluntarily, without any compulsion, solely with the aim of serving Your Majesty against the enemies of the Kingdom of Portugal. In this manner they are like myself who, even if white-headed, possesses sufficient strength to wield a sword and carry a lance in Your Majesty's Service and defense of the fatherland.

I also give to Your Majesty some other news, which seems most miraculous to me, which I received after I had left Macao.

The Portuguese who remained behind in Manila later received the same news of the Restoration of the Kingdom of Portugal by way of the Spaniards, who then began treating them severely. But the God who watches over us so warped the judgment of Manila's Governor that he believed the promises of the merchants who said they would surrender Macao to him. For this purpose he immediately dispatched General Dom João Claudio on a ship to take over Macao. The General was accompanied by seventy Castilians serving as military officers, along with numerous Portuguese residents and their capital, totaling more than 600,000 gold coins to help finance expenses of the garrison and related necessities.

They all disembarked in Macao with as much self-confidence as if they had been in Seville when the Spanish General was immediately confined in a house where he is closely guarded. The others were being held in the forts of Macau, their money placed in security and the ship seized. This was, in short, an event which reflected the great glory of Macao as well as the Portuguese nation.

Thanks and praise are due to God our Lord for these great marvels as the primary and principal cause, but earthly Kings are not absolved from rewarding the persons whom the same Lord took as instrument and secondary cause in the execution thereof—more especially in my case, as Your Majesty sent me for this purpose to such far distant regions. And thus I am very sure that Your Majesty will reward my services with the grants that I expect from his Royal magnanimity, honoring my sons who are the riches which I cherish most. And, if owing to my unlucky star, Your Majesty should think that I do not deserve anything, I yet will not fail to exult in the glory of the willingness with which I exposed myself to such manifest perils by sea and land in the course of such a lengthy journey. Finally, I mention the love with which, like a loyal servant of Your Majesty, I passed through fire and sword for the sole purpose of securing obedience to Your Majesty in every region, and resolve to continue in his Royal service until the last breath of my life.

The Dutch have captured the fortress of São Salvador from the Spaniards, and have completely expelled them from the island of Formosa, between China and Japan.

The have also sent warships to intercept the military forces which go from the City of Manila to the fortresses of Ternate in the Moluccas. If they succeed in this, it should be very easy for them to capture all those places with the fleet which they sent and other precautionary measures, which come at an opportune time for us, since the Spaniards will be so preoccupied with this war that they will be unable to go and rescue their compatriots in Macao.

The citizens remain in arms, ready for any event, firmly resolved to die at the foot of their bulwarks, acclaiming Your Majesty as our true King and native Lord.

May God carry me before Your Majesty's eyes so that I may explain at greater length all the occurrences which happened in the progress of my mission. God guard Your Majesty's life for many years, and give him always the victory over his foreign and domestic foes. From this island of Saint Helena on the 12th April, 1643.

With all the necessary licenses.

In the Office of Domingos Lopes Rosa. Year 1643.

Lisbon 20th November 1643.

(*Signed*) Pinheiro   (*Signed*) Coelho

Appendix D

The Organic Statute of Macau

Law No. 1/76—February 10, 1976 (with amendments Law No. 13/90, May 10, 1990)

Under provisions 1 and 2 of Article 6, Constitutional Law No. 5/75 of March 14, 1975, I promulgate the following by order of the Revolutionary Committee as a Constitutional Law:

CHAPTER I—PRELIMINARY

Article 1   The territory of Macau shall comprise the city of Santo Nome de Deus de Macau and the two islands of Taipa and Coloane.

Article 2   The territory of Macau shall be organized as a corporation in which the people enjoy civil rights and, except as provided otherwise in the Constitution of the Republic of Portugal and this Constitution, the right of self-government in administration, economy, finance and legislation.

Article 3

1) With the exception of the courts of law, the sovereignty of the Republic in this territory shall be represented by the Governor.

2) The powers to deal with matters relating to foreign relations, international agreements or conventions, and the powers to represent Macau shall be vested in the President. He may delegate to the Governor the power to handle matters concerning the territory only.

3) Before delegation of power to implement any international agreement or convention in the territory, as provided in the preceding clause, the advice of the local government must first be sought.

CHAPTER II — THE GOVERNING BODY

SECTION 1: PRELIMINARY

Article 4   The governing body of the territory of Macau shall be the Governor and the Legislative Council. The Governor shall be advised by a Consultative Council.

Article 5   The Legislative Council and the Governor shall be responsible for legislation.

Article 6   The Governor, with the assistance of the Secretaries for Administration, shall be responsible for the implementation of laws.

SECTION 2: THE GOVERNOR

Article 7

1) The Governor shall be appointed by the President, and powers shall be conferred upon him by the President.

2) Prior to the appointment of the Governor, local residents shall be consulted, through the Legislative Council and representatives of basic social organizations.

Article 8   In the scale of civil service, the Governor shall have a rank equivalent to that of a Minister in the Government of the Republic.

Article 9

1) When the Governor is not in Macau, the President of the Republic shall designate a person to discharge the relevant duties. However, in the meantime, the Governor may appoint a person from among the Secretaries for Administration and the Commander of Public Security Force to act as the Governor.

2) In the absence of the Governor, the longest serving Secretary for Administration shall be the Acting Governor until a person has been appointed Governor by the President of the Republic.

Article 10   The Governor may not leave the territory without the prior consent of the President of the Republic.

Article 11

1) Apart from his representative capacity in general, as prescribed in Article 3, the Governor has the following additional powers:

    a. to represent the territory in internal relations. However, a delegate may be appointed by law to discharge certain functions.

    b. to sign laws and orders and to promulgate the same;

    c. to define the internal security policy for the territory, ensure that it is implemented and to be responsible for the execution in terms of the organization, operation and discipline;

    d. in the event the public order of any place within the Macau territory is seriously threatened or affected by any riot, to take the necessary and appropriate measures to restore order swiftly upon the advice of the High Security Committee. In the course where it is necessary to temporarily restrict or terminate any constitutional rights, freedoms and protections, the advice from the Legislative Council shall be sought first, and the President of the Republic must be notified forthwith whenever it is possible.

e. to present to the Constitutional Courts for determination of any laws promulgated by the Legislative Council in contravention of the Constitution or against the law;

f. to present to the Congress of the Republic any recommendation as to amendments or substitution of this Law and to comment on the recommendations for amendments made by the Congress of the Republic; and

g. to exercise all other powers under the Law.

2) Regulations requiring the signature of the Governor shall be considered null and void if they are not so signed.

Article 12

1) The powers to deal with the external security of the territory shall be vested in the President of the Republic.

2) The powers, as prescribed above, may be delegated.

Article 13

1) The legislative authority of the Governor shall be exercised by means of orders and shall consist of all matters which have not been reserved to the Republic or to the Legislative Council. This shall not contravene the requirement under Article 31.

2) It shall also be the duty of the Governor to legislate if the Legislative Council has granted such authorization or has been dissolved.

3) The exclusive authority of the Governor shall complement the basic law of the Republic and promulgate any regulation for the organization and operation of any administrative organ.

Article 14

1) Legislation which is authorized by law shall state its terms of authorization, its scope and period of its validity. Such period of validity may be extended.

2) Legislative authorization shall not be exercised for more than once, but such authorization may be selectively applied.

Article 15

1) Save for laws promulgated under Article 13, Item 13, all other laws shall, after their promulgation, undergo ratification upon the request of six members of the Legislative Council within the immediate five subsequent meetings of the Legislative Council after the said promulgation.

2) If ratification is refused, the law shall be null and void on the date when the decision of the Legislative Council notice is published in the official Bulletin. If the refusal for ratification is based on the contravention of the constitution, this law or any regulation promulgated by the authorities of the Republic which are not to be contravened, Article 40, Item 3 shall be observed.

3) Ratification may be granted after amendments are made. In this case, the order in question shall continue to be in force unless a resolution to terminate its operation is made by two-thirds of the active members of the Legislative Council.

Article 16

1) The administrative powers of the Governor which have not been conferred upon the sovereign body of the Republic by the Constitution or by this law are as follows:

a. To conduct the general policy of the territory;

b. To coordinate the entire public administration;

c. To execute the laws and other legal documents in force in the territory;

d. To ensure the freedom of judicial authorities so that they may carry out their duties fully and independently;

e. To administer the finances of the territory;

f. To define the structure of the monetary and financial markets, and to control their activities;

g. To deny entry to or to expel, in accordance with the law, any Portuguese national or foreigner whose presence would seriously affect internal or international peace and order. The party involved shall have the right to appeal to the President of the Republic.

2) In the exercise of his administrative power, the Governor shall ensure that orders issued by him are published in the Government Gazette and, depending on their nature, other instructions may also be published if necessary.

Article 17

1) Secretaries of Administration, whose number shall not exceed seven, shall be appointed and dismissed by the President of the Republic, upon nomination of the Governor.

2) In the scale of civil service, the Secretaries of Administration shall have a rank equivalent to that of Deputy Ministers of the Republic.

3) If the power of the Governor is suspended, the Secretary of Administration shall continue to discharge his duties until he is replaced.

4) A Secretary of Administration shall exercise the administrative powers delegated to him by written order of the Governor or in accordance with any administration regulation under Article 13, Item 3.

Article 18   During their terms of office, the Governor and the Secretaries of Administration may not concurrently take another public post or engage in any private activity.

Article 19

1) Acts which are not lawfully vested in the Governor and the Secretaries for Administration may be revoked, modified or suspended.

2) Lawful acts may also be revoked, modified or suspended, based upon a claim of illegality and within a period established by law for appeal or until the granting of the appeal.

3) The aforesaid rule shall be applicable to ratification, reform or

amendment of all illegal acts of the Governor and the Secretaries of Administration.

4) Administrative acts of the Governor or the Secretaries of Administration may be contested by interested parties based upon incompetence, usurpation or abuse of power, error or violation of the law, of regulations, or of administration contract.

5) Appeals against the judgments and decisions of the Governor and the Secretaries of Administration are to be ruled on by the High Court of Appeal. Such appeals must be lodged within forty-five days of the announcement of such judgments and decisions.

Article 20

1) The Governor is politically responsible to the President of the Republic.

2) The Governor and the Secretaries of Administration are civilly and criminally responsible to the law courts for their actions.

3) Civil and criminal actions in which the Governor and the Secretaries of Administration are parties while still in office shall be settled in the District of Lisbon, unless another tribunal has jurisdiction. Such tribunal shall not be from Macau.

SECTION 3: LEGISLATIVE COUNCIL
SUB-SECTION 1: ORGANIZATION

Article 21

1) The Legislative Council shall be composed of 23 members, chosen as follows from among those citizens qualified to be electors:

    a. seven appointed by the Governor from among residents who enjoy recognized prestige in the local community;

    b. eight elected by direct universal suffrage; and

    c. eight elected by indirect suffrage.

2) The Council shall elect its President and Vice President by secret ballot from among its members. The former may delegate the presidency to the latter, and such delegation shall be automatic whenever the President is absent from the Council.

Article 22

1) The tenure in office of the Deputies shall be of four years' duration, commencing from the day of the first Legislative Council meeting after the election to the day of the first meeting of the Legislative Council after the next election, but this shall not affect the termination of individual appointments made.

2) Vacancies that shall occur during the four-year period, if to be filled, shall be filled according to law depending on the vacancies, by means of designation (appointment) or supplement election to take place within sixty days after their [the vacancies] verification, except when the term of tenure in office shall expire during this interim period.

3) In a case such as that described above in Article 22, Item 2, the Deputies will serve until the end of the same four-year period.

Article 23

1) The local law court is responsible for counting the ballots and for announcing the result of the elections. The names of the successful candidates shall be published in the Government Gazette.

2) The result of the elections shall be made known by the law court at least eight days before the first meeting of the Council and, in the event of a supplementary election, the result shall be made known fifteen days after the election.

Article 24

1) Each Legislative term shall have four sessions.

2) The period between each session shall not exceed eight months.

3) The Legislative Council shall extend the term of the Legislative term, to enable matters raised in the meeting to be resolved in the extended meeting.

Article 25

1) For reasons of public interest, the President of the Republic may dissolve the Legislative Council upon the advice of the Governor and, in these circumstances, a new election will be held.

2) Full justification for the advice to dissolve the Legislative Council must be given and should be made known to members of the Legislative Council.

3) Upon assembly of the Legislative Council and the commencement of the new legislative term, the period of its existence shall include the period from the date which the new Legislative Council was formed to the date of the termination of that legislative term at the point of the election date.

Article 26

1) Councilors shall be immune from prosecution for opinions and votes in the exercise of their mandates.

2) Without the authorization of the Legislative Council, its members may not be detained, arrested or imprisoned except in the case of a major crime, or any similar crime, and an arrest on the spot.

3) Whenever a member of the Legislative Council is charged with any criminal or civil offense, it is the duty of the judge concerned to so inform the Legislative Council so as to enable the latter to consider whether or not the member concerned should be suspended from duties.

Article 27

1) A member of the Legislative Council:

    a. shall not act as a juror, judge or witness without the prior consent of the Legislative Council. The decision to give consent shall be made after a hearing with the member concerned;

    b. shall be deferred from all military and civil obligations while the Legislative Council is in session; and

    c. is entitled to receive all materials, reports and Government publications pertaining to his duties.

2) A member of the Legislative Council is entitled to an identification card, a special passport, and such remuneration as may be fixed by the Legislative Council.

Article 28   A member of the Legislative Council may resign by serving a written declaration to this effect.

Article 29

1) A member of the Legislative Council may lose his office under the following circumstances:

a. any reason of incompetence or prohibition of holding concurrent posts as prescribed by law; and

b. if he has been absent from the Council sessions five times consecutively or a total of fifteen times.

2) The right of declaring the suspension of any member rests with the Legislative Council itself.

Article 30

1) The functions of the Legislative Council are:

a. to supervise the observation in the territory of regulations under the Constitution, this law and all other laws, as well as to submit to the Constitutional Court of all the regulations issued by the Governor to ascertain their validity;

b. to submit to the Republic of any recommended amendments or substitutions of this law, and to express any views on the recommendations made by the Governor and the Congress of the Republic on the same purpose;

c. to enact laws on matters which are not reserved to the sovereign body of the Republic nor to the Governor, but this shall not contravene Article 31 hereof;

d. to approve the enactment of laws by the Governor;

e. to refuse ratification or amendment in pursuant to Article 15, to examine orders made by the Governor except for those laws which are promulgated under the exclusive authority of the Governor;

f. to formulate the social, economic and financial policies of the territory;

g. to approve the Government's collection of revenue from the territory and future Government expenditures before December 15 of each year, and to lay down in relevant regulations the principles of budgeting to be followed by departments to whom no specific amount has been voted under the laws or existing contracts.

h. to permit the Governor to borrow money according to law and to undertake other credit activities, including the furnishing of guarantees under conditions mentioned in Article 63;

i. to issue opinions in the cases referred to in Article 3, Item 3; and in Article 11, Item 1, letter (d).

j. to recognize and verify the seating of its members;

k. to elect a standing committee and to make internal regulations and policy; and

l. to advise on all matters concerning the territory, either on its own initiative or on the instructions of the Government of the Republic or the Governor.

2) The further functions of the Legislative Council are:

    a. to supervise the activities of the Governor, the Secretaries and the Government;

    b. to examine the territory's statements of account of each financial year, for which an auditor's certificate and report and other essential data for reference should be prepared by a competent court;

    c. to vote no-confidence motions against the Government. These must contain a detailed exposition of the reasons which justify them and must immediately advise the President of the Republic and the Governor; and

    d. to execute all other functions granted under the law.

Article 31

1) The Legislative Council is authorized to legislate for:

    a. identity and capacity;

    b. rights, freedom and protection;

    c. crimes, punishments, security sanctions and its compulsory requirements and also the laying down of procedure for criminal litigation;

    d. punishment for contravention of the law and regulation, crime for breach of administrative order and general systems on all related procedures;

    e. public use and public levying;

    f. leasing;

    g. grants to be made by the Governor;

    h. to stipulate the essential features of the tax system of the territory—the application and rate of each tax, and to establish the terms for the granting of tax exemptions and other concessions;

    i. the standards of the currency and measurements;

    j. the boundaries of local administrative districts;

    l. outline of the local administrative legal system, including local finances;

    m. the legal system regulating the relationship between the control administrative organ and the local administrative organ, and matters concerning the dissolution of the local administrative organ by the governor;

    n. the protection of public bodies and subjects, and civil liabilities of the Executive Council;

    o. the guidelines for public enterprise;

    p. the guidelines for local public administration; and

    q. to set up new grades and new titles in the civil service, to amend the tax regulations for these grades, and to set the remuneration of administrative personnel.

2) The Legislative Council shall have exclusive power to legislate for the following: Councilor codes, its own electoral system, the conditions of electors, the registration of voters and the qualifications of electors; also the definition of the social benefit represented in the indirect election, election procedure, election date and all related matters.

3) Save for authorization made to the Governor, matters under Article 31, Item 1, letters (g), (h), (j), (l), (m), (p) and (q), detention, residential search, confidentiality of private communication, unfixed imprisonment periods and security sanctions, together with their requirements, shall be the function of the Legislative Council.

4) Letters (a), (d), (e), (f), (i), (n) and (o) under Article 31, Item 1 are matters which may be promulgated jointly by the Governor and the Legislative Council.

5) Letters (b) and (c) under Article 31, Item 1 may be promulgated jointly by the Governor and Legislative Council on the basis that these be no contravention of the second part of Article 31, Item 3.

Article 32 In pursuant to its authority, the Legislative Council shall commence meeting on the fifth working day after the release of the document as to its assembly.

Article 33

1) Ordinary meetings of the Legislative Council may be called by the Chairman or at the request of not less than six Councilors.

2) Extraordinary meetings of the Legislative Council may be called by the Chairman or one-half of the Councilors to discuss items mentioned in the notice of convocation.

Article 34 At a legislative meeting, the presence of more than one-half of the Councilors shall comprise a quorum.

Article 35

1) General meetings of the Legislative Council shall be public, unless the Chairman or any Councilor proposes otherwise, in the public interest.

2) The Legislative Council may form permanent committees or temporary committees for specific purposes.

Article 36

1) Decisions of legislative meetings shall be passed by majority vote, but shall not affect the following.

2) The following decisions shall require a two-thirds majority:

a. cases in which the Governor fails to execute bills approved by the Legislative Council; and

b. cases referred to in Article 15, Item 3; Article 26, Item 3; decisions made under Article 30, Item 2; in Article 30, Item 1, letter (h); and in Article 31, Item 2, letters (a), (b), (c), (p) and (q).

3) In case of a tie, the Chairman shall have the deciding vote.

Article 37

1) The Governor may, at any time, attend sessions of the Council, but without the right to vote.

2) The Chairman may, on his own initiative or in compliance with the request of any Councilor, invite persons other than members of the Legislative Council, especially those knowledgeable about items under review, to attend legislative meetings or meetings of committees set up under Article 35, Item 2. These persons shall not have the right to vote.

Article 38

1) Legislative Councilors may:

a. submit written inquiries on any action of the Governor or the territory's administration so that explanations may be made to the public; and

b. obtain, consult or order information, independently of Council procedure, from any corporation or department of public affairs.

2) Requests for explanations, or inquires made in accordance with Item 1 above, may not be refused unless they concern matters of national security. Departments may not so refuse without the previous authorization of the Governor.

Article 39   The right to initiate bills shall be vested jointly in the Governor and in the Councilors, as provided in Council regulations.

Article 40

1) Proposals and bills approved by the Legislative Council shall become laws, and they shall be sent to the Governor so that he, within fifteen days from the date of reception, shall sign them and have them published.

2) In cases of disagreement, the law in question shall be referred back to the Legislative Council for review. If a majority of the active Councilors in pursuant to Item 2 of Article 36 confirms the law, the Governor may not refuse publication.

3) If, however, the disagreement is based on a claim of unconstitutionality or breach of the guidelines of the authorities of the Republic and, if the bill has been passed by the majority provided for, it shall be sent to the Constitutional Court to determine whether there is any unconstitutionality or breach of the guidelines of the authorities of the Republic. This decision shall be binding upon the Legislative Council and the Governor.

Article 41

1) The courts, when handling cases submitted to them, shall not follow any regulation which is unconstitutional or in contravention of this regulation.

2) If the sovereign authority of the Republic issues any law applicable to the territory in pursuant to Article 72 and such is in contravention of the laws made by the Macau territory Administrative authorities, and if the former involves matters under Article 31, Item 1, letters (a) to (f), (i), (n) and (o), the former shall prevail over the latter. When, in view of the special circumstances of the territory, the latter does not contravene with the content of the former, such provision shall not apply.

Article 42

1) The regulations of the Legislative Council shall provide for:

a. the composition and duties of the Legislative Council Standing Committee;

b. the organization of necessary committees;

c. the voting system;

d. the advance notice required for agenda items;

e. the conditions for the submission of bills and the time allowed for discussion;

f. the procedures for the final drafting of laws approved by the Council;

g. the time limits for the drafting of bills and opinions;

h. the rights, immunities and privileges of Legislative Councilors; and

i. all other matters essential to the work of the Legislative Council.

SUB-SECTION 2: CONSULTATIVE COUNCIL

Article 43   The Consultative Council shall be presided over by the Governor or his substitute, or any Councilor delegated by the Governor.

Article 44

1) The Council shall consist of five elected and five appointed members; their terms shall be four years.

2) The elected members shall be selected by groups as follows:

a. two by the territory's executive organizations; and

b. three by groups representing interest of the society.

3) The appointed members shall be named by the Governor from among citizens of recognized merit and prestige, who shall fulfill their functions during four-year terms.

Article 45

1) Elected members referred to above under Article 41, Item 2. Substitute members are also elected in order to take over for any elected members who may be unable to take the post.

2) Substitutions for appointed members shall be under the authority of the Governor.

Article 46   All Councilors shall be accorded the same prerogatives and privileges as the Legislative Councilors.

Article 47   The election system referred to in Article 44, Item 2, in particular the conditions of the electors, the registration, the qualifications, the definition of the representation, the election procedure and the date shall be set by law.

Article 48

1) The Council shall issue opinions on all general matters related to the Government and administration of the territory which are submitted to it by the Governor.

2) The Council must be consulted on the following matters:

a. bills which the Governor introduces to the Legislative Assembly;

b. proposed orders to be issued by the Governor;

c. regulation of the execution of legal documents in force in the territory;

d. definition of the general guidelines of economic, social, financial and administrative development in the territory;

e. refusal of entry rights to nationals or foreigners because of public interest, and orders of expulsion, according to law, when such presence may jeopardize internal or international order. Appeal may be brought to the President of the Republic; and

f. all matters in pursuant to the law.

3) The council shall formulate its own regulations.

Article 49

1) The Council shall meet whenever it is convened by the Governor. It may function only when a majority of its members are present.

2) Resolutions of the Council shall be passed by a majority of the Councilors who are present. The Governor may vote only in case of a tie.

3) Opinions on proposals for laws and orders shall be issued within the time set by the appropriate regulation or within the time limit set by the Governor, if the matters are considered urgent.

4) Opinions of the Consultative Council shall not be binding.

Article 50

1) Meetings are not open to the public. The Secretaries of Administration and other civil servants designated by the Governor for each individual case may attend, but without the right to vote.

2) The Governor may invite to attend the meetings, without the right to vote, persons who, by the special competence, can contribute useful information to matters under discussion.

Article 51

1) Macau territory possesses its own judicial system which enjoys its self-autonomy, serving the characteristic features.

2) The guideline of the Judicial system of Macau shall be made by the Congress of the Republic.

Article 52 On the administration of Justice, the Courts of Macau shall uphold the Rule of Law, to prevent any contravention of law in order to resolve any public and private interest disputes.

Article 53

1) The Courts in Macau are independent and are subject only to the law.

2) The independence of the Courts in Macau are ensured by the non-removal of the judges and not to be bound by any order or directive. This does not apply to the obligation to follow the decisions made under an appeal by the Superior Courts.

3) If the judge is appointed by a fixed term, it is guaranteed that no removal can be made during the term.

4) The judge is not liable for the decision made. This does not apply for matters under the law.

5) The body of the prosecutions subject to the law makes its own regulations and enjoys self-autonomy.

CHAPTER III—FINANCE

Article 54 The territory of Macau, possessing liabilities and assets, shall act in accordance with the relevant laws and honor its obligations and liabilities arising out of its acts or contracts. The Macau Government shall have the power to handle its assets and revenue.

Article 55   Territorial property of Macau shall include: vacant land, or land which is not within the system of private property or the public domain, and other movable and immovable property which belongs to no one within the limits of the territory or which may be acquired, or legal property outside the territory, especially dividends and other types of income to the territory.

Article 56

1) The territory's finances shall be controlled by a budget prepared and planned in accordance with the law.

2) The budget shall be a single volume, including all revenue and expenditures, together with various foundation funds and budgets from offices with autonomous power where such budgets shall be separately prepared in detail as stipulated by law.

3) The budget must provide for revenue sufficient to cover expenses.

Article 57

1) The budget shall be prepared every year as instructed by the Governor in accordance with the law.

2) If for any reason the budget cannot take effect at the beginning of the financial year, the collection of revenue set for unspecified times or for the period of the new budget shall proceed according to pre-existent law and, regarding ordinary expenditures, one-twelfth of the budget of the previous year and of the credits authorized during that year shall continue temporarily in force in order to meet ordinary expenses and new permanent obligations which may be incurred.

Article 58

1) The revenue of Macau shall be reported in the laws in force or in bills which may be issued by the respective legislatures.

Article 59   Revenue may be collected which has been authorized in legal form and which is written into the budget tables, with provisions for what is created or authorized at a later date.

Article 60

1) The following shall be financial obligations of the Republic in relation to the territory of Macau:

a. expenses related to the Republic's various offices in Macau and concessions in the territory guaranteed by the Republic;

b. total or partial subsidies to maritime or air transport organizations and other operations of communication among other territories of the Republic and the territory of Macau;

c. subsidy to the expenses of the region's security forces; and

d. grants to the Oriental Catholic Mission and subsidies to recognized Catholic missionary organizations, educational establishments and centers for personnel.

2) The following shall be financial obligations of the territory of Macau:

a. interest, repayment of loans and other financial obligations resulting from contracts or legislation;

b. expenses of Government offices, including travel expenses for the staff, expenses for materials and other expenses in connection with the operation of the offices.

c. expenses for the development of the territory, including legal and contractual obligations for concessions or public works to accomplish this purpose;

d. pensions for retired personnel, calculated at a rate proportional to their length of service in Macau;

e. expenses related to the production of currency; and

f. subsidies granted by the Government of Macau to organizations which maintain regular services in the public interest in the territory and other institutions.

3) Expenditures which have not been listed in the budget may not be carried out. Obligations may not be contracted, nor payments made, which exceed the budgetary allotments.

4) The sums authorized for certain expenses may not be applied in ways different from what is indicated in the budget or other legislation.

Article 61

1) The territory of Macau may contract loans for extraordinary uses in economic development, redemption of other loans, necessary increases in public territory or urgent matters regarding security or public safety.

2) While forming to the preceding provisions, the territory of Macau may contract internal loans or external loans which do not require special guarantees, and may carry out other credit operations.

3) The territory of Macau may raise money necessary to supplement the revenue of a financial year by means of floating debts but, before the end of the financial year concerned, arrangements should be made for settling such liabilities or money should be appropriated from the public treasury for such settlement.

4) When the issuing bank of Macau operates, it shall be the same as the bank for the territory.

5) The territory of Macau may not reduce, to the detriment of holders of titles, the capital and interest of established public debts. It may, however, convert them according to law.

Article 62

1) Debts from deposits in the treasury of the territory of Macau, or in its credit establishments, may not be subject to forced consolidation.

2) The following shall not be invalidated by time limits:

a. the creditor's equity in the national treasury and credit institutions designated by the Governor as past or future liabilities of Macau; and

b. the territory of Macau's claim as a creditor on the credit institutions mentioned above in Article 62, Item 2, letter (a).

Article 63

1) The territory of Macau may contract loans and carry on internal or external credit operations through public institutions or private organizations established in the territory when such financing has as its object enterprises

or projects of manifest interest for the territory's economy or when the territory's share justifies the contracting of such a guarantee.

    2) The guidelines regarding the process of the granting of loans, their execution and guarantees, shall be established by the legislative body concerned.

Article 64 Review of the accounts of administrative bodies and corporations of public utility, as well as audit functions for acts and contracts under the authority of territory offices, shall be the duty of the Administrative Tribunal.

Article 65

    1) The annual accounts of the territory compiled and reported by the Department of Finance shall be submitted to the judgment of the Administrative Tribunal within the legal time-period and deadline.

    2) The Governor shall be responsible for the submission of accounts to the Administrative Tribunal within the legal time-period.

Article 66 In case of disagreement between the Macau Government and the Administrative Tribunal in examination and approval of accounts, an appeal may be lodged with the Ministry of Audit of the Republic, whose decision shall be final.

CHAPTER IV—ADMINISTRATION OF THE TERRITORY

SECTION 1: PUBLIC DEPARTMENTS

Article 67 Public departments in Macau belong to the territory and may organize themselves into autonomous bodies with or without the status of a corporation.

SECTION 2: CIVIL SERVANTS

Article 68 Personnel of public departments, regardless of rank, are part of the organization of the territory of Macau and are only subject to the control and supervision of the departments concerned.

Article 69

    1) Personnel of offices under the sovereignty of the Republic or any self-autonomous organization of the territory, at their request or consent, with the permission of the department heads concerned or the relevant lawful authorities, as well as the consent of the Governor, may serve in Macau for regular periods. Under such circumstances, this service will be legally regarded as actual periods of service in their original office at their original rank.

    2) The personnel referred to above in Item 1, Article 69, at their request and with the consent of the department heads concerned or the relevant authorities, may serve in offices in Macau, but the right of appointment to a new office rests with the Governor.

Article 70

1) Personnel serving in offices in Macau, at their request and with the consent of the Governor, together with the approval of the Government of the Republic or any relevant lawful authorities, may serve in fixed terms in accordance to each individual case, at any sovereign offices of the Republic or self-autonomous organization in the territory. Under such circumstances, this service will be legally regarded as actual service in their original office at their original rank.

2) Such personnel, at their request and with the consent of the Governor of Macau, may be transferred to offices under the sovereignty of the Republic or any self-autonomous organization in the territory. Appointment to new offices shall be made by an effective appointment of the Governor.

Article 71 Franchise companies, and companies to which Macau contributes more than fifty percent of the capital, must have their headquarters and executive offices in Macau.

Article 72

1) Ordinances promulgated by offices under the sovereignty of the Republic which are to be applied to Macau and which stipulate publication in the Republic Gazette, should be so published and the dates of such publication should be recorded.

2) Laws and ordinances take effect only after being published in the appropriate Government Gazette, with the exception of laws and ordinances whose terms require immediate application. Whatever the circumstances, publication shall be made in one of the first two issues of the Government Gazette after the arrival of the Republic Gazette.

3) In the case of laws and ordinances requiring immediate implementation, and in other emergencies, their texts shall be transmitted by telegram to be immediately published in the Government Gazette or its supplement. In that case, the document will take effect from the date of publication of the telegram.

Article 73 Unless otherwise stated, ordinances will take effect in Macau five days after their publication in the Government Gazette.

Article 74

1) Any necessary replacement, deletion or addition in this law shall be inserted in a suitable place.

2) Any amendment to this law shall together be published with the new version.

Article 75 The President of the Republic, upon receiving the opinion of the Congress and the Government of the Republic, shall determine when to provide the Courts in Macau the right of final adjudication.

(Signed) **Francisco da Costa Gomes, President of the Republic**

Appendix E

Chronology of Events Relating to Macau

1152   Establishment of Zhongshan County (China) and Macau under its administration.

1277   Duan Zong, the young emperor of the South Song Dynasty, together with 50,000 followers, reached Macau to avoid attack by Mongolians. The beginning of inhabitation in Macau.

1488   A-Ma Temple is built.

1498   Vasco da Gama reaches Goa in India.

1510   Alfonso de Albuquerque of Portugal occupies Goa.

1511   Portuguese occupy Malacca.

1513   Jorge Álvares reaches Tuen Mun (an island near Hong Kong) and begins trading with China.

1513   Jorge Álvares, treasurer of the Malacca trading post, reaches Tuen Mun and becomes the first Portuguese to enter southern China and explore possible trading with China.

1515   Portuguese trader Rafael Perestrelo leads second mission from Malacca to the southern China coast and up the Pearl River towards Guangzhou.

1517   Lopo Soares de Albergaria, viceroy of Goa, appoints Tome Pires as a special envoy of Portugal commissioned to seek trading relations and settlement rights with the Chinese. Pires sails to Guangzhou with a fleet headed by Fernão Peres de Andrade and is granted permission to travel on to Beijing.

1519   A Portuguese expedition, led by Simão Peres de Andrade, builds a fortification on Neilingding Island in the Pearl River Delta near Macau. Without seeking Chinese permission, he builds a fenced barrier of sharp poles and a gallows and attacks Chinese vessels. China retaliates by arresting Tome Pires and placing him in a Guangzhou prison, where he dies in 1524.

1521   Pressure from China forces the Portuguese to leave Neilingding Island. The Chinese also close Guangzhou to foreign trade, but the Portuguese continue trading illegally in small ports of Zhejiang and Fujian provinces, particularly the towns of Quanzhou and Ningbo.

1530   China reopens Guangzhou to foreign trade, except to the Portuguese.

1535 Foreign trade office of China relocates in Macau.

China allows Portuguese ships to moor on occasion in Macau.

1542 Chinese officials force the Portuguese to end illegal trading at Quanzhou and Ningbo, after which they move farther south to the islands of Shangchuan and Lampacau, not far from Macau.

Portuguese expedition "discovers" Japan and begins developing trade with Japanese.

1549 Father Francis Xavier, a Portuguese Jesuit, arrives in Japan, hoping to convert the Japanese to Christianity.

1552

December

After two years of introducing and promoting Catholicism in Japan, Father Francis Xavier sails for Macau. He becomes ill and dies en route on the island of Shangchuan, off the southern China coastal province of Guangdong.

1553 Portuguese traders begin settling at Macau.

1554 Leonel de Sousa, representing Portugal, signs an agreement with a Chinese official of Guangdong province permitting the Portuguese to resume trading at Guangzhou.

1555 Father Melchior Nunes Carneiro, a Lisbon Jesuit, arrives in Macau en route to Japan. He returns in 1568 and founds hospitals for both Chinese and Portuguese, establishes an institution to treat leprosy, and opens the Santa Casa de Misericordia "to provide for all the poor." In addition, Father Nunes Carneiro was instrumental in the 1576 establishment of the diocese of Macau.

The total population of Macau is estimated at 400.

1556 Portuguese poet Luís de Camões is assigned to Macau, where he writes the famous nationalistic epic poem *Os Lusiadas* (*The Lusiads*).

Portuguese successfully battle pirates at sea near Macau, impressing Chinese authorities.

1557 Portuguese obtain the leasehold of Macau by paying annual fees.

Foundation of Macau as a Portuguese settlement under the formal name "City of the Name of God, Macau."

1564 Jesuits reach Macau in greater numbers, influencing future generations through educational and charity work.

Population of Macau is estimated at 900.

1568 Portuguese successfully defend the seas around Macau against major attack by pirates, afterwards gaining permission from China to construct fortresses on the tiny peninsula.

1569 Nagasaki in Japan becomes a trading post for Portugal.

1573 Portuguese in Macau begin paying ground rent to Chinese government.

Chinese construct a barrier gate, or "border" gate (Portas do Cerco), at the narrow isthmus between Macau and mainland China.

1576 Pope Gregory XIII issues a papal bull formally founding the diocese of Macau and pledges to establish more than 600 dioceses in Asia.

1578 King Dom Sebastião of Portugal is killed at age 24 in the battle of Alcacer Quibir in Morocco. His death leads to the Union of Crowns uniting Portugal and Spain.
Poet Luís de Camões, after living in near poverty for two years, dies in Lisbon.

1580 The dual monarchy is established, uniting the Portuguese and Spanish Crowns.
Macau enters a sixty-year period of trading activity and world prominence known as its "golden age."

1582 Portuguese signs a land-lease with China covering Macau, agreeing to pay an annual rent of 500 taels of silver to Zhongshan County.
Matteo Ricci, an Italian member of the Jesuit order and student of mathematics and astronomy, arrives in Macau.

1583 Establishment of the Municipal Senate (later Senado da Camara), Macau's oldest local political institution.
Leonardo de Sá becomes the first bishop of the diocese of Macau.

1584 Father Matteo Ricci of the Jesuit order arrives in Macau to prepare for establishing Christian missions in China.

1586 The viceroy of Goa approves Macau's status as a self-governing city, based on municipal rules governing the Portuguese city of Evora.

1587 King Philip II of Spain and Portugal designates Macau as "City of the Name of God in China" (Cidade de Nome de Deus na China).

1594 Jesuits establish the Madre de Deus School in Macau.

1597 Madre de Deus School in Macau formally becomes a university.

1601 Dutch ships first appear at Macau, seeking permission to trade with China.

1602 São Paulo Church is built in Macau, adjacent to the Jesuit College of São Paulo.
Dutch forces turned back after an "exploratory" attack on Macau.

1603 Dutch forces again turned back after a minor attack on Macau.

1604 First serious invasion of Macau by Dutch military ships ends in failure.

1605 Portuguese build defensive city wall at Macau without Chinese permission.

1607 Second invasion of Macau by Dutch ships again ends in failure.

1622 Dutch fleet attempts third invasion of Macau, the strongest incursion to date, but is humiliated by Portuguese defenders under Captain-Major Lopo Sarmento de Carvelho.

1623 Captain-General Dom Francisco Mascarenhas becomes Macau's first full-time governor.

1627 Small Dutch fleet again unsuccessful in fourth attempt to invade Macau.

1631 Holland seizes Malacca, severing the trade route between Goa and Macau and adversely affecting Portuguese trade.

1637 British fleet under the command of Captain John Weddell arrives at Macau en route to Guangzhou, seeking to engage in trade with China.

1640 Dual monarchy of Portugal and Spain ends after "sixty years' captivity" as the Duke of Braganza becomes King João IV of Portugal.

1641 Antonio Fialho Ferreira leaves Lisbon as a "royal envoy" to deliver news of the Restoration to Macau, arriving on the last day of May in 1642 after a sixteen-month journey by sea.

1642 Macau pledges loyalty to King João IV of Portugal and participates in ten weeks of celebration.

1654 Portuguese King João IV formally proclaims Macau as "City of the Name of God, There Is None More Loyal" (Macau: Cidade do Nome de Deus na China, Não Há Mais Leal). The inscription was placed on a monument near the entrance of the Loyal Senate. Macau's governor during 1850–57 added his own inscription to the Royal proclamation: "In the name of the King, our Sovereign Dom João IV, the Captain-General of this fortified town, João de Sousa Pereira, ordered this notice to be displayed as a witness to the great loyalty of its people."

1685 Chinese end Portuguese monopoly on trading with China by opening four ports to foreign trade, including one at Macau with an official customs office.

1717 China issues imperial decree that Chinese ships will be restricted to trading only at Macau and Japan, significantly increasing Macau's importance as a trading port.
Chinese officials prohibit British and French ships from trading at Guangzhou, but give them permission to anchor at Taipa Island near Macau.

1746 China, which has attempted to suppress Christianity on the mainland since 1723, expands its persecution of Christians to Macau.

1762 Religious conflict in Europe leads to expulsion of the Jesuits from Macau, three years after suppression of the Jesuit Society in Portugal.

1773 Britain expands opium sales at Chinese ports in Guangdong Province.

1785 British artists Thomas Daniell and William Daniell visit Macau and sketch Oriental landscapes.

1799 China bans opium for the first time.

1802 Britain fails in an attempt to invade Macau in an effort to "protect" the Portuguese enclave "from French attack." Threatened intervention by China subsequently leads to Britain's withdrawal.

1808 The British again occupy Macau but leave under the pressure of Chinese threat.

1810 The Portuguese Crown designates Macau's Municipal Senate as the Loyal Senate (Leal Senado).

1825 British artist George Chinnery arrives in Macau, the only acclaimed European artist to live permanently in the Portuguese enclave.

1835 Fire destroys Macau's Jesuit College of São Paulo (St. Paul) and much of the adjacent São Paulo Church.

1839 Imperial Commissioner Lin Tse-hsu of China takes strong action to prohibit opium trade in Macau. Events lead to First Opium War between Britain and China.

1842   British defeat Chinese in First Opium War. Hong Kong is ceded "in perpetuity" to Great Britain in the Convention of Nanking (Nanjing). China opens the ports of Guangzhou, Amoy, Foochow, Ningbo, and Shanghai to foreign trade.

1844   The Treaty of Wangxia (Sino-American Treaty of Friendship and Trade) is signed in Macau, formally establishing trading relations between China and the United States.

1845   Macau is declared a free port by Portugal's Queen Maria II, who appoints Portuguese naval officer João Ferreira do Amaral as governor.

1846   Governor João Ferreira do Amaral of Macau initiates expansionist policies, even taxing local Chinese residents of the Portuguese enclave.

1849   Under the direction of Governor João Ferreira do Amaral, officials in Macau tax incoming ships, expand their territory beyond its "border," devastate Chinese graveyards to build new roads, and demolish the Chinese customs office, expelling its officer.
        Macau Governor João Ferreira do Amaral is assassinated and beheaded by seven mainland Chinese posing as beggars. His death is followed by a vengeful retribution against a nearby Chinese fortress by Vicente Nicolau de Mesquita (the Hero of Passaleong).

1851   Portuguese seize Taipa, an island just south of the Macau peninsula.

1852   Portuguese and British engage in the coolies trade.

1862   Treaty of Tientsin (Tianjin) between Portugal and China is negotiated by the French ambassador. The treaty is intended to confirm recognition of Macau as a Portuguese colony.

1864   China refuses to ratify the Treaty of Tientsin (Tianjin), but makes no change in Portugal's administration of Macau.

1873   Portuguese bans coolie trade in Macau.
        Kiang Wu Hospital is established at Macau.

1874   Portuguese demolish the old barrier gate (Portas do Cerco) and build a new one.

1886   Dr. Sun Yat-sen, founder of the Chinese Republic, is born in Zhongshan County, which comprises Macau and surrounding areas.

1887   Conclusion of negotiations on the Treaty of Friendship and Trade between China and Portugal (Luso-Chinese Treaty), which confirms the perpetual occupation of Macau by the Portuguese. Treaty evades the question of border delimitation.

1888   Luso-Chinese Treaty of Friendship and Trade is ratified by China and Portugal, guaranteeing that "Portugal will forever administer Macau."

1890   Portuguese integrates nearby Green Island (Ilha Verde) into Macau's territory.

1892   Dr. Sun Yat-sen graduates from Hong Kong College of Medicine for Chinese and works as a doctor in Kiang Wu Hospital at Macau.

1902   The first bank is established in Macau.

1909   China and Portugal negotiate unsuccessfully in Hong Kong in efforts to determine the official border of Macau.

1911   Establishment of the Macau Chinese Chamber of Commerce in Macau.

1928   Expiration of the 1887 Luso-Chinese Treaty (also known variously as the Lisbon Agreement or the Treaty of Beijing). The treaty is renewed but still avoids the issue of Macau's border delimitation.

1934   Portuguese government grants monopoly rights to casino gambling in Macau to the Tai Xing Company syndicate, which opens its first casino in the Central Hotel near Macau's Loyal Senate.

1937   Japan invades China in the years leading to World War II.
       Chinese refugees flee to Macau to escape from Japanese invaders.

1945   Mainland Chinese refugees living in Macau return to China following Japan's surrender and the end of World War II.

1948   Air traffic (by seaplane) begins between Macau and Hong Kong but ends promptly when a plane crashes.

1949   Founding of the People's Republic of China, ending China's Civil War.
       Nan Guang Trading Company becomes China's only commercial and political representative in Macau.

1951   Korean War breaks out.
       Macau is designated as a "province," joining the United Nations embargo against China (because of China's involvement in the Korean War).

1952   "Barrier Gate Incident" leads to Chinese restriction on food imports to Macau.

1953   Monument is raised in Macau honoring Jorge Álvares, who in 1513 was the first European to arrive in China from the sea (making port on Neilingding Island, three miles off the Chinese coast in the Pearl River Delta).

1955   The term *Macao* officially becomes *Macau* in Portuguese.
       Portugal formally declares Macau to be an "overseas province."

1957   Exports from Macau are declared to be duty-free to Portuguese territories, by order of Portugal.

1961   Portugal declares Macau to be a tourist center, with the authority to establish gambling.

1962   Casino rights in Macau are granted exclusively to the Macau Tourism and Entertainment Company (Sociedade de Turismo e Diversões de Macau, or STDM).

1966   Conflict between Macau police and local leftists develops into violent demonstrations.

1967   Spillover from the Cultural Revolution in the People's Republic of China disrupts daily life in Macau.
       China and Portugal sign a secret agreement promising reasonable Chinese cooperation in return for continued Portuguese administration of Macau.

1972   Sovereignty over Macau is claimed by China in letter to the United Nations.

1974   Military revolution in Portugal.

1976   New Portuguese constitution provides for Macau to be governed by the "Organic Statute for Macau" (Estatuto Organico de Macau, or EOM), providing for election of some members of its Legislative Assembly (Assembleia Legislativa). In addition, Portugal proposes changing Macau's designation as a Portuguese colony to a "territory under Portuguese administration."

1977   Macau's currency is tied directly to the Hong Kong dollar.

1979   China and Portugal negotiate a second secret agreement affirming Macau as "a Chinese territory under Portuguese administration." Diplomatic relations are established between Portugal and China.

1981   The University of East Asia, the only university in Macau, is established by the Ricci Island West Company.

1984   The governor of Macau, Vasco Fernando Leote de Almeida e Costa, dissolves the enclave's Legislative Assembly following a dispute over the legislature's authority to amend his decrees without his final approval.

The Nan Guang Trading Company, China's only official commercial and political representative in Macau, is formally divided into the Nan Guang Company (political) and Nan Guang Trading Company (commercial).

1986   Negotiations begin between China and Portugal on the future of Macau.

Macau's Legislative Assembly approves extending until 2001 the casino monopoly license of the Macau Tourism and Entertainment Company.

1987   China and Portugal agree on terms of the Sino-Portuguese Joint Declaration on Macau.

March 26

The Sino-Portuguese Joint Declaration on Macau is initialed by representatives of China and Portugal.

April 13

Officials of China and Portugal sign the Sino-Portuguese Joint Declaration on Macau, providing for Chinese sovereignty over Macau on December 20, 1999.

Portugal assures full Portuguese citizenship rights for ethnic Chinese residents of Macau and their descendants after 1999.

April 18

Portugal again assures the Macanese of their right to Portuguese citizenship, saying that under Portuguese law nationality will be transmitted by bloodline instead of place of birth. China warns that ethnic Chinese in Macau cannot hold dual nationality after 1999.

September 21

China's official news agency, Xinhua, opens an office in Macau.

1988   Formation of the Basic Law Drafting Committee to prepare a constitution-like document for Macau after its 1999 transfer to China.

February

The Macau government assumes jurisdiction over the University of East Asia.

1989 Formation of the Basic Law Consultative Committee, designed to help provide for a smooth transition of Macau to China in 1999.

1990 Governor Carlos Melancia of Macau resigns from office after being implicated in a corruption scandal.

November

President Mario Soares of Portugal visits Macau, hoping to boost morale and demonstrate his personal concern for the residents of the enclave.

1991 Public opinion is requested on the Basic Law for Macau.

East Asia Airlines begins regular helicopter service between Macau and Hong Kong.

March

General Vasco Rocha Vieira, a Portuguese minister with special responsibility for the Azores Islands, is named by Portuguese President Mario Soares of Portugal as the new governor of Macau.

November

The Macau International Airport Corporation awards contracts worth U.S. $500 million for runway construction and land reclamation required for Macau's new airport.

1992 Submission of the revised draft Basic Law to the Standing Committee of the National People's Congress in Beijing.

Establishment of the Supreme Court of Justice, Macau's highest court of appeal, subject neither to Lisbon nor Beijing.

1993 Final draft of the Basic Law of Macau is presented to Beijing for approval.

March 31

National People's Congress in Beijing adopts final draft of Basic Law for Macau.

1994 Thirtieth anniversary of the Macau Grand Prix.

1995 The new Macau International Airport opens for business.

1999

December 20

Macau becomes a "special administrative region" of the People's Republic of China.

2049

December 20

Expiration of the basic law for Macau, a constitutional document in which China guaranteed 50 years of autonomy, capitalism and continued fundamental rights after taking effect on December 20, 1999.

Notes

Chapter 1

1. R. D. Cremer, ed., *Macau: City of Commerce and Culture* (Hong Kong: UEA Press, 1987), p. vii.
2. Cremer, *Macau,* p. 27.
3. Elfed Vaughan Roberts, Sum Ngai Lin, and Peter Bradshaw, *Historical Dictionary of Hong Kong and Macau* (Metuchen, N.J.: Scarecrow Press, 1992), p. 297.
4. Cremer, *Macau,* p. 9.
5. E.V. Roberts, *Historical Dictionary of Hong Kong and Macau,* p. 291.
6. Cesar Guillen-Nuñez, *Macau* (Hong Kong: Oxford University Press, 1984), p. 4.

Chapter 2

1. *Los Angeles Times,* April 7, 1984, p. A1.
2. Cesar Guillen-Nuñez, *Macau* (Hong Kong: Oxford University Press, 1984), p. 5.
3. C. R. Boxer, ed., *South China in the Sixteenth Century* (Glasgow: University Press, 1953), p. xxxii.
4. Ibid.
5. Guillen-Nuñez, *Macau,* p. 57.
6. Ibid.
7. Ibid., p. 1.
8. R. D. Cremer, ed., *Macau: City of Commerce and Culture* (Hong Kong: UEA Press, 1987), p. 10.
9. Leonard Bacon, trans., *The Lusiads of Luiz de Camões* (New York: Hispanic Society, 1950), p. xxi.
10. C. R. Boxer, *Fidalgos in the Far East, 1550–1750* (London: Oxford University Press, 1968), p. 65.
11. Cremer, *Macau,* p.39.
12. Guillen-Nuñez, *Macau,* p. 39.
13. Cremer, *Macau,* p. 40.
14. Guillen-Nuñez, *Macau,* p. 6.

15. Cremer, *Macau,* p. 41.
16. Guillen-Nuñez, *Macau,* p. 10.
17. Boxer, *Fidalgos,* p. 217.
18. Ibid.
19. Ibid.
20. Ibid., p. 218.
21. Ibid.
22. Guillen-Nuñez, *Macau,* p. 14.
23. Paul Hibbert Clyde, *The Far East: A History of the Impact of the West on Eastern Asia* (Englewood Cliffs, N.J.: Prentice-Hall, 1964), p. 86.
24. Cremer, *Macau,* p. 46.
25. Guillen-Nuñez, *Macau,* p. 15.

Chapter 3

1. R. D. Cremer, ed., *Macau: City of Commerce and Culture* (Hong Kong: UEA Press, 1987), p. 30.
2. Cremer, *Macau,* p. 11.
3. Cesar, Guillen-Nuñez, *Macau* (Hong Kong: Oxford University Press, 1984), p. 11.
4. Ibid.
5. Ibid.
6. Ibid.
7. Leonard Bacon, trans., *The Lusiads of Luiz de Camões,* (New York: Hispanic Society, 1950), p. xxix.
8. Ibid.
9. C. R. Boxer, *Fildagos in the Far East, 1550–1750* (London: Oxford University Press, 1968), p. 40.
10. Ibid.
11. Ibid., p41.
12. Richard Louis Edmonds, comp., *Macau* (Oxford: Clio Press, 1989), p. xxxiv.
13. E.V. Roberts, Sum Ngai Lin, and Peter Bradshaw, *Historical Dictionary of Hong Kong and Macau,* p. 289.
14. Cremer, *Macau,* p. 43.
15. George Bryan Souza, *The Survival of Empire: Portuguese Trade and Society in China and the South China Sea, 1630–1754* (Cambridge: Cambridge University Press, 1986), p. 26.
16. Ibid., p. 23.
17. P.H.M. Jones, *Golden Guide to Hongkong and Macau* (Rutland, Vt.: Charles E. Tuttle, 1969), p. 368.
18. Malyn Newitt, ed., *The First Portuguese Colonial Empire* (Exeter, England: University of Exeter, 1986), p. 56.
19. The term *fidalgo,* derived from the Portuguese designation *filho d'algo,* specifically referred to a person of aristocratic background, literally "sons of somebody." Elfed Vaughan Roberts, Sum Ngai Lin, and Peter Bradshaw, *Historical Dictionary of Hong Kong and Macau,* p. 296.

20. Boxer, *Fidalgos,* p. 218.

21. Roderich Ptak, ed., *Portuguese Asia* (Stüttgart: Steiner, Verlag, Wiesbaden GMBH, 1987), p. 87.

22. Ibid., p. 105.

23. A ca.1600 Macau-to-Nagasaki freight document reprinted in C. R. Boxer's *The Great Ship from Amacon* (1959) lists raw silk, colored fine silk, embroideries and brocats, common gold, fine gold, musk, white ceruse, cotton thread, cotton cloth, quicksilver, lead, tin, China root, rhubarb, licorice, white sugar, and black sugar. Cremer, *Macau,* p. 33.

24. Boxer, *Fidalgos,* p. 12.

25. Ibid., p. 16.

26. Souza, *Survival of Empire,* p. 173.

27. Frank Welsh, *A History of Hong Kong* (London: HarperCollins, 1993), p. 25.

28. Cremer, *Macau,* p. 77.

29. J. M. Braga, *Early Medical Practice in Macau* (Macau: Agencia de Turismo, 1935), p. 12.

30. Ibid.

Chapter 4

1. Cesar Guillen-Nuñez, *Macau* (Hong Kong: Oxford University Press, 1984), p. 16.

2. P.H.M. Jones, *Golden Guide to Hongkong and Macau* (Rutland, Vt.: Charles E. Tuttle, 1969), p. 355.

3. C. R. Boxer, *Fidalgos in the Far East, 1550–1750* (London: Oxford University Press, 1968), p. 76.

4. Ibid., p. 79.

5. Ibid., p. 80.

6. Ibid.

7. Ibid.

8. Ibid.

9. Ibid., p. 81.

10. Ibid.

11. Ibid., p. 83.

12. R. D. Cremer, ed., *Macau: City of Commerce and Culture* (Hong Kong: UEA Press, 1987), p. 77.

13. Boxer, *Fidalgos,* p. 143.

14. Ibid.

15. Guillen-Nuñez, *Macau,* p. 22.

Chapter 5

1. Richard Louis Edmonds, comp., *Macau,* (Oxford: Clio Press, 1989), p. xx.

2. C. R. Boxer, *Fidalgos in the Far East, 1550–1750* (London: Oxford University Press, 1968), p. 139.

3. Ibid.

4. Ibid., p. 140.

5. Ibid., p. 147.

6. Ibid., p. 151.

7. Ibid.

8. Ibid., p. 154.

9. Frank Welsh, *A History of Hong Kong* (London: HarperCollins, 1993), p. 12.

10. Paul Hibbert Clyde, *The Far East: A History of the Impact of the West on Eastern Asia* (Englewood Cliffs, N.J.: Prentice-Hall, 1964), p. 104.

11. The number 13, matching the 13 members and orifices of the human body, was of great symbolic value for the Chinese. Henry and Sydney Berry-Hill, *Chinnery and China Coast Paintings* (Leigh-on-Sea: England: F. Lewis, 1963), p. 35.

12. Clyde, *Far East,* p. 104.

13. Ibid.

14. Berry-Hill, *Chinnery,* p. 35.

15. The word *Hoppo* was derived from the Cantonese-dialect *hoi poi,* which itself was an abbreviation of the Mandarin-dialect *yueh hai kuan pu.* The Hoppo was officially the superintendent of the South Sea customs, a position of unique power in China's commerce with other countries which had existed since the eleventh century. Welsh, *History of Hong Kong,* p. 27.

16. Ibid.

17. Ibid.

Chapter 6

1. Cesar Guillen-Nuñez, *Macau* (Hong Kong: Oxford University Press, 1984), p. 63.

2. Henry and Sydney Berry-Hill, *Chinnery and China Coast Paintings* (Leigh-on-Sea, England: F. Lewis, 1970), p. 32.

3. R. D. Cremer, ed., *Macau: City of Commerce and Culture* (Hong Kong: UEA Press, 1987), p. 56.

4. Ibid., p. 59.

5. Henry and Sydney Berry-Hill, *George Chinnery, 1774–1852: Artist of the China Coast* (Leigh-on-Sea, England: F. Lewis, 1963), p. 37.

6. Berry-Hill, *Chinnery and China Coast Paintings,* p. 29.

7. Berry-Hill, *George Chinnery,* p. 37.

8. Guillen-Nuñez, *Macau,* p. 63.

9. Berry-Hill, *Chinnery and China Coast Paintings,* p. 29.

10. Berry-Hill, *George Chinnery,* p. 41.

11. Ibid., p. 49.

12. Ibid., p. 38.

13. Patrick Conner, *George Chinnery, 1774–1852: Artist of India and the China Coast* (Woodbridge, Suffolk, England: Antique Collectors Club, 1993), p. 290.

14. William C. Hunter, *Bits of Old China* (Taipei: Chéng-wen, 1966), p. 273.

15. Berry-Hill, *George Chinnery,* p. 13.

Chapter 7

1. Jack Beeching, *The Chinese Opium Wars* (New York: Harcourt Brace Jovanovich, 1975), p. 27.

2. Cesar Guillen-Nuñez, *Macau* (Hong Kong: Oxford University Press, 1984), p. 41.

3. R. D. Cremer, ed., *Macau: City of Commerce and Culture* (Hong Kong: UEA Press, 1987), p. 14.

4. Guillen-Nuñez, *Macau*, p. 41.

5. Paul Hibbert Clyde, *The Far East: A History of the Impact of the West on Eastern Asia* (Englewood Cliffs, N.J.: Prentice-Hall, 1964), p. 122.

6. William F. Beazer, *The Commercial Future of Hong Kong* (New York: Praeger, 1978), p. 13.

7. Frank Welsh, *A History of Hong Kong* (London: HarperCollins, 1993), p. 71.

8. Beeching, *Chinese Opium Wars*, p. 54.

9. Ibid.

10. Welsh, *History of Hong Kong*, p. 71.

11. Ibid.

12. Cremer, *Macau*, p. 74.

13. Beeching, *Chinese Opium Wars*, p. 29.

14. Henry and Sydney Berry-Hill, *Chinnery, 1774–1852: Artist of the China Coast Paintings* (Leigh-on-Sea, England: F. Lewis, 1963), p. 42.

15. Beeching, *Chinese Opium Wars*, p. 30.

16. Ibid., p. 24.

17. Ibid., p. 28.

18. Ibid., p. 25.

19. Ibid., p. 26.

20. Ibid.

21. Ibid. Historian Jack Beeching describes the opium product as follows: "Chests of Patna opium, each containing 40 balls of crude opium, a juice-like thick treacle, enclosed in a shell of dried poppy petals—about the size of an apple dumpling—were sold by auction in Calcutta at prices about four times the cost of production. During ten days of its annual life-cycle, the seed-box of the white poppy exudes a milky juice of extraordinary chemical complexity, not yet fully understood, and from this is derived a bitter, brown, granular power: commercial opium.

22. Henry and Sydney Berry-Hill, *Chinnery and China Coast Paintings* (Leigh-on-Sea, England: F. Lewis, 1970), p. 35.

23. Beeching, *Chinese Opium Wars*, p. 39.

24. Ibid., p. 36.

25. Ibid., p. 42.

26. Ibid.

27. Clyde, *Far East*, p. 117.

28. Guillen-Nuñez, *Macau*, p. 42.

Chapter 8

1. *Los Angeles Times*, April 14, 1987, p. A1.
2. Paul Hibbert Clyde, *The Far East: A History of the Impact of the West on Eastern Asia* (Englewood Cliffs, N.J.: Prentice-Hall, 1964), p. 84.
3. Elfed Vaughan Roberts, Sum Ngai Lin, and Peter Bradshaw, *Historical Dictionary of Hong Kong and Macau* (Metuchen, N.J.: Scarecrow Press, 1992), p. 320.
4. Cesar Guillen-Nuñez, *Macau* (Hong Kong: Oxford University Press, 1984), p. 45.
5. Ibid., p. 46.
6. R. D. Cremer, ed., *Macau: City of Commerce and Culture* (Hong Kong: UEA Press, 1987), p. 157.
7. Ibid.
8. Ibid., p. 53.
9. Guillen-Nuñez, *Macau,* p. 46.
10. Roberts, *Historical Dictionary of Hong Kong and Macau.*
11. Ibid., p. 305.
12. Cremer, *Macau: City of Commerce and Culture,* p. 17.
13. Guillen-Nuñez, *Macau,* p. 48.
14. Ibid., p. 81.
15. Cremer, *Macau,* p. 81.
16. Harold Z. Schriffrin, *Sun Yat-sen and the Origins of the Chinese Revolution* (Berkeley: University of California Press, 1968), p. 20.
17. Ibid., p. 31.
18. Ibid.
19. Roberts, *Historical Dictionary of Hong Kong and Macau.*
20. Schriffrin, *Sun Yat-sen,* p. 32.
21. Ibid., p. 33.
22. P.H.M. Jones, *Golden Guide to Hongkong and Macao* (Rutland, Vt.: Charles E. Tuttle, 1969), p. 363.
23. Guillen-Nuñez, *Macau,* p. 65.
24. Ibid., p. 66.
25. Ibid., p. 67.
26. Cremer, *Macau,* p. 17.
27. Ibid., p. 18.
28. Jones, *Golden Guide,* p. 364.
29. Christopher Rand, *Hongkong: The Island Between* (New York: Alfred A. Knopf, 1925), p. 97.
30. Roberts, *Historical Dictionary of Hong Kong and Macau.*
31. Ibid.

Chapter 9

1. *New York Times*, April 8, 1982, p. A2.
2. P.H.M. Jones, *Golden Guide to Hongkong and Macao* (Rutland, Vt.: Charles E. Tuttle, 1969), p. 364.

3. Ibid.

4. Christopher Rand, *Hongkong: The Island Between* (New York: Alfred A. Knopf, 1925), p. 102.

5. Jones, *Golden Guide,* p. 364.

6. Dick Wilson, *Hong Kong! Hong Kong!* (London: Unwin Hyman, 1990), p. 84.

7. Ibid.

8. Ibid.

9. Ibid.

10. Rand, *Hongkong,* p. 81.

11. Ibid., p. 85.

12. Wilson, *Hong Kong,* p. 131.

13. Kevin P. Lane, *Sovereignty and the Status Quo: The Historical Roots of China's Hong Kong Policy* (Boulder, Colo.: Westview Press, 1990), p. 67.

14. *New York Times,* March 16, 1959, p. A9.

15. "Rightists" were characterized by the Communist China leadership as individuals who lacked enthusiasm for the establishment of communes and the "Great Leap Forward" to increase agriculture production and who showed an inability to make the full effort demanded by the mass-movement social and economic programs. *New York Times,* November 15, 1959, p. A22.

16. Ibid.

17. Ibid., p. A25.

18. Austin Coates, *Invitation to an Eastern Feast* (New York: Harper & Brothers, 1955), p. 268.

Chapter 10

1. *New York Times,* December 17, 1966, p. 15.

2. Joseph Cheng, ed., *Hong Kong: In Search of a Future* (Hong Kong: Oxford University Press, 1984), p. 28.

3. There have been numerous attempts to describe, explain, and analyze China's Great Proletarian Cultural Revolution. According to Jean Daubier: "The Chinese Cultural Revolution set as its basic and ultimate goal the remaking of the human spirit." (*A History of the Chinese Cultural Revolution,* p. 13). Editors Molly Joel Coye and Jon Livingston wrote: "The essential goal of the Cultural Revolution, as expressed by Mao, was to prevent the Chinese leadership from becoming a Soviet-style bureaucratic ruling class." (*China, Yesterday and Today,* p. 390). Mao Zedong, in a 1962 speech, said: "The object [of the Great Proletarian Cultural Revolution] is to solve the problem of world outlook and eradicate revisionism." (*People's China, Social Experimentation, Policies, Entry onto the World Scene, 1966 through 1972,* edited by David Milton, Nancy Milton and Franz Schurmann).

4. *New York Times,* December 4, 1966, p. A1.

5. Stuart R. Schram, ed., *Quotations from Chairman Mao Tse-tung* (New York: Frederick A. Praeger, 1967), p. 7.

6. Ibid.

7. Ibid., p. 37.

8. Ibid., p. 45.
9. Ibid., p. 44.
10. Ibid., p. 47
11. Ibid., p. 48.
12. Ibid., p. 60.
13. Ibid., p. 65.
14. Ibid., p. 102.
15. *New York Times,* December 6, 1966, p. A8.
16. *New York Times,* December 4, 1966, p. A1.
17. Ibid.
18. Ibid.
19. Ibid., p. A3.
20. *New York Times,* December 5, 1966, p. A1.
21. Ibid., p. A5.
22. Ibid.
23. *Asia Yearbook 1968*, p. 230.
24. *New York Times,* December 5, 1966, p. A5.
25. *New York Times,* December 13, 1966, p. A1.
26. *London Times,* May 13, 1967, p. 1B.
27. Ibid.
28. Ibid.
29. *New York Times,* May 22, 1967, p. A19.
30. *New York Times,* May 23, 1967, p. A4.
31. *London Times,* May 25, 1967, p. A1.
32. *New York Times,* June 1, 1967, p. A16.
33. *New York Times,* March 3, 1962, p. A5.
34. *New York Times,* March 4, 1962, p. A19.
35. Ibid.
36. Ibid.
37. Ibid.
38. *New York Times,* June 21, 1962, p. A5.
39. Ibid.
40. Ibid.

Chapter 11

1. *Free China Review,* March 1990, p. 54.
2. *New York Times,* June 21, 1962, p. A5.
3. *Asia Yearbook 1977*, p. 221.
4. Tom Gallagher, *Portugal: A Twentieth Century Interpretation* (Manchester, England: Manchester University Press, 1983), p. 202.
5. Joseph Cheng, ed., *Hong Kong: In Search of a Future* (Hong Kong: Oxford University Press, 1984), p. 66.
6. *New York Times,* December 5, 1974, p. A13.
7. Ibid.
8. *New York Times,* April 2, 1975, p. A5.

9. Christopher Rand, *Hongkong: The Island Between* (New York: Alfred A. Knopf, 1925), p. 93.

10. *Asia Yearbook 1972*, p. 228.

11. Ibid.

12. *Asia Yearbook 1974*, p. 209.

13. Ibid.

14. Robin Hutcheon, *Chinnery: The Man and the Legend* (Hong Kong: *South China Morning Post*, 1974), p. viii.

15. *Asia Yearbook 1981*, p. 186.

16. Ibid.

17. Ibid.

Chapter 12

1. *London Times*, May 25, 1985, p. 4.

2. Steve Shipp, *Hong Kong, China: A Political History of the British Crown Colony's Transfer to Chinese Rule* (Jefferson, N.C.: McFarland, 1995), p. 51.

3. *Far Eastern Economic Review*, August 30, 1984, p. 14.

4. Ibid., p. 15.

5. *London Times*, February 4, 1985, p. 5.

6. *London Times*, May 23, 1985, p. 6.

7. *Los Angeles Times*, May 24, 1985, p. 5.

8. Ibid.

9. *New York Times*, May 24, 1985, p. A7.

10. Ibid.

11. Elfed Vaughan Roberts, Sum Ngai Lin, and Peter Bradshaw, *Historical Dictionary of Hong Kong and Macau* (Metuchen, N.J.: Scarecrow Press, 1992.), p. 299.

12. R. D. Cremer, ed., *Macau: City of Commerce and Culture* (Hong Kong: UEA Press, 1987), p. 157.

13. Ibid., p. 160.

14. *Asia Yearbook 1980*, p. 225.

Chapter 13

1. *Los Angeles Times*, April 14, 1987, p. A5.

2. R. D. Cremer, ed., *Macau: City of Commerce and Culture* (Hong Kong: UEA Press, 1987), p. 20.

3. *London Times*, October 23, 1986, p. 9.

4. *London Times*, April 14, 1987, p. 11A.

5. *London Times*, March 27, 1987, p. 9.

6. Ibid.

7. *Asia Yearbook 1988*, p. 174.

8. *New York Times*, June 8, 1986, p. A7.

9. *London Times*, June 2, 1987.
10. *Asia Yearbook 1988*, p. 174.
11. *Forbes*, July 20, 1992, p. 177.
12. *Asia Yearbook 1987*, p. 184.
13. Ibid.
14. *Business Week*, January 19, 1987, p. 98.
15. Dick Wilson, *Hong Kong! Hong Kong!* (London: Unwin Hyman, 1990), p. 108.
16. Ibid.
17. *Business Week*, January 19, 1987, p. 99.
18. *London Times*, March 25, 1987, p. 10.
19. Ibid.
20. *Far Eastern Economic Review*, December 2, 1993, p. 61.
21. Ibid.
22. Ibid.
23. *Asia Yearbook 1988*, p. 173.

Chapter 14

1. *Asia Yearbook* 1995, p. 161.
2. *Aviation Week*, January 28, 1991, p. 47.
3. *Macau Travel Talk*, May 1995, p. 11.
4. Ibid.
5. *Macau Travel Talk*, July 1995, p. 3.
6. *Asia Yearbook 1992*, p. 150.
7. *Wall Street Journal*, January 7, 1993, p. A10.
8. *Hong Kong Standard*, August 22, 1996, p. A1.
9. *Wall Street Journal*, October 12, 1993, p. A16.
10. Ibid.
11. *Asia Yearbook 1991*, p. 154.
12. Ibid., p. 155.
13. Ibid.
14. Ibid., p. 148.
15. Ibid.
16. *Wall Street Journal*, February 5, 1992, p. A8.
17. *Travel/Holiday*, April 1992, p. 87.
18. Ibid.
19. *Pacific Affairs*, Spring 1993, p. 7.
20. Ibid., p. 8.
21. Ibid., p. 20.
22. *Los Angeles Times*, April 4, 1995, p. C1.
23. Ibid., p. C4.
24. Ibid.

Bibliography

Books

Adley, Robert. *All Change Hong Kong*. Poole, Dorset, United Kingdom: Blandford Press, 1984.

Bacon, Leonard, trans. *The Lusiads of Luiz de Camões*. New York: Hispanic Society, 1950.

Beazer, William F. *The Commercial Future of Hong Kong*. New York: Praeger, 1978.

Beeching, Jack. *The Chinese Opium Wars*. New York: Harcourt Brace Jovanovich, 1975.

Berry-Hill, Henry, and Sydney. *Chinnery and China Coast Paintings*. Leigh-on-Sea, England: F. Lewis, 1970.

_____. *George Chinnery, 1774–1852: Artist of the China Coast*. Leigh-on-Sea, England: F. Lewis, 1963.

Blaustein, Albert P., ed. *Constitutions of Dependencies and Special Sovereignties*. Dobbs Ferry, New York: Oceana Publications, 1994.

Boxer, C. R. *Fidalgos in the Far East, 1550–1750*. London: Oxford University Press, 1968.

_____. *Four Centures of Portuguese Expansion, 1415–1825: A Succinct Survey* Johannesburg: Witwatersrand University Press, 1965.

_____. *Portuguese Conquest and Commerce in Southern Asia, 1500–1750*. London: Variorum Reprints, 1985.

_____. *The Portuguese Seaborne Empire 1415–1825*. New York: Alfred A. Knopf, 1969.

_____. *Portuguese Society in the Tropics: The Municipal Councils of Goa, Macau, Bahia and Luanda, 1510–1800*. Madison: University of Wisconsin Press, 1965.

_____, ed. *Macau Three Hundred Years Ago* (Macau na Época da Restauração). Macau: Imprensa Nacional, 1942.

_____, ed. *South China in the Sixteenth Century*. Glasgow: University Press, 1953.

Braga, J.M. *The Beginnings of Printing at Macao*. Lisbon: Centro de Estudos Históricos Ultramarinos, 1963.

_____. *Early Medical Practice in Macau*. Macau: Agencia de Turismo, 1935.

Carney, Daniel. *Macau*. New York: Kensington Publishing Corp., 1985.

Chang, Ming K., and David J. Clark, eds. *The Hong Kong Basic Law: Blueprint for "Stability and Prosperity" Under Chinese Sovereignty?* Armonk, N.Y.: M. E. Sharpe, 1991.

Cheng, Chu-yuan. *Behind the Tiananmen Massacre: Social, Political and Economic Ferment in China.* Boulder, Colo.: Westview Press, 1990.

Cheng, Joseph, ed. *Hong Kong: In Search of a Future.* Hong Kong: Oxford University Press, 1984.

Chung-tu Hsueh. *Revolutionary Leaders of Modern China.* New York: Oxford University Press, 1971.

Clarence-Smith, Gervase. *The Third Portuguese Empire, 1825–1975: A Study in Economic Imperialism.* Manchester, England: Manchester University Press, 1985.

Clewlow, Carol, and Robert Storey. *Hong Kong, Macau & Canton: A Travel Survival Kit.* Hawthorn, Victoria, Australia: Lonely Planet Publications, 1989.

Clyde, Paul Hibbert. *The Far East: A History of the Impact of the West on Eastern Asia.* Englewood Cliffs, N.J.: Prentice-Hall, 1964.

Coates, Austin. *Invitation to an Eastern Feast.* New York: Harper & Brothers, 1955.

Conner, Patrick. *George Chinnery, 1774–1852: Artist of India and the China Coast.* Woodbridge, Suffolk, England: Antique Collectors Club, 1993.

Cottrell, Robert. *The End of Hong Kong: The Secret Diplomacy of Imperial Retreat.* London: John Murray, 1993.

Coye, Molly Joel, and Jon Livingston, eds. *China: Yesterday and Today.* New York: Bantam Books, 1979 (2nd ed.).

Cremer, R. D., ed. *Macau: City of Commerce and Culture.* Hong Kong: UEA Press, 1987.

Daubier, Jean. *A History of the Chinese Cultural Revolution.* New York: Vintage Books, 1974.

Dos Passos, John. *The Portugal Story: Three Centuries of Exploration and Discovery.* Garden City, New York: Doubleday, 1969.

Edmonds, Richard Louis, comp. *Macau.* Oxford: Clio Press, 1989.

Fodor. *Fodor's Southeast Asia.* New York: Fodor's Travel Publications, 1993.

Fox, Grace. *British Admirals and Chinese Pirates, 1832–1869.* London: Kegan Paul, 1940.

Gallagher, Tom. *Portugal: A Twentieth-Century Interpretation.* Manchester, England: Manchester University Press, 1983.

Grant, Maurice Harold. *A Dictionary of British Landscape Painters: From the 16th Century to the Early 20th Century.* Leigh-on-Sea, England: F. Lewis, 1952.

Grantham, Alexander. *Via Ports: From Hong Kong to Hong Kong.* Hong Kong: Hong Kong University Press, 1965.

Guillen-Nuñez, Cesar. *Macau.* Hong Kong: Oxford University Press, 1984.

Hillard, Katharine, ed. *My Mother's Journal: A Young Lady's Diary of Five Years Spent in Manila, Macau and the Cape of Good Hope, From 1829–1834.* Boston: George H. Ellis, 1900.

Hungdah Chiu, Y. C. Jao, and Yuan-li Wu, eds. *The Future of Hong Kong: Toward 1997 and Beyond.* New York: Quorum Books, 1987.

Hunter, William C. *Bits of Old China.* Taipei: Ch'eng-wen, 1966.

Hutcheon, Robin. *Chinnery: The Man and the Legend.* Hong Kong: South China Morning Post, 1974.

Jones, P.H.M. *Golden Guide to Hongkong and Macao.* Rutland, Vt.: Charles E. Tuttle, 1969.

Kane, Robert S. *Hong Kong at Its Best: With Macau and China's Top Three Cities—Beijing, Shanghai, Guangzhou (Canton)*. Lincolnwood, Illinois: Passport Books, 1992.

Kelly, Ian. *Hong Kong: A Political-Geographic Analysis*. London: Macmillan, 1987.

Lane, Kevin P. *Sovereignty and the Status Quo: The Historical Roots of China's Hong Kong Policy*. Boulder, Colo.: Westview Press, 1990.

Lethbridge, David G., ed. *The Business Environment in Hong Kong*. Hong Kong: Oxford University Press, 1984.

Lieberthal, Kenneth. *Governing China: From Revolution Through Reform*. New York: W.W. Norton, 1995.

Livermore, H. V. *A New History of Portugal*. London: Cambridge University Press, 1966.

Maitland, Derek. *The Insider's Guide to Hongkong*. Edison, N.J.: Hunter, 1988.

Mallalieu, H. L. *The Dictionary of British Watercolour Artists up to 1920*. Woodbridge, Suffolk, England: Antique Collectors Club, 1983.

Marques, A. H. de Oliveira. *History of Portugal*. Vol. 1, *From Lusitania to Empire*. New York: Columbia University Press, 1972.

_____. *History of Portugal*. Vol 2, *From Empire to Corporate State*. New York: Columbia University Press, 1976.

Milton, David, Nancy Milton, and Franz Schurmann, eds. *People's China: Social Experimentation, Politics, Entry onto the World Scene, 1966 through 1972*. New York: Vintage Books, 1974.

Milward, Peter, ed. *Portuguese Voyages to Asia and Japan in the Renaissance Period*. Tokyo: Renaissance Institute, 1994.

Mushkat, Miron. *The Economic Future of Hong Kong*. Boulder, Colo.: Lynne Rienner, 1990.

Newitt, Malyn, ed. *The First Portuguese Colonial Empire*. Exeter, England: University of Exeter, 1986.

Parkes, Carl. *Southeast Asia Handbook*. Chico, Calif.: Moon, 1990.

Passport. *Hong Kong*. Lincolnwood, Illinois: Passport Books, 1986.

Patrikeeff, Felix. *Mouldering Pearl: Hong Kong at the Crossroads*. London: George Philip, 1989.

Posner, Gerald L. *Warlords of Crime: Chinese Secret Societies—The New Mafia*. New York: McGraw-Hill, 1988.

Ptak, Roderich, ed. *Portuguese Asia*. Stuttgart: Steiner, Verlag, Wiesbaden GMBH, 1987.

Rand, Christopher. *Hongkong: The Island Between*. New York: Alfred A. Knopf, 1925.

Ride, Edwin. *British Army Aid Group: Hong Kong Resistance, 1942–1945*. Oxford: Oxford University Press, 1981.

Roberti, Mark. *The Fall of Hong Kong: China's Triumph and Britain's Betrayal*. New York: John Wiley, 1994.

Roberts, Elfed Vaughan, Sum Ngai Lin, and Peter Bradshaw. *Historical Dictionary of Hong Kong & Macau*. Metuchen, N.J.: Scarecrow Press, 1992.

Roberts, Gerald. *China, Japan & the Asian Nics: Hong Kong & Macau, Singapore, South Korea, Taiwan—Economic Structure and Analysis*. London: Economic Intelligence Unit, 1988.

Robinson, R.A.H. *Contemporary Portugal*. London: George Allen & Unwin, 1979.

Russell, Jacqui, ed. *Fodor's Southeast Asia.* New York: Fodor's Travel Publications, 1993.

Schiffrin, Harold Z. *Sun Yat-sen and the Origins of the Chinese Revolution.* Berkeley: University of California Press, 1968.

Schram, Stuart R., ed. *Quotations from Chairman Mao Tse-tung.* New York: Frederick A. Praeger, 1967.

Scott, Ian. *Political Change and the Crisis of Legitimacy in Hong Kong.* London: Hurst & Co., 1989.

Segal, Gerald. *The Fate of Hong Kong.* New York: St. Martin's Press, 1993.

Shipp, Steve. *Hong Kong, China: A Political History of the British Crown Colony's Transfer to Chinese Rule.* Jefferson, N.C.: McFarland, 1995.

Sobel, Lester A., ed. *Portuguese Revolution, 1974–76.* New York: Facts on File, 1976.

Souza, George Bryan. *The Survival of Empire: Portuguese Trade and Society in China and the South China Sea, 1630–1754.* Cambridge: Cambridge University Press, 1986.

Sullivan, Michael. *The Meeting of Eastern and Western Art: From the Sixteenth Century to the Present Day.* Greenwich, Conn.: New York Graphic Society, 1973.

Sung, Yun-Wing. *The China-Hong Kong Connection: The Key to China's Open-Door Policy.* Cambridge: Cambridge University Press, 1991.

Sutton, Thomas. *The Daniells: Artists and Travelers.* London: Bodley Head, 1954.

Tsai, Jung-fang. *Hong Kong in Chinese History: Community and Social Unrest in the British Colony, 1842–1913.* New York: Columbia University Press, 1993.

Viviano, Frank. *Dispatches from the Pacific Century.* Reading, Mass.: Addison-Wesley, 1993.

Welsh, Frank. *A History of Hong Kong.* London: HarperCollins, 1993.

Wesley-Smith, Peter. *Unequal Treaty, 1898–1997: China, Great Britain and Hong Kong's New Territories.* Oxford: Oxford University Press, 1980.

Wheeler, Tony. *South-East Asia on a Shoestring.* Hawthorn, Victoria, Australia: Lonely Planet Publications, 1992.

Wilson, Dick. *Hong Kong! Hong Kong!* London: Unwin Hyman, 1990.

Periodicals

Asian Affairs
Associated Press
Aviation Week
Beijing Review
Business Week
Case Western Reserve Journal of International Law
China Quarterly
China Report
Chinese Social and Political Science Review
Far Eastern Economic Review
Forbes
Free China Review
Gourmet

Hong Kong Law Journal
London Times
Los Angeles Times
Macau Travel Talk
Maclean's
New York Times
Pacific Affairs
Reuters
South China Morning Post
Travel/Holiday
Wall Street Journal

Index

"Adeste Fideles" 50
ADIM *see* Association for the Defense of the Interests of Macau
Africa 11, 34, 41
Aguiar, Joaquim Antonio de 66
Agustinians
Akihito, Emperor 125
Alcácer-Quibir (Morocco) 34
Alemão, João 24
Alexander, William 56
All Circles Compatriots 94
Allom, Thomas 58, 60
Almeida e Costa, Vasco de 103, 105–6, 112
Almeida Santos, Dr. Antonio de 96
Álvares, Jorge 13
Álvares Cabral, Pedro 11
A-Ma Temple 18–21, 60
anti–Rightest campaign 86
APIM *see* Association for the Promotion of the Instruction of the Macanese
APIM Business School 75
Apostle of the Far East *see* Xavier, Father Francis
Apostolic Administrator of the Far East Missions *see* Carneiro, Father Nunes
Aquino, Jose de 83
Arab countries 12
Armed Forces Movement 95
Arriaga, Miguel de 64, 65
Asia 1, 3, 17, 26, 36, 38, 43, 50, 57, 74–76, 82, 84, 86, 97, 111, 118
Asian language influences 78
Associated Press 88
Association for the Defense of the Interests of Macau (ADIM) 95
Association for the Promotion of the Instruction of the Macanese (APIM) 75

Australia 97
Azores 11, 125

Balzac, Honoré de 61
Banco Nacional Ultramarino 98
Bangkok (Thailand) 84
Bank of China 98
Baptist del Monte, Father John 26
Baptista, Marciano 62
Barbosa Medina, Dr. Rui 107
Barra Bill 41
Barrier Gate *see* Portas do Cerco
Basic Law (Hong Kong) 102
Basic Law (Macau) 2, 4, 110–11
Basic Law Consultative Committee (Macau) 110
Basic Law Drafting Committee (Macau) 110
Batavia 43
Beeching, Jack 64, 67, 68
Beijing (China) 14, 16, 28–29, 31, 41, 54, 64, 87–89, 95–97, 103–5, 107–8, 110–11, 118, 120, 126
Bela Vista Hotel 109
Belem Palace 105
Bengal (India) 68
Berrio (ship) 12
Berry-Hill, Henry 59, 63
Berry-Hill, Sidney 59, 63
Bishop's Residence 46
Boca Tigris (Tiger's Mouth) 53, 58
Bogue (Humen) 53
Bomporto Fort *see* Nossa Senhora do Bomporto Fort
Bonavia, David 90
Borget, Auguste 61–62
Boston 62
Boxer, C. R. 35, 38, 44, 49, 52

Bradshaw, S. 60
Braganza (Portugal) 50
Brazil 11, 37
Britain *see* Great Britain
British consulate (Macau) 89–91
British East India Company 40, 51–53, 60, 67–68, 70
British Parliament 65, 70
British travel permit office (Macau) 90–91
Buddhism 19, 24, 31

Cacilhas Beach 44–45
Calcutta (India) 59, 61–62
caldeirao (tax) 39
Calicut (India) 12
Camara Municipal das Ilhas 111–12
Cambodia 23
Camões, Luís de 22–23, 35, 100
Canton *see* Guangzhou
Cantonese 78
Cape Bojador
Cape of Good Hope 11, 38
Cape of Storms 11
Cape Verde Islands 11
capitalism 92, 107
Capone, W. H. 58
Carlos I, King 78
Carneiro, Father Nunes 26, 35
carracks *see* nãos do trato
Castle Peak 13
Catalina flying boats 84
Catholic church 24, 66, 82
Catholicism 24, 26, 31, 42, 91
Cavaco Silva, Anibal 108–9, 120, 123, 125
Celebes Islands 48
Central Hotel 104
Chang Te, Emperor 14
Chiang Kai-shek 89
Children's Meals Society 82
China *see* People's Republic of China; Republic of China
China and Britain 82
China trade paintings 57–59, 61
La Chine et les Chinois 61
Chinese Chamber of Commerce (Macau) 89, 92, 104
Chinese chess 117
Chinese Civil War 2, 82, 85, 107
Chinese Empire 31
Chinese House of Bishops 82

Chinese language 29–30, 110
Chinese New Year 96, 113
Chinese Republic 76–77
Chinese-Western Apothecary
Ch'ing dynasty *see* Manchu dynasty
Ching-hu Hospital (Macau) 76
Chinnery, George 54, 56, 58–63, 100
Chinnery School 59, 61–62
Christianity 24–25, 28, 40, 46
Chu Yuan 15–16
Ch'uen-pi Fort 53
Church of St. Maria 26
Church of São Lázaro 26
Church of São Lourenço (St. Lawrence) 28, 60–61
Church of São Paulo (St. Paul) 28–29, 45, 47
Church Times 82
Cidade de Nome de Deus da China *see* City of the Name of God in China
City of the Name of God in China (Cidade de Nome de Deus da China) 37, 51
Coates, Austin 41, 86
Cochin 12, 23
Coelho do Amaral 75
Cohin 38
Co-hong 53–55, 65
Coimbra University (Portugal) 28
College of Medicine for Chinese (Hong Kong) 76
Coloane Island (Macau) 8, 25, 79–80, 97–98, 105, 112, 117, 122
Columbus, Christopher 13
Communism (China) 24, 73, 82, 84–94, 102, 104, 107, 120
Concorde 123
Confucius 30–31, 68
Consoo Hall 54
Cook, Captain James 56
Corpus Christi 72
Council of Government 72
country traders 68
country wallahs 68
Court of Qianlong 56
Coutinho Docem, Dom Diogo 52
Cremer, Rolf Dieter 32
Crown Prince Luis Filipe 78
Cultural Institute of Macau 128
Cultural Revolution (China) *see* Great Proletarian Cultural Revolution

Daniell, Thomas 56
Daniell, William 56
De Albuquerque, Afonso 12, 24, 26, 47
Deng Xiaoping 102, 107–8, 110, 121;
  one country, two systems 107, 121
Denmark 53
Dias, Bartholomeu 11
dictatura 78
diocese of Funai 36
diocese of Macau 26, 35–36
Diogo de Pantoja, Father 28
Diogo Pinto, Antonio 123
Dom Henrique the Navigator 11
Dom João de Almeida 35
Dom Leonardo de Sá 35
Dom Manoel I, King 35
Dom Pedro V Theatre 74
Dom Sebastião, King 34
Dom Theodosio, Prince 51
Domingos de Sousa 24
Dominicans 30–31
Dona Luisa de Guzman 50
Dona Maria Hill 19, 71
Dona Maria I 55
Drury, Admiral William 64
Dual Monarchy *see* Union of Crowns
Dublin (Ireland) 58
Duke of Braganza 50
Dunn, Nathan 54
Dutch East Asia Company (VOC) 42,
  47–49
Dutch West Indies Company 49

Eanes, Antonio Ramalho 103–6, 110, 112
Eanes, Gil 11
East Asia Airlines 121
East Indies 23, 46, 68
East-West Apothecary 77
Edmonds, Richard Louis 50
Egidio, Nuno Melo 105
Elements of Geometry of Euclides 31
Elliot, Captain Charles 65, 70
emperor's merchant 53–54
England *see* Great Britain
English language 76
Estatuto Organico de Macau (EOM)
  see Organic Statute for Macau
Estoril Hotel 90
Estoril-Sol Group 116
Europe 3, 11, 42, 50, 56–57, 64, 74, 81,
86, 88, 105, 128
European Community 108, 111
European Union *see* European Com-
  munity
Evora (Portugal) 37
Executive Council (Macau) 92

Factories, the 66–67
Factory Street 54
Far East 1, 11–12, 23–24, 32–33, 35–36,
  42, 49, 51, 58, 66, 105
Far East Missions 26
Far Eastern Economic Review 121
Fa-tee Flower Gardens 57
Ferreira do Amaral, Governor João 71–
  73, 75, 125
Fialho Ferreira, Antonio 50–51
fidalgo 37–38
Figuierdo, Octavio 89
First Bar 53
Fischer, S. 57
Fleming, Ian 87
Flores (Lesser Sunda Islands) 48
Fok, C. Y. 71
foreign devils 32
foro do chao 71
Formosa *see* Taiwan
Fourth of July 97
fragrant mountain 21
France: 61; and China 53, 67; and
  Macau 3, 123
Franciscans 31
Franco, João 78
French Revolution 66
Frias dos Santos, Adelino 122
Friendship Bridge 123
Fróis, Father Luís 26
Fujian province (China) 13, 15–16
Funai (Japan) 36

Gago, Baltasar Father 26
galiotas (small trading ships) 39
Gallagher, Tom 95
Gama, Jaime 103
Gama, Paolo da 11–12
Gama, Vasco da 11–13, 23
Gan Baoshi 64
Garcia Leandro, Colonel José Eduardo
  96, 105

Gaspar de Cruz, Friar 18, 24
Germany 34
Ghost of Macau *see* Teizeira, Father
  Manuel 17, 26, 127
Goa (India) 12, 17–18, 23–24, 26, 28,
  33, 37–39, 47, 52, 55, 60–61
Gonzalez, Father Gregorio 25
Goddess of Mercy 19
Gonzaga Gomes, Luís 100
Government House (Macau) 52, 83, 87
Grand Canal (China) 79
Great Britain: 51, 63, 97; and China 1-
  4, 39–40, 52–53, 56, 62, 64–68,
  70–71, 89–91, 95–96, 102, 107, 116;
  and France 3; and Holland 42, 44;
  and Hong Kong 1–4, 61–62, 64–66,
  71, 95–96, 102, 107, 111, 121; and Joint
  Declaration (Hong Kong) 1, 3–4, 102,
  107, 116; and Macau 2–3, 42, 53, 56,
  63–65, 70, 72, 81, 84, 89–91, 98, 108,
  123; negotiations on Hong Kong 1,
  102, 107, 108; and Portugal 3, 11, 40,
  72, 89, 108
Great Hall of the People 108
Great Proletarian Cultural Revolution
  2, 87–91
Green Island 19–20, 76
Green Island Cement Company 76
Greek language 28
Guangdong province (China) 13, 15,
  17, 32, 66, 72, 75–76, 81, 92
Guangxi province (China) 66
Guangzhou (Canton) 14, 17, 32–34,
  38–40, 42, 52–58, 60–62, 65–68, 70,
  76–77, 88, 92, 103
Gudin, Jean-Antoine-Theodore 61
Guia Fort 45–46, 52, 64
Guia Hill 19, 59, 71, 75
Guia Lighthouse 75
Guillen-Nuñez, Cesar 19, 34, 42, 56,
  60
Guimarães, Governor Isidoro Francisco
  73–75, 98, 104
Guy Fawkes Day 97

Hainan Island 57, 67
haitao 17, 18, 32
Hall, Bishop Ronald 82
Haoching Bay (Macau) 16
Heang-Shan Fort 57

Hermitage of our Lady of Hope 26
Hero of Passaleong *see* Nicolau de
  Mesquita, Lieutenant Vincente
Hilliard, John 62
Hilliard, Katherine 62
Hirado (Japan) 43
History of the Future 23
Ho, Stanley 105, 110, 113–16, 118, 123
Ho Yin 88, 91–92, 95, 97, 104
Holland: and China 39, 42–43, 46, 48,
  64, 67; and Great Britain 42, 44
  and India 43; and Japan 43, 46, 48;
  and Macassar 48; and Macau 2–3,
  42–46, 48; and Malacca 47, 52; and
  Portugal 39–40, 42–46, 49, 51; and
  Spain 51
Holy House of Mercy 26
Hong Kong: 14, 58, 61–63, 72, 75, 81,
  87–91, 98, 100, 116; and China 1–4,
  65–66, 71, 83–84, 92, 95–96, 107, 116,
  121; and Chinese Cultural Revolution
  87–91; and Great Britain 1–4, 61–62,
  64–66, 71, 95–96, 102, 107, 111, 121;
  and Macau 1–4, 72, 75–76, 82–84,
  86, 90, 92–93, 95, 97–100, 104–6,
  109, 113, 115–18, 120–23, 128; and
  Joint Declaration (Hong Kong) 1,
  3–4, 102, 107–9, 111, 116, 120; and
  Joint Declaration (Macau) 1, 4, 102,
  108–9, 111, 116; negotiations (China
  and Britain) 1, 102, 107; size 1; popu-
  lation 1; as trading center 3; transi-
  tion to China 1, 4, 121
Hong Kong, China 1
Hong Kong and Macau Affairs Office
  125
Hong Kong and Shanghai Banking
  Corporation 97
Hong Kong General Medical Council 76
Hong Kong Motor Sports Club 118
Hong Kong Social Welfare Council 82
Hong Kong University 114
hongs 53
Hongs of Canton 67
Hoppo 54–55, 71–72, 125
Hospital of St. Raphael 26
Hotel Lisboa 98, 113
Hou Qua II 54, 57
"Hou Qua's Tea Gardens and Pleasure
  Pavilions on Hainan Island" 57
House of Braganza 64

Hsu, Immanuel 107
Huang Hua 95
Huangpu 58
Humen *see* Bogue
Hunter, William C. 73
Hutcheon, Robin 100

Iberia 42
Ilha Verde *see* Green Island
India 11–13, 23–24, 33–34, 41, 43, 49, 56, 59, 61–62, 64, 68, 86
Indian language influences 78
Indochina 36, 38
Indonesia 48
Inner Harbor 19, 23, 58, 60, 66, 71, 75–76
Inquisition 42
International Institute for Software Technology 124
International Monetary Fund 84
Investment and Immigration Act of 1995 121
Ions, Norman 89–91
Italy 12, 28, 34, 45, 56

Jackass Point 67
Japan: and China 15, 34, 38–39, 42, 81; and Great Britain 43; and Holland 43, 46, 48; and Hong Kong 114; and India 13; and Jesuit brotherhood 24–26, 36; and Macau 13, 37–39, 41–43, 76, 81, 84, 98, 114–15; and Portugal 15–17, 33–34, 37–40, 42–43, 47, 64, 81, 125; and Spain 40
Jardine, William 61, 66
Jesuit brotherhood 1, 23–26, 28–31, 35–36, 41, 43, 45, 47, 72, 75, 79
Jesuit College (Macau) see Madre de Deus College
Jesuit College (Rome) 28
Jiaqing, Emperor 65
João, Prince-Regent 66
João II, King 11
João IV, King 50, 51
João VI, King 66
Joint Declaration (Hong Kong) 1, 3–4, 102, 107–9, 111, 116, 120
Joint Declaration (Macau) 1–4, 102, 108–11, 115–16, 118–20

Ka Ho Harbor 117
Kagoshima (Japan) 24
Kai-Tak Airport 84
Kam Pau-said 65
Kaohsiung (Taiwan) 118
Kemble, John 90–91
Kent (England) 90
Keppel, Captain Henry 72
Klee, Paul 83
Korea 36
Korean War 2, 82, 84, 115
Koxinga 46
Kun Iam Temple 18–19, 69
Kuomintang 82, 89, 93, 104
Kyushu (Japan) 36

Lake Tai (China) 79
Lam Qua 61
Lampacau Island 15, 17, 24
lanteas (lighters) 38
Lappa Island (China) 14, 81, 86
Largo de Senado *see* Leal Senado Square
Latin America 128
Latin culture 128
Latin language influences 28, 79
Laureiro, Adolfo 76
Leal Senado da Camara (Loyal Senate) 35, 37, 55, 66, 73, 104, 111–12
Leal Senado Square 60, 66, 85, 96
Lee, Mary 102
Legislative Assembly (Macau) 92, 95, 103–5, 109–13, 121, 125, 127
Lei Tim-Oi, Deaconess florence 82
Lemos e Faria, Bernardo Aleix 64
Leonel de Sousa, Captain-Major 17, 18, 32
Leonor, Queen Dona 26
Lesser Sunda Islands 38, 48
Li Peng 110, 127
Li Xiannian 108
"Licentiate in Medicine and Surgery of the College of Medicine for Chinese, Hong Kong" 76
Lin, Prof. T.K. 11
Lin-Font (Lotus Temple) 18
Lin Tsu-hsu, Imperial Commissioner 70
lingua de Macau see Macanese language

Lisbon (Portugal) 12–13, 17, 23, 26, 32, 33, 50–52, 71, 95–97, 104–6, 110, 112, 116, 125–27
Lisbon Agreement *see* Luso-Chinese Treaty of Trade and Friendship
Lobo, Roger 84
Lobo da Silveira, Dom Sebastião 51, 52
London 54, 56, 60–61, 82, 91, 123
London Times 90
Los Angeles Times 128
Lotus Temple (Lin-Font) 18
Lou Lim Iok Garden 79
Low, Harriet 62
Low, William Henry Sr. 62
Loyal Senate *see* Leal Senado da Camara
Lu Ping 125
Luís de Camões Grotto and Garden 23, 60, 117
Luís de Camões Museum 100, 122
Luiz, Infante Dom 17
The Lusiads see *Os Lusiadas*
Luso-Chinese Treaty of Trade and Friendship 74, 80

Ma Man-kee 110
Macanese 55, 64–65, 73, 75, 78, 86, 106, 110–11
Macanese language 78
Macartney, George 56
Macassar 48
A Macao Narrative 41
Macau: 14–15, 75, 92; agriculture 3, 19, 82; architecture 1, 28, 58, 66, 78, 86; art and artists 2, 54, 56–63, 69, 78, 81, 128; and Basic Law (Macau) 2, 4; and China 1–4, 32–33, 41, 45, 47–48, 53, 55, 57, 64–66, 71–74, 78–98, 100–12, 116–20, 122–25, 127; and Chinese Cultural Revolution 2, 87–91; citizenship (Portuguese) 4, 108–09, 111; culture 1, 74, 116, 128; description 3, 13, 18–21, 32, 41, 45–46, 48–49, 51, 56, 58, 60, 71, 74–76, 82–84, 86–87, 95, 97–98, 113, 122–23, 125, 128; economy 1–4, 73–74, 79, 86, 97–98, 103–6, 108, 113, 115–17, 120–23, 125, 127–28; exports 3, 98, 123–24; fishing 3, 19, 71, 75; food 1, 85, 92; and France 3, 123; gambling 3, 73, 97–99, 104–5, 112–17, 121, 123; gold trading 84, 92; and Great Britain 2–3, 42, 53, 56, 63–65, 70, 72, 81, 84, 89–91, 98, 123; handover 1–4, 108, 110, 115, 128; health care 26–28, 41, 76–77, 92; and Holland 2–3, 42–46, 48; and Hong Kong 1–4, 72, 75–76, 82–84, 86, 90, 92–93, 95, 97–100, 102, 104–6, 109, 113, 115–18, 120–23, 128; industry 3, 75–76, 97–98, 123–24; and Japan 13, 37–39, 41–43, 76, 81, 84, 114–15; and Jesuit brotherhood 1, 24–26, 28, 31, 35–36, 41, 79; and Joint Declaration (Hong Kong) 1, 3–4, 109, 111; and Joint Declaration (Macau) 1–4, 102, 108–11, 115–16, 118–20; and Korean war 2, 82, 84, 115; land reclamation 3, 20, 76, 105, 122, 127; and Macassar 48; and Malacca 17–18, 24, 26, 33, 37–38, 41, 47–48; negotiations (China and Portugal) 1–4, 97, 102–4, 107–10, 112, 116; and Organic Statute 2, 94–95, 105; and the Philippines 33–35, 39, 48, 50; politics 1, 35–37, 52, 55, 66, 71, 78, 92, 95–96, 103, 106, 109–12, 120, 124–25, 127; population 1, 3, 18, 34, 41, 48–49, 78, 81, 86, 91–92, 100, 103, 106, 109, 111, 115; and Portugal 1–4, 11, 13, 16–18, 25, 32–34, 37–43, 46–53, 55, 64–66, 72–75, 78–81, 84–85, 87–89, 94–98, 102–12, 115–16, 119–21, 125, 127–28; and Portuguese Restoration 1, 50–51; postage stamps 85, 100; and secret agreements (China and Portugal) 94–95, 103; size 1–3, 41, 95, 122; and Spain 3, 104; tourism 3, 97–100, 104, 113, 116–18, 121, 124; as trading center 1, 3–4, 11–13, 15–18, 26, 32–35, 37–43, 47–48, 50, 52–53, 55, 62, 65, 70; transition to China 1–4, 110–11, 121, 125–28; and World War II 2, 81–84
Macau, China 1, 120
Macau-Chinese Enterprises Association 124
Macau City Hall 88
Macau Cultural Centre 122
Macau Federation of Trade Unions 88
Macau Ferry Terminal 122
Macau Grand Prix 100, 117

Macau Grand Prix Museum 118
Macau International Airport 4, 97,
  105, 111–12, 117, 121–25, 127
Macau International Airport Company
  123
Macau Land Registry and Map
  Department 122
Macau Post Office 85
Macau Public Works Department 78
Macau Struggle Committee 94
Macau Tourism and Entertainment
  Company 104–5, 113, 115–16, 118, 123
Macau Tourist Information Bureau 98
Macedo Pinto, Fernando de 118
MacGregor, Greg 86
Machado Pinto, J. 64
Madeira 11
Madras (India) 59
Madre de Deus College (Macau) 31, 43
Mage Temple (Ma-Kok Temple) 56
Ma-Kok Temple *see* Mage Temple
Malabar Coast 23
Malacca 12–15, 17–18, 24, 26, 33,
  37–38, 41, 47–48, 111
Malacca Trading Post 13
Malaya 12
Malaysia 41, 106
Manchu dynasty 47, 55, 77
Mandarin Chinese 110
Mandarin Oriental Hotel 122
Mandarins 35
Manila (the Philippines) 33–35, 39,
  48, 50
Manoel I, King 11
Manoel II, King 78
Mao Zedong 87–91
Margulhão, Álvaro 24
Mascarenhas, Francisco 45
Mascarenhas, Jorge de 14
Matheson, James 61
Mediterranean region 12, 41
Melancia, Carlos 112, 124–25
Mercedes-Benz 113
Mexico 33–34
Ming dynasty 18–19, 47
ministry of interterritorial coordination
  (Portugal) 96
Misericordia 52
Misericordia Brotherhood 26–28
Mok Lai Meng 94
Moluccas (islands) 42

Monaco Grand Prix 118
Mong-Ha Hill 19
Montanha Russa Hill 19
Monte Fort 42, 46–47
Moorish Barracks 75
Moors 28, 34
moradores 36
Morocco 34
Mota Cerveira, Carlos Armando da 89
Municipal Council of the Islands *see*
  Camara Municipal das Ilhas
Municipal Senate *see* Senado da
  Camara
Museu de Vinho 116
My Mother's Journal 62

Nabo, Francisco 125
Nagasaki (Japan) 33–34, 37, 39, 43
Nam Kwong company 118
Nam Tung Bank 97–98
Nanjing (China) 14
Nantou (China) 13
nãos do trato (carracks) 37–39
Napier, Lord William 65–66
Napoleon 64
Natal (southern Africa) 52
National People's Congress 92, 104, 110
Negro slaves 44–45
Neilingding Island 13
Neo-Confucianism 31
Netherlands see Holland
New York City 54, 96
New York Times 86
Ngai Mei-cheong, Gary 128
Nicolau de Mesquita, Lieutenant
  Vicente 72–73
Ningbo (China) 15–16, 24, 73
Nobre de Carvalho, Brigadier 89,
  97–98, 100
Nogueira, Estevao 24
Nossa Senhora do Bomparto Fort 46,
  64
Nunes Barreto, Father Melchior 24, 26

Oita (Japan) 36
Old China Street 61
Old Prostestant Cemetery 100
opium trade 67–70, 79–80, 82
Opium Wars 2, 58, 61–62, 71, 79

Oporto (Portugal) 112
Organic Statute for Macau 2, 94–95, 105
Oriental Scenery 56
Ormuz 12
Os Lusiadas 23
Our Lady of Fátima 81
Our Lady of Grace 28
Our Lady of Hope 28
Our Lady of the Angels 28
Our Lady of the Rosary 28
Our Lady of the Visitation 28
Outer Harbor 41, 84, 86, 122
ouvidor 37

pai-lou 78
Palace Santa Sancha
Paris (France) 61, 106, 123
Paris Foreign Missions 31
Passaleong Fort 73
Patane Hill 19
Pearl River 6, 13, 19, 38, 40–41, 57, 65–67, 86, 90, 98
Pearl River Delta 21, 113
Penha Church 46
Penha Hill 19, 41, 46, 58
Peninsula of the Sea Mirror 21
People's Daily 85
People's Republic of China: 61, 92; and Denmark 53; economy 1, 4; and France 53, 67; and Great Britain 1–3, 39–40, 42, 52–53, 56, 62, 64–68, 70–71, 89–91, 95–96, 102, 107, 116; and Holland 39, 42–43, 46, 48, 64, 67; and Hong Kong 1–4, 65–66, 71, 83–84, 92, 95–96, 107, 116, 121; and Hong Kong transition 1, 3–4; and Japan 15, 39, 42; and Jesuit brotherhood 24–25, 28–31, 36, 45; and Joint Declaration (Hong Kong) 1, 3–4, 102, 107, 116, 120; and Joint Declaration (Macau) 1–4, 102, 108–11, 115–16, 118–20; and Macau 1–4, 32–33, 41, 45, 47–48, 53, 55, 57, 64–66, 71–74, 78–98, 100–5, 107–12, 116–19, 120-25, 127; and Macau transition 1–4, 102–04, 116; and Malacca 12, 14; and negotiations on Hong Kong 1, 102, 107; and negotiations on Macau 1–2, 4, 103–4, 107–10, 112; and the Philip-

pines 67; and Portugal 1–4, 13–18, 23, 25, 32–35, 38–43, 47, 52, 64–66, 72–74, 80, 85, 87–89, 94–97, 102–5, 107–12, 125–27; and Russia 53; and Spain 67; and Sweden 53, 67; trading with Portugal 1, 3, 13–18, 24, 32–34, 38–42, 52–55; and United States 53, 67, 69, 82, 91
Peres de Andrade, Fernão 14
Peres de Andrade, Simão 14
Perestrelo, Rafael 13
Perez, Father Francisco 26
Pescadores Islands 46
Philadelphia 54, 73
Philip II, King 34–35, 37, 48
Philippines 33–35, 39, 48, 67
Pimenta 23
Pinto, Brother André 26
Pinto, Governor Silveira 70
Pinto Machado, Dr. Joquim 112, 124, 125
piracy 3, 15–16, 18, 34, 39, 41, 43, 64–65, 73
Pires, Tome 13–14
Pollard, Edward 90–91
Ponta da Amizade *see* Friendship Bridge
Pope Gregory XIII 35
Porto Exterior *see* Outer Harbor
Porto Interior *see* Inner Harbor
Portas do Cerco (Barrier Gate) 32–33, 55, 71–73, 89, 92, 101, 123
Porter, Jonathan 128
Portugal 79, 92; and Brazil 11; and China 1–4, 13–18, 23, 25, 32–35, 38–43, 47, 52, 64–66, 72–74, 80, 85, 87–89, 94–97, 102–5, 107–12, 116, 125–27; exploration in Asia 1, 11–13, 23, 37; and France 3, 64; and Great Britain 3, 11, 40, 72, 89; and Holland 39–40, 42–46, 49, 51; and Italy 12; and Japan 15–17, 33–34, 37–40, 42–43, 47, 64, 81, 125; and Joint Declaration (Macau) 1–4, 102, 108–11, 115–16, 118–20; and Macassar 48; and Macau 1–4, 11, 13, 16–18, 25, 32–34, 37–43, 46–53, 55, 64–66, 72–75, 78–81, 84–85, 87–89, 94–98, 102–12, 115–16, 119–21, 125–28; and Malacca 12–15, 17–18, 24, 26, 33, 37–38, 41, 47–48; and negotiations on Macau

1–2, 4, 102–4, 107–10, 112, 116; and Spain 34–35, 37, 40, 50–51, 66; trading with China 1, 3, 13–18, 23–24, 32–34, 38–43, 52–55; trading with Europe 12, 42; trading with India 11–12, 24, 33, 37–39, 47; trading with Japan 33–34, 37–39
Portuguese Civil Code 75
Portuguese Crown 2, 11–12, 17, 23, 26, 34, 37–38, 50–52, 64, 78
Portuguese India 12, 26, 37, 47
Portuguese language 78, 110
Portuguese Restoration 2, 50–51
Portuguese Revolution 79, 95
Portuguese tea 128
Pousada de São Tiago 126
Praia Grande 41, 56, 58–60, 74–75, 83, 98, 110
Prinsep, Mary 62
Prinsep, William 61, 62
Protestantism 72
Protin Qua 61
Protocol of Lisbon 32

Qianlong (China) 56
Quanzhou (China) 13, 15
"Queen of the World: Mother of Portugal, Guard Macau" *see* "Rainha do Munco: Mae de Portugal, Amparai Maca"
Quotations from Chairman Mao Tse-tung 87–88

Radio Vila Verde 94
"Rainha do Munco: Mae de Portugal, Amparai Maca" 81
Rand, Christopher 83, 98
Reijersen, Captain Cornelis 43–44
Republic of China 89, 96, 107
Repulse Bay (Hong Kong 116
Restoration (Portugal) 2,
Rho, Father Jeronimo 45
Ribeiro, Avenida Almeida 66
Ricci, Father Matteo 28–31
Rice, Edward E. 91
The Rise of Modern China 107
Rightist opportunists 86
Rocha Vieira, General Vasco 125–27
Rolls-Royce 113

Rome 19
Royal Academy 60–61
Rua da Felicidade 82
Runcie, Archbishop 82
Russell and Company 62, 73
Russia 53

Saigon (Vietnam) 84
St. Dominic's Church 30
St. Francis Xavier Chapel 25
St. Ignatius of Loyola 24
St. John the Baptist 44
St. Paul's College 72
St. Raphael's Hospital 41
Sale Marques, José Luís de 128
Salim, Salim A. 95–96
Sanchez, Father Alfonso 36
Santa Casa da Misericordia 26–27
Santa Maria 115
Santo Agostinho 60
São Domingos Square 60
São Francisco Fort 44, 46, 64, 75
São Gabriel (ship) 12
São Geronimo Hill 19
São Lourenço Street 60
São Paulo Hill 19
São Rafael (ship) 12
São Tiago Fort 43, 45–46
Sarmento de Carvalho, Lopo 44–45
Scotland 62
Scottish tea 128
Sé Cathedral 28
Second Bar 53
Seminary of São José (St. Joseph) 28, 75, 79, 127, 128
Seminary of São Paulo (St. Paul) 28, 36, 43, 47
Senado da Camara (Municipal Senate) 35, 36–37, 48, 52
"Settlement or Port of the Name of God in China" 37
Shangchuan Island 15, 24
Shanghai 58, 79, 81, 89, 91, 103
Shenzhen 120
Shortlands Tavern 90
Shun Tak Shipping 113
Siam 38
Sian (steamer) 81
Silva, Bishop F. Pedro da 38

Silva Mendes, Manuel da 78
Singapore 106
Sino-British Joint Liaison Group 102
snakeboats 100
Soares, Father João 26
Soares, Mario 12, 112, 123, 125
Soares de Albergaria, Lopo 14
Sociedade de Turismo e Diversoes de
    Macau (STDM) *see* Macau Tourism
    and Entertainment Company
Society of Jesus 24
Solor (Lesser Sunda Islands) 38, 48
South America 11
South China Sea 16, 32, 48, 73, 86
Southeast Asia 3, 75, 84
Spain: 67; and Holland 42–43, 51; and
    Macau 3, 104; and Portugal 34–35,
    37, 40, 50, 51, 66
Spanish Basques 104
Spanish Crown 50–51
Special Administrative Regions 102,
    108–9, 120
Special Economic Zones (China) 4,
    120, 123
Spice Islands 24, 33
spice trade 12–13, 18, 33, 38, 40, 48
Standing Committee (National People's
    Congress) 104
Star Ferry Riots 87
Stewart, Lucretia 128
Street of Happiness *see* Rua da Felici-
    dade
Street Sleepers Society 82
Summers, James 72
Sun Yat-sen 76, 77
Suzhou (China) 79
Swatow region (China) 82
Sweden 53

Tai Xing Company 104
Taipa Island (Macau) 4, 71, 79–80,
    87, 97, 105, 111–12, 117, 121–23,
    125
Taipei Trade and Tourism Office
    (Macau) 125
Taiwan (Formosa) 36, 46, 89, 93, 96,
    107, 117, 118, 121
Tamão 13–14
Tanzania 95
Taoism 31

Tavares Bocarro, Manuel 39, 45
Teixeira, Father Manuel 17, 26, 127
Teledifusão de Macau 94
Tempest, Rone 128
Temple, Archbishop 82
Tiananmen Square 111
Tianjin *see* Treaty of Tientsin
Tidore (Moluccas) 42
Tiger's Mouth *see* Boca Tigris
Timor (Lesser Sunda Islands) 38, 48
Toit, Paul du 118
trading fairs 38, 40
Travel/Holiday 127–28
Treatise on Geometry 31
Treatise on the Celestial Bodies 31
Treaty of Beijing *see* Luso-Chinese
    Treaty of Trade and Friendship
Treaty of Friendship and Trade 69
Treaty of Tientsin (Tianjin) 74
Trench, David 90
Truce of Antwerp 43
Trumbull, Robert 92
Tuen-mun 13, 14
Ty-lok-to Fort 53
Typhoon Rose 98

Union of Crowns 34–35, 45, 50–51,
    66
United Nations 82, 84, 95–96, 107
United Nations Special Committee on
    Colonialism 95
United Nations University 124
United Press International 93
United States 53, 62, 65, 67, 69–70,
    72, 81–82, 91, 98, 105
United States Department of State 91

Valignano, Father 25
Vatican 36
Vaz Freire, Diogo 52
vereadores 36
Vereenigde Oost-Indische Compagnie
    (VOC) *see* Dutch East India Com-
    pany
Vicenta da Rocha, Carlos 75
Viceroy (Canton) 65
Victoria Harbor (Hong Kong) 75
Vieira, António 23–24
Vietnam 84, 114

Wangxia 55
Wangxia Hill 71
Wan-li, Emperor 18–19, 28, 31
Wang Po 17, 18, 2
Watson, Elizabeth 63
Watson, Thomas Boswall 62–63
Webber, John 56
Weddell, Captain John 40
Wellesley, Lord 64
Welsh, Frank 53, 55, 65
West Indies 23
Westlake, Michael 121
Whampoa 53, 56–57
Wilson, Dick 84
Work on Trigonometry 31
World War II 2, 81–82, 84
Wu, Gordon 118
Wu Xuegian 103

Xavier, Father Francis 24–25
Xinhua 103, 119–20

Yorkshire (England) 40, 90
Youngjiang River 15
Yuan dynasty 18

Zelandia Castel Fort 46
Zhao Ziyang 103, 108, 120
Zhejiang province (China) 15–16
Zhongshan County (China) 21, 76, 81
Zhou Ding 120
Zhou Nan 107, 108
Zhuhai province (China) 4, 123, 128